Tudor London Visited

TUDOR LONDON VISITED

Norman Lloyd Williams

CASSELL

First published in the UK 1991
by Cassell Publishers Ltd
Villiers House
41/47 Strand
LONDON
WC2N 5JE

Distributed in the United States
by Sterling Publishing Co., Inc.
387 Park Avenue South, New York, NY 10016-8810

Distributed in Australia
by Capricorn Link (Australia) Pty Ltd
P.O. Box 665, Lane Cove, NSW 2066

British Library Cataloguing in Publication Data for this title is available upon
request from the British Library

ISBN 0–304–31239–6

Typeset by Columns of Reading

Printed and bound in Great Britain by Mackays of Chatham

Contents

Preface

This book begins with a guide to London at this time of crisis, and brings the reader up to date with people and affairs. Up to 6 July 1553, Thursday. Then it follows the odd paths we took towards salvation from our problems.

It is told in the present tense, a tense rarely used by historians unless they are Carlyle. I have used it in order to remind myself, as well as the reader, of how ambiguous with possibilities was the present of these over-judged protagonists of the 1550s, Northumberland, Mary, and the rest.

I thank my son Dr Perry Williams and my old and very valued friend Raymond O'Malley for much and good advice.

Norman Lloyd Williams

Introduction

Tudor London, July 1553, we English were in trouble.

Europe, civilized, saw us as barbarians. We were rich, with a fine city which had the world's biggest church and most beautiful bridge, but we had sold up our monasteries and smashed our altars and holy images.

We loved four things: heresy; making and selling woollen cloth, much of it of poor quality; despising foreigners; beer.

Visitors found they could not understand a word in Londoners' twisted mouths. We had lovely women, but independent and dowdy, and some good inns. When we ate we belched.

A bloody-minded lot: arrogant, unstable, vindictive, and so foggy-brained we could not possibly deal with our crisis. On the other hand, Londoners and other English Protestants were pretty sure we were God's Chosen People.

Our crisis. Sixteen-year-old King Edward VI, a very Protestant young man, was about to die. He would be succeeded by a very Catholic middle-aged spinster, the kindly, clothes-loving, devout, tough Princess Mary, who was daughter by a Spanish mother of the same father, our much-married national hero Henry VIII. When Mary Tudor became queen she would wipe out the Protestant Reformation of Henry VIII and Edward VI, attacking heresy as vigorously as it had been attacked in Spain, the Netherlands, France.

Or else there would be a coup to put another Protestant on the throne. It would be led by the head of Edward's government, an unpopular nobleman with soft brown eyes, John Dudley, Duke of Northumberland, and would be followed by civil war. This would be accompanied by invasion on Princess Mary's behalf by her Catholic cousin, Charles V, Holy Roman Emperor, who ruled Spain, the Netherlands, almost all the rest of Europe outside France, and the gold and recently discovered silver of the Americas as well. Invasion by Charles V would be accompanied by a competing one, by his enemy Henri

II, Catholic King of France, which would be on behalf of anyone unlikely to be Charles's puppet.

Religious and patriotic killing on a large scale. Bloodshed had been foretold by the most violent storms in living memory. Blood-red hailstones had fallen on London gardens. God save the English![1]

I

Visit to Crisis London

1

Gravesend to Greenwich Palace and Billingsgate

i

For a visitor the best entry from the Continent is by Rye, on the Sussex coast, then overland to Gravesend at the head of the Thames estuary. An alternative, taking ship direct to Gravesend, is not advised: although the ship will pick up a pilot to take it up the estuary, the widespread and shifting sands are virtually unmarked by the English and exceedingly dangerous.

From Gravesend it is 26 miles up the Thames to London. A wherry with two Gravesend oarsmen costs 2s, but it is quite respectable and comfortable to go in a barge, which takes up to twenty-four passengers at 2d a head. Gravesend watermen row the barges as well as the wherries: they have a monopoly.

On the morning tide along with the barge there may be English coasters, and ships from Antwerp, Bordeaux, Spain. Most ships coming to London are only 80 or 100 tons, but some are 200 or more, and more than half are English.

Piloting up the river is another monopoly, shared by a fellowship based on Dover and another (Trinity House) based on Deptford. Monopolies, it will be noticed, are everywhere in England. This one is said to reduce losses through bad piloting, and to be good for security, confining knowledge of the channels to these identifiable groups of natural-born Englishmen. Foreign shipmasters, especially from the Hanseatic ports of north Germany, detest not being allowed to provide their own pilots, nor even to choose fellowship pilots they trust. English arrogance, say the Germans.

Pilots have to navigate in the Thames by landmarks. To provide buoys in the Thames, as in the estuary, is a duty of the Lord Admiral which is traditionally neglected. Traditionally un-neglected is the Lord Admiral's perquisite: the monopoly of supplying ships with ballast. Tradition, neglect of duties, and insistence on perquisites are all, one notices, everywhere in

England. By regulation of the City of London (regulations also are everywhere in England) this ballast has to be dug out of the river, because the Thames is becoming silted.

Across the estuary, half a mile north, is another optimistic Thames defence: the blockhouses of Tilbury, which, if they have guns, shot, powder and men, can crossfire with the Gravesend fort, if that also has guns, shot, powder and men. It is said that Edward's Council has just had all available guns carted off to the Tower of London.

As the barge leaves Gravesend a passenger sees, west or a little north of west across the flat, marshy, thinly inhabited country, the pinnacles and towers of Greenwich Palace. It is the favourite palace of Edward 'by the grace of God King of England, France and Ireland'. When a young French doctor, named Etienne Perlin, heard him so announced he almost died, he says, of indignation. However, by July 1553 Edward is in practice king of only England, Calais and Ireland. He used to have Boulogne also, taken in the last of Henry VIII's wars, but the Council and its President, the Duke of Northumberland, have sold it back to France. 'Treachery!' say Londoners.

Before the barge reaches Greenwich it comes, around a few bends, to the naval dockyards of Woolwich, where there are several large ships dating from Henry's time, but they are not manned. Neither are two smaller ships on the opposite bank. In spite of the crisis.

But something has been done. Northumberland and the Council have been flirting with the French as a potential counter to Charles V. And they have sent half a dozen ships out of the Thames to the East Anglian coast, to forestall any attempt to waft Princess Mary from her house in Norfolk to Charles in Brussels, his capital. When she was six he signed a contract to marry her; he is now fifty-three, she thirty-seven.[1]

ii

One more hairpin bend and on the left, facing north, is the lovely long red-brick palace, *Placentia*, Pleasance. The royal standard is flying, a Tudor custom whenever the sovereign is in residence.

On Sunday, 2 July, a crowd came to the square in front of the gatehouse, at the side of the banqueting hall, because the King was expected to show himself, as he had a few days before. He did not, and they were told to come again on the Tuesday, when there was again a crowd, but a Gentleman of the Privy Chamber came out and said the air was too chill. Edward has not been seen for a week. Has he been poisoned by the Duke of Northumberland? The question was asked.

4

He is still alive, but his death when it comes may well be kept as secret as possible for a few days, as was Henry VIII's. He is a fair boy, a little shorter than average, with high shoulder blades. Grey eyes. What sort of boy? Not strong but quite active. Intelligent, although Catholics would say he has been over-influenced by Protestant tutors. Why should Henry have given him tutors far to the left of his own convictions? To be sure his successor would not let in the Pope.

King Edward has been most affected by Sir John Cheke (reddish face, yellow beard), an irrepressible reformer: he presses for a reformed pronunciation of Greek, the phonetic spelling of English, and the expulsion from English of all foreign words. His devotion to principle and his benevolence and diligence inspire, and are inspired by, the King's own pertinacious sanctity.

But the King is his own man. Protestantism makes for conscientiousness, not docility. And a Tudor king is a king is a king. Edward is not yet of full age but he is not a cipher. He can hold his own. When the great Italian mathematician Cardano visited last year, Edward questioned him on planetary motions. Cardano granted him condescending half-truths. Edward would not be put down. Cardano was impressed: 'The miraculous boy . . . he led me among the stars.'

Not a cipher, and not pig-headed to extremity. When his Archbishop of Canterbury and Bishop of London were sent to him by the Council – without notice, to prevent his being briefed beforehand by Cheke – to say that Princess Mary's obstinacy in having Mass sung in her chapel should, after all, be given in to, and gave good political reasons, Edward gave reasons why it should not, quoting the ultimate authority for political and every other kind of action, Scripture. His respected and beloved Archbishop Cranmer and Bishop Ridley came again: it would be dangerous to anger the Emperor, they said, because he was just then not fighting the French and could invade England. Edward said no. They came again: it would be only for the time being. He burst into tears. So did they. Not until this third appeal did he give way, and was then right to give way.

His sickness has been with him most of this year. He has a wracking cough, and brings up a black sputum which smells beyond measure. He is in constant fever; plasters keep being applied to his shaven head; his legs and belly have badly swelled.

Palace routines continue. First dinner at 10 a.m., first supper at 4 p.m. Less important persons sleep at night on truckle beds put up in this room or that passage; important persons have two-room suites. Everyone who passes through the Presence Chamber bows to the empty chair of state. All are expected to attend the services in the chapel, which are according to the new

5

Prayer Book of 1552, with simple Reformed music composed by Christopher Tye, Thomas Tallis and John Shepherd, Gentlemen of the Chapel Royal.

Where is the chapel? It is not the building surmounted by upstanding pinnacles, behind the main building: that was Henry's armoury. It is not the building with little pointed windows and a very slim flèche, at the west end of the main buildings: that was Henry's carpenter's shop. The chapel is at the eastern end of the main building, with rounded windows. The carpenter's shop used to be the church of the Franciscans, whose priory adjoined the palace. Twenty years ago Princess Elizabeth was christened there, receiving by Henry's command instant precedence over Princess Mary.

Surely Elizabeth should accede then, and since she is almost certainly Protestant there should be no religious problem? It is not so simple. The Council, which under normal conditions meets fairly equably three times a week, has had very worried sessions these last three weeks, since 16 June when Edward's death was finally accepted as imminent.[2]

iii

The trouble is that, as circumstances changed, Henry changed his commands and did not tie up loose ends. Mary was heir as long as her mother, Catherine of Aragon, was his wife. Then Elizabeth was his heir as long as Ann Boleyn was his wife. Then he had Parliament declare both Mary and Elizabeth bastards, and so ineligible. Then he had Parliament leave it to him to decide the succession, and they were to confirm whatever he decided.

He decided, and Parliament confirmed: the Crown was to go, after his only legitimate son Edward and Edward's progeny, to Mary (Henry's daughter by a marriage which by Act of Parliament never existed) and Mary's progeny; if there were no progeny, then to Elizabeth (uncertainly fathered daughter of an officially adjudged whore, whose marriage to Henry was by Act of Parliament 'utterly void and of none effect') and Elizabeth's progeny; if there were no progeny then to descendants of Henry's younger sister (ignoring his elder sister's), that is to say to progeny of Frances, Duchess of Suffolk (ignoring Frances herself), the eldest of her three girls being Jane Grey. The descendant of Henry's elder sister, with a greater claim than Frances or Jane, is Mary of Scotland, but he excluded a Scot (as he could if he wished: in matters of succession, genealogy is relevant but not decisive) because she would be in the pocket of France (and sure enough eleven-year-old Mary Queen of Scots is already affianced to the Dauphin).

A ridiculous kettle of fish? Why be King of England, or the English Parliament, if you cannot make a kettle of fish?

6

By Act of Parliament confirming Henry's decision, the crown will go to Catholic Mary. She will do what Henry most did not want, bring back the Pope. She will destroy Protestantism, she will marry some Catholic foreigner, she will cause economic chaos by making everyone who has monastic lands (almost every landowner in the country) give them back.

The crown cannot go to Mary, and the King does not want it to go to Elizabeth either. If the older bastard is excluded should one not also exclude the younger? Doubt about a monarch's birth lays up trouble. The King wants a male monarch (in England a female monarch has been unknown), so Edward has decided to skip both bastards and devise the crown to the male progeny of Frances, or failing such a male, to the male progeny of her daughters, Jane, Catherine and Mary – a succession absolutely secure in birth and the Protestant religion.

Unfortunately there are no such male progeny, nor of any of the seven non-Scottish descendants of Henry VII, so Edward has had to amend his plan and nominate Jane herself (excluding Frances, as had Henry – because she was unlikely to produce male children? Or was just unpopular? Or her husband was too feeble to be a king?) Jane has now been safely married to Guildford Dudley, youngest son of John Dudley, Duke of Northumberland. This plan may or may not have been Edward's own invention, but it is certainly his pride and delight, and he has pressed it on the Council with all his royal power.

When his devise (not 'device', a tricky plan, but 'devise', a bequeathing) showed a path through the impasse, and the Council achieved unanimity upon it, the faces of Councillors were noted by the French ambassador to clear and they feasted rejoicing. Edward had letters patent drawn up and witnessed here at Greenwich by the Council and the law officers. And he made the Council individually swear and sign an oath to see that his devise was carried out. That was two weeks ago.

The crisis is solved then? No. The devise is not legal until Parliament has ratified it; Parliament does not meet until 20 September; Edward is unlikely to live so long. Why cannot Parliament meet earlier? Because instead of being prorogued at the end of its session in March, so that it could be recalled quickly (at that time no one was thinking in terms of Edward's almost immediate death), it was dissolved; new elections will be necessary and will take time.

Does temporary illegality matter? It matters if it matters. It could legitimize rebellion. Two-thirds of the population outside London are still Catholic and might object to an illegal thrusting aside of their Catholic princess.

Mary quickly heard of the devise, as did Charles's ambassador, Jan

Scheyfve. He was horrified. He wrote to Charles that the unscrupulous, ambitious Northumberland was behind the plot against Mary; that everyone said he had already poisoned Edward; that the plot was opposed in Council by the Lord Treasurer, Sir William Paulet, Marquis of Winchester, and by the Earl of Arundel and others, including the law officers; that Northumberland had been governing as if he had absolute authority, often dispatching business with his own hand, not trusting even his personal secretary (a Catholic incidentally), and that he had men ready to seize Mary the moment the King died.

How reliable is Scheyfve in all this? Like other ambassadors in England he has not learned the language: it would be useless in another posting. He tries to show inside knowledge but his information comes from rumours, servants, very junior officials, axe-grinders and the disgruntled, and whenever the Council do not confide in him he is filled with suspicion and supposition. And prejudice.

But he is probably right about Paulet, Arundel and the law officers: they would have been failing in their duties if they had not expressed the obvious objections to the devise. When the lawyers' objections jeopardized the hard-won unanimity, Northumberland is said to have raised his voice. He also would have been failing in his duty had he not.[3]

iv

One might expect the bedroom in which Edward is dying to be on the sunny side of the palace, the other side overlooking the gardens, but medical opinion does not favour the sun.

To see the garden side, with the maze which has water channels in place of hedges, one must go up to Duke Humphrey's Tower on the hill behind the palace. From there one has in the foreground the park where Edward has often ridden and shot with his young friends and Northumberland. And west, across the bends of the river, one sees London less than 5 miles away, like the boss on a targe, the boss having a spike, which is the spire of St Paul's, the tallest spire in Christendom. And there is the Tower of London, and in the Pool the cross-hatching of mast-tops and sailyards, 'like a naked wood in the wintertime'.

The barge leaves Greenwich, passing a couple of the King's (unmanned) ships and then, round the next bend, comes to Deptford, his principal dockyard, Henry's creation, like Woolwich. The dockyard is very dependent on Hanse imports from the Baltic for its masts and hemp. Since such ships as could be manned as well as readied have been sent round to East Anglia, there are rather fewer ships than usual in front of Deptford.

Almost opposite, on the north bank, is the pleasant village of Limehurst, or Limehouse, with a few of the King's (unmanned) ships, and another seamen's town, Ratcliffe. It was from Ratcliffe that two months ago Sir Hugh Willoughby set off with three ships for the frozen north of Norway, to look for a passage to the silks and spices of the Far East, and to new markets, it is hoped, for woollen cloth. Next to Ratcliffe is miserable Wapping-in-the-Woze, with its gallows planted well out in the river for the hanging of sea-criminals.

Then, around a bend, for a stretch there is no habitation on either side, but London fills the eye in front. On the right, beyond St Katharine's Hospital (not a medical hospital but one of the few remaining religious communities), the Tower of London commands for the King this river approach to London and commands London itself. The shipping clusters towards this north bank. Beyond, London Bridge with its tall houses conceals what is immediately up-river. But nothing can conceal St Paul's, its huge octagonal steeple standing up from the massive cruciform body.

Now that Tower of London, is it as great a fortress as in medieval history and the people's imagination? With enough guns and mines any old-fashioned castle can be taken sooner or later, but for practical local purposes the Tower is strong. There is a wide moat, and behind it a double shield of walls strengthened by a dozen towers, and within the double shield the square Norman keep, the erstwhile-whitewashed White Tower.

Within the last few days Lord Admiral Clinton has been put in charge, and very competent he is (except in the matter of buoys), instead of the valiant but Catholic and seventy-four-year-old Sir John Gage. There are sometimes guns on the top of the White Tower, and always a number on the quay. The Tower is the King's main store of arms and artillery, and with the recent strengthening the guns should be enough for any emergency, but the arms are not all in good condition.

The Tower, like other large stone buildings, serves a number of functions. It contains the Jewel House, which stores the King's plate as well as his jewels, and it is thither that so much gold and silver have gone from the churches (which for Reformed services no longer require very much), but not sufficient to balance the royal accounts. King Edward has to borrow on the Antwerp market at 14 per cent (a reputable merchant can borrow at half that), although he pays his debts, unlike Charles V, who, nevertheless, is borrowing at the same rate. It looks as though Edward is paying too much, but Sir Thomas Gresham who acts as his agent in Antwerp says he would be paying more if Gresham were not so industrious and clever.

In a row of buildings on the far side of the White Tower is the Mint, from

9

which Henry VIII raised a good deal of revenue by debasing the currency. The experts, and the inexperts with social consciences, declared this was a bad thing, so the Council under Northumberland tried to amend matters two years ago by reducing the value of the debased silver testoon from sixpence to its intrinsic value of fourpence, and the silver groat from fourpence to threepence. The man in the street felt he had been robbed, and instead of prices falling, as the Council and the experts and publicists predicted, they rose, presumably owing to loss of confidence. All a trick, it was said, of Northumberland's.

On prices the Council legislates and legislates, but they rise and rise. Why? Experts and interested parties now blame the profiteering of middlemen; the growth of sheep instead of corn; speculation; and avarice. In fact, inflation is Europe-wide, and there are several unrecognized factors: increased population; increased availability of gold and silver; increased use of bills of exchange; increased use of foreign coins; increased velocity of circulation.

The Tower also contains the King's zoo, just inside the entrance, where one can see two lions, a pelican and a unicorn, but one must tip. As also in order to see the arms museum started by Henry. As well as fortress, safe deposit, mint, zoo and museum, the Tower is a traditional but little-used royal palace. The King's Lodgings are between the White Tower and the river, not roomy or comfortable or in good repair, and used only for a few days at the beginning of a reign. But the roses in the Privy Garden are famous.

The smell of the moat is famous too. It is the summer bane of prisoners lodged in rooms and cells in and under the towers, but not as bad as the winter cold. One of the present prisoners who always finds the winter cold trying is the eighty-year-old Duke of Norfolk, imprisoned by Henry VIII for treason. A younger man, also imprisoned by Henry, is Edward Courtenay, aged twenty-seven, who has been there since he was twelve, guilty of proximity to the line of succession. The most famous of the other prisoners is Stephen Gardiner, the ex-Bishop of Winchester, who obeyed Henry in repudiating Rome and dissolving monasteries, but came to his sticking place when the Mass was attacked after Henry's death. He is seventy, 'nostrils like a horse, ever sniffing the wind', and has suffered leg-pulling in the Tower from a visiting Protestant, Catherine Bertie, lively young Dowager Duchess of Suffolk.

There ought also to be Cuthbert Tunstall, 'man of invincible moderation', ex-Bishop of Durham, nearly eighty, but, like some others, he has been moved elsewhere by Northumberland and the Council to make room for more guards. Now, what about this Northumberland who governs 'as if he had absolute authority'?[4]

V

John Dudley, Duke of Northumberland, is now fifty. Well built, and with the gentle eyes he has passed to his fourth son, Guildford, he has long been famed for energy, and for readiness and charm of speech. He has always been a remarkable fighting man. In his youth his conspicuous courage in war and his skill in joust drew attention at Henry's court. He had no strings to pull; he moved up step by step, by his own ability and others' lack of it, right up to Commander-in-Chief of Henry's land forces and Admiral of his fleet.

He has repeatedly won battles for his country. In Scotland at Musselburgh, when the English horse were in confusion and the whole English army likely to break up, he kept his men in order and in heart, and so directed an attack that in the end it was the Scots who were shattered. At Boulogne when the Dauphin, with a bigger force of (it is said) the best troops in France, broke into and took the lower town, he filled his own men with such spunk they drove the French right out. In Norwich in 1549, when the town looked lost to Kett and his rebels, who had defeated the Earl of Northampton, he had his officers kiss one another's swords and swear to fight to the death, and they held on for two days until German mercenaries arrived.

With his combination of physical courage, military verve, and reliability in military administration he is without equal as a soldier in his generation of Englishmen. If the devise has to be imposed or defended by force, Northumberland is the man to do it.

Has he been a capable head of government? Ten years ago, when he was first charged with some civil administration, he said he was not the man for it, and apologized to the Council for constantly consulting them. Nevertheless, he found himself successfully involved in civil government. He was on good terms with his fellow Councillors and had a good public reputation. By the time of Henry's death he was the most important man in the Council, except his old friend Edward Seymour, who became Lord Protector and Duke of Somerset.

When there is no longer an adult king, a leader quickly arouses jealousy. The Councillors became hostile to Somerset, whose populist policies made him immensely popular but who overplayed the autocrat and ignored the Council's advice. Northumberland, with his Norfolk victory fresh upon him, was the Council's inevitable leader in trying to bring Somerset to co-operative sanity; but Somerset would not be saved, and finally there seemed no alternative but execution. Execute the people's hero and you are the people's villain. And you are the new leader, new target for jealousy.

Under Northumberland the Council has been restored to orderly routines and begun to govern the country. Council-government is unprecedented, and not what England has liked, but until Edward's majority the only alternative has been another Somerset, which could not be tolerated. Northumberland has played the uncongenial Council game seriously, constantly trying to get the Council to make up its mind. His letters are full of 'I desire the Council's opinion on . . .', 'Pray get the answer of the Lords, and send me an answer I may subscribe . . .'. Councillors' names and signatures are always in accord with conventional precedence: his own is never first, but after those of the Archbishop of Canterbury, the Lord Chancellor and the Lord Treasurer. Window-dressing? Not of a form common among dictators. Not window-dressing.

Without an adult king the frictions and stresses of the last few years of Protestant radicalism and economic difficulty have made the Council, and especially its President, unpopular and untrusted. He had been hoping that Edward would take over full kingship later this year, two years before the traditional age.

As to how far he is driven by single-minded ambition. . . . He is ambitious, of course, but his ambition is usually double-minded, not single. The devise can be seen as his plot to bring the crown into his own family; or that result can be seen as a happy but secondary sequel to fulfilling the King's desire to save his religious revolution from anti-Christ. Certainly the benefit the devise will bring to Northumberland's family should make him the ideal man to carry it through.[5]

vi

Charles V's Scheyfve has been impressed by the power in Northumberland's hands, as no doubt will be the special envoys he is expecting from Charles. These envoys, charged with helping Mary to the throne, are led by Simon Renard, a good-looking, clever fellow, who is to act pander on behalf of Prince Philip. Charles has decided, he says, he is too old now to marry Mary, and his son must board her. When the envoys arrive and receive Scheyfve's assessment of the situation, and look at the Tower, they will agree with Scheyfve: when Edward dies, Mary must lie low – on no account must she proclaim herself Queen and give Northumberland an excuse to seize her.

Ah, these foreign affairs experts and their assessments! There are arms in the Tower and some guards have been added, but where is there any considerable force? The King's Guard is small, and the still smaller body of gentlemen known as Pensioners are a personal guard, largely ceremonial. There is no standing army. German mercenaries were employed to help put down the rebellions of 1549, and again were brought in last year in case there was trouble over Somerset's execution, but they have been sent home, because there is no money. For the same reason every garrison and every ship's crew is minimal. The militia and the Lords Lieutenant of the counties could be raised against a foreign invader, but could they against an English princess, by an unloved Council and its unloved President? Councillors' own retainers and relatives, totalling a thousand or two (Northumberland has recently been licensed to keep 500 servants in his livery, the Duke of Suffolk 300, and the others smaller numbers), are his largest reliable force, reliable if the Councillors and he are fully at one. As for active support from the French, which Scheyfve believes he is promised, an envoy of Charles sees Henri under every bed, as an envoy of Henri sees Charles.

vii

The Gravesend barge is among the anchored and moored ships: on the port side Southwark, with St Thomas's Hospital, which is run by the City, and the Bridge House where the City keeps material for repair of the Bridge, and stores wheat against a shortage; on the starboard the King's Custom House – half-timbered, a great gable at either end, a broad wharf in front – and private wharves and quays, and Billingsgate dock, the destination.

A ship – if there is room and enough water (there is a difference of 15 or 20 feet between high and low tides) – may tie up at Billingsgate or a quay, but it is more likely to anchor in midstream and discharge into lighters or barges. The ship's master goes to the Custom House to swear an oath as to his cargo and its owners; foreign owners (except, it always used to be, the Hanse) pay more than English. He may have difficulty finding his Customs man: the offices have overflowed into neighbouring houses, and the officers are casual in their time-keeping. The Customer when found, makes entries in his book. The master waits. The Customer comes aboard and checks the cargo. He expects a sweetener to expedite these slow matters and cast a benevolent eye on declared quantities. Corruption is endemic.

If lighters are needed lightermen come aboard, but they are not found too easily today because some have been pressed for the King's ships, and others have fled for fear of being pressed. A ship's crew is capable of discharging cargo into a lighter, but the lightermen have the monopoly. The Customs man watches. The lighter in due course makes for a wharf, or awaits still water in order to shoot the Bridge.

On the wharves and quays there is more checking and measuring, and at last the assessment of duty. Duty is proportional to value, and the value of oil, say, is found by the Customer in his rate book to be £4 a tun (a barrel), as it was in the last rate book of 1507, and perhaps before. Its present value is £30 a tun. A ton of iron is rated at £2. This value too is way out of date: it should be £26.

Then the porters get to work, or do not get to work. Many cargoes are in barrels so that they can be rolled over the quay, and then carried or driven in carts to their destination. Or they may be left out in the rain, especially, the French say, if they are French.

What do ships bring to London? English coasters bring grain, fish, salt, coal, wool; other ships pepper, ginger, sugar, wine, fruit, vegetable oil, woad and alum for the cloth industry, masts and ropes, and manufactured goods – copper kettles and pans, armour, weapons, clocks and watches, glass, paper, needles, pins, beads, buckles, brooches, and gloves. But not hats or caps, the import of which has just been banned, to protect the English industry.

What do they take away? Cloth, cloth, cloth. Cloth makes up three-quarters of the value of all English exports, and almost all of it through London. Do Merchant Adventurers have a monopoly? Yes – the only Englishmen who can export woollen cloth though London are Merchant Adventurers. No – they do not have a monopoly because foreigners export twice as much, especially the Italians and the Hanse.

Merchant Adventurers send almost all their cloth to two month-long fairs at Antwerp, at Whitsun and in late August, and two at Bergen-op-Zoom (20 miles north of Antwerp), at Easter and in early November. In June the 100 or 200 Merchant Adventurers who went to the Whitsun fair at Antwerp began to trickle back, and are still trickling back, with purchases for their wives and friends if not for their businesses. London merchants do not import much: most of them leave that to foreigners.

Other exports? Raw wool and wool-yarn, important but much decreased in importance with the rise of cloth exports. The wool goes from London to Calais, the English port nearest the continental market. Calais has the monopoly as a port, and the Merchants of the Staple have the monopoly of the business.

Other English exports, such as lead, tin, saffron and skins – all primary products – come out largely through London, although their production centres are far away. London, you note, has the country's foreign trade pretty well sewn up, but the greater part of it is in the hands of businessmen from more developed countries.

If the barge is not yet alongside, it is well to avert the eyes from the great clamour, great confusion, great delay, great thieving of the London wharves, quays and Customs, and look upstream, beyond the shipping, to the structure which others besides young Perlin think 'the most beautiful bridge in the world'.[6]

viii

Is it really so beautiful? No. But it functions with vigour, and it has age and character. Most of the houses straddle the roadway, which is 15 feet wide, and either stand wholly on the 4-foot strip on either side, or else extend on to a pier, or are supported on struts projecting over the water. The houses towards the north end fetch the best rents. There are shallow shops on the ground floor, and stalls in front on the road: milliners, hosiers, haberdashers, silk mercers. Women buy sober materials in the 1550s: the Reformed Religion disapproves of colour and gold thread. Shoppers and pedestrians are in danger from horses, carts, cattle, but there are one or two nooks in which to take refuge.

People and animals are everlastingly falling in the water. There is an alderman living on the Bridge, William Hewett, a clothworker, who is going to marry his daughter to one of his erstwhile apprentices who saved her when, three years old, she fell out of a window. Hewett says, 'Osborne saved her, Osborne shall enjoy her.' Animals which fall off the Bridge are the perquisite of the Constable of the Tower.

Towards the north end there is a thirteenth-century stone building which looks like a chapel, with two storeys of Gothic windows. That is a grocer's house and shop, with the lower part his store. It used to be a chantry dedicated to St Thomas Becket where one could have Masses sung for one's dead, but it is four years since chantries went the way of monasteries. Incidentally one should not say 'Saint' Thomas Becket in 1553 – Henry unsainted him for his disrespect to a king.

The Bridge is considered a pleasant place to live. There is a breeze, and little stench, and a splendid view especially from the west side. The famous swans which embellish the view are supposed to stay above the Bridge and be plucked once a year for the King's upholstery. If any of the hundreds and hundreds slip through the Bridge, they, like commoner animals, become the perquisite of the Constable of the Tower. The Thames is fairly clear, and full of fish. Above the Bridge, wheeling in the air, there is usually an assemblage of scavenging red kites.

There are also disadvantages. The river receives refuse from houses and wharves, and blood and offal from butchers (who are supposed to dispose of them only at high tide), and excreta from little huts perched over the water at some of the wharves and lane-ends. And there is the noise. At five in the morning in summer the gates at each end are opened, dues are paid for entry of produce and for wheelage and passage, and cattle and carts clatter over. Mercifully there are no iron-clad wheels, which are against regulations. For several weeks the guards at these gates, as on all the city gates, have been doubled.

A little to the north of the southern gatehouse, which can be identified by its single chimney, one can see a handrail. It runs along the edge of a drawbridge which used to be raised to let ships through to Queenhithe in the days when it was as busy as Billingsgate is now. It has not been raised in the last fifty years because passage of the Bridge has become too difficult for anything but barges, lighters and wherries.

Newcomers always have the drawbridge tower pointed out to them because at the top, stuck on poles, are the heads of traitors, parboiled and tanned so as to last. Perlin declares you hardly find an English nobleman whose parents did not have their heads chopped off. Himself, he would rather be a swineherd and keep his head. Northumberland's father, Edmund Dudley, was a very able swineherd to Henry VII but, to gratify the swine, Henry VIII beheaded him. However, he permitted the head to be buried, so Northumberland, a boy of six at the time, did not see his father's head on the Bridge.[7]

ix

Before disembarkation it is useful to imagine a bird's-eye view of the city. The walls enclose a rectangle ½ mile from north to south, 1 mile from east to west. That is all. There is a mild hill in the western half, and a mild hill in the eastern; the paved-over Walbrook runs in the mild valley between. From its headquarters at Guildhall, which is north of the rectangle's centre, the City controls the wards within the walls and, less tightly, some wards outside the walls, but not the suburbs beyond.

Two miles south-west of Guildhall, on the shining highway of the Thames, speckled with shipping, wherries and swans, is Westminster, independent of London. It is a city and contains the King's palace of Whitehall, his Courts of Justice and his Exchequer, and the church and precinct of the old abbey of Westminster, but it is small.

With bird's-eye view one would look down on the dwellings, mostly rented, of 90,000 Londoners. Almost all the houses are lath and plaster, with timber frames and brick foundations. They are tiled – no thatch by City regulation – so there is much red. And much grey, of cobbled main streets, unmade lanes, stone city walls and gatehouses, the 100 or more parish churches with their steeples and towers, and the other large stone buildings put up by kings, nobles and Church. And much green, of small plots behind almost all the houses, of Companies' gardens and bowling greens, and of rich men's gardens and orchards with summerhouses and bowling greens. The gardens and orchards of the twenty-three major religious institutions have largely come on the market in the last fifteen to twenty years but not all have yet been built on. And most churchyards are still green (and headstoneless) although a few have recently been built over with tenements.

There is a great north–south road – from Cambridge – entering the city at Bishopsgate and crossing the Bridge into Southwark; and a great east–west road – from East Anglia – entering at Aldgate and issuing at Newgate on its way to Uxbridge and Oxford.

If, scarcely landed, one is asked for an opinion of London, one says, no doubt: 'Very busy, very handsome.' And of the English? They do not seem so unstable as one has heard, if they are indeed given to monopoly, regulation, conservatism.

And the crisis? The precautions against disorder seem very slight: anywhere on the Continent there would be a greater show of force. But perhaps they are enough: the devise seems sensible, there could hardly be a better man than Northumberland in control, and there are no overt signs of opposition. There is nothing to dissuade one from making straight for an inn and dinner. In the afternoon one might come back to Billingsgate and take a wherry westward, beyond the city to Whitehall Palace.[8]

2

Billingsgate to the Three Cranes and Whitehall Palace

i

At Billingsgate, does one call a waterman? No. The river at the Bridge is compressed by twenty piers (or rather by the starlings which surround the piers) into twenty-one little rapids. There can be a difference of 5 feet between the levels on the two sides of the Bridge. During every flood tide there are two hours when boats are prohibited altogether from passing under it. If a boat capsizes, the waterman is holding on to an oar and saves himself; his passenger is not and does not. Royalty and those who are just plain sensible pass under the Bridge only when there is still water at the turn of the tide. The most cautious do not even then: 'Wise men go over and fools go under London Bridge.'

So, walk along Thames Street (cobbled, a runnel along the middle) to the Three Cranes and take a wherry from there. Or go by mule along Thames Street, for dignity and avoidance of muck, but to walk is the usual thing. But first, walk a few steps eastwards, and turn up Hart Lane. Halfway up, on the right, is the hall of the Bakers' Company. The Livery Companies are so fundamental to London that it is worth visiting one before all else, not a leading Company like the Mercers' or Grocers' or Drapers', but a middling one. The Bakers' is about the twenty-fifth of the sixty Companies, immediately below the Brewers', Scriveners and Butchers', and above the Poulterers', Stationers' and Innholders', Girdlers' and Barber-Surgeons'.

Bakers' Hall stands back from the lane round a little paved courtyard, part brick, part timber and plaster. There is a garden with a whitewashed wall, where sometimes a gardener at 8d a day works at training the vines and tidying the thyme, rosemary and eglantine. It has a paved walk, and benches, and a bowling alley. A modest, pleasing garden. The garden of a more important Company is bigger, but the Drapers', for example, is spread all over with cloths drying and bleaching (which destroy the garden borders and knots), and is taken over on Sundays by the general public, who eat the fruit.

All the master bakers and journeymen bakers of London's sixty bakeries are members of the Company, and hence freemen of the City; citizens, not 'foreigners'. Master bakers can be members of the senior division of the Company, the livery; journeymen of the junior, the yeomanry. The livery controls the Company, and the Company controls the making and selling of bread in London, subject to overriding regulation by the City.

The weight of the 1d loaf is set by the City in accordance with the price of wheat. The week before last the 1d loaf became bigger: thirty-two loaves per quarter of wheat instead of thirty-seven.

Bakers say that the price is too low and the City exploits them. Their allowance for overheads, which is fed into the price-fixing formula, has remained the same for ten years although costs have risen. It took decades of agitation to get the allowance raised ten years ago; presumably it will take more decades to get it raised again. The formula itself was arrived at three centuries ago.

They say that while the bigger bakers get bigger the smaller get more into debt to their flour-suppliers and cannot meet the membership dues of the livery, but this has the air of being very ancient grumble. The popular belief is that all bakers do well for themselves: after all, when they buy flour their pound weight has 14½ ounces in it, but when they sell bread it has only 12 ounces.

Perlin, the young Frenchman, finds London bread good bread, and the white whiter and cheaper than in Paris. Every loaf is stamped with the baker's seal so that it can be traced back to source if underweight or poor in quality. Bread can be delivered to the house, or bought at bakers' places of business or in the streets at a few specified places, but it cannot be hawked around until after 9 a.m., that is to say until after the bakers have had the best of the market.

In any other trade, freemen hold the exclusive right to sell wholesale or retail in London, but bread is a special case because the city needs the bread cooked by 'foreigners'. At about five in the morning at this time of year, as soon as the gates open, the wives and servants of 'foreign' bakers bring their cartloads or basketloads into the city. From St Albans they come in through Newgate, from Tottenham through Bishopsgate, from Stratford through Aldgate. Others row in from Ratcliffe, Limehouse, Deptford, and stand by the waterside at Billingsgate or Queenhithe. 'Foreign' bakers feel the Company is over-strict with them on weight and quality. It is as great a crime for 'foreign' bread to be over-weight as under-weight: the loaves have to be thirty-eight to the quarter of wheat, smaller than Company bread so as not to sell so readily.

19

The Company is motivated by the interest of its members, particularly its senior members, but it also has feeling for the organism of which it is part, the City, and is regulated by the City.[1]

ii

Return to Thames Street. The lanes from Thames Street down to the river are narrow, dirty, lined with stables and petty warehouses, with latrines and ruffians, and they are almost level. The lanes on the north side of Thames Street (running like Hart Lane up to the next east–west street, which is Tower Street/Eastcheap), are steeper but just as narrow.

So goods are conveyed from and to the wharves with much clogging of the lanes, much noise. It is done by porters and carmen, starting work at about five in summer and earning 8d or 10d a day. The porters unload on to the wharf or quay and then, without a vehicle, take the goods to a warehouse or market, or to an inn-yard for a country carrier. A carman has a horse-drawn two-wheeled cart, shaped for the small wharves and narrow lanes. The number of cars is fixed by the City, so if you want to be a carman you have to buy or be given somebody's car-room.

These unskilled workers feel their jobs at risk from wandering unemployed, of whom there are many. Copying preachers and social reformers, who are talking much of social justice, the poor blame unemployment on enclosures of arable and common land, and they blame enclosures on Northumberland and the Council. The great period of enclosures is in fact thirty or forty years in the past and there are few being made now, but that makes no difference. Did not the good Duke of Somerset try to stop enclosures? Did not Kett and his men of Norfolk try to stop enclosures? Did not Northumberland have Somerset's head cut off, and put down Kett and slaughter his men?

Besides, peace has been made with France and Scotland so that thousands of soldiers have been paid off. Good King Harry did not disband his army, he went gloriously to war. He took Boulogne. Northumberland sold Boulogne back to the French, *sold* it, and probably pocketed the money. He is in league with the French: one night he and the Duke of Suffolk were stopped by the Watch, and where were they going so secretly? To the French ambassador's lodging in the Charterhouse. So the common people say. And they do not want the French, the old enemies, any more than Emperor Charles and his Inquisition.

Continue along Thames Street. Opposite the masts of Billingsgate there is, on the right, St Mary Hill lined with merchants' houses, and three lanes further, Pudding Lane coming down from the meat market (mostly pork) of Little Eastcheap and with butchers' sheds for scalding hogs. The butchers' filth is thrown into Pudding Lane (there are prescribed hours), whence it is channelled across Thames Street and to a jetty over the river, where there is a shed for getting rid of it at high tide.

Street cleanliness is the responsibility of every householder: he is supposed to sweep and cleanse the street every day up to the channel in the middle, at seven in the evening in summer.

Then on the left, St Magnus's church, its images defaced, and the Bridge. On the right Fish Street, with shops and taverns and fishmongers' houses, leading up to Leadenhall; and further on the right, a lane leading up to the Eastcheap meat market and the Boar's Head Tavern.

Then on the left more narrow lanes leading down to Fish Wharf (which has the usual privy hanging over the Thames), some 'fair houses for merchants', and Fishmongers' Hall. The Fishmongers are fourth in precedence of all the Companies, below the Mercers, Grocers and Drapers, roughly equal with the Goldsmiths.

Then the Old Swan Brewery, and a very narrow lane down to Old Swan Stairs, and the old stone building called Coldharbour. For the last year Coldharbour has been the London house of Francis Talbot, Earl of Shrewsbury. Shrewsbury, who is President of the Council of the North, is not one of the very new aristocracy, and not of the Reformed Religion, but he has gone along with Northumberland. He signed the letters patent for Jane's succession, and he swore the bond to see it carried out.

Now, after a couple of defaced churches, the Steelyard, where merchants of the Hanse live fortress-bound without fraternizing with the natives. Four acres, portcullised gateway, with double-headed eagle and Imperial flag; a fine hall with magnificent carvings and paintings (two murals by Holbein). To the Steelyard wharves the merchants of Cologne, Hamburg, Lubeck and Danzig import the products of North Germany, Scandinavia and the Baltic: linen and wax, steel and metallic manufactures, Rhine wine, caviare, wheat and rye, ropes, masts and hemp. And from them go English minerals and a quarter of England's exports of woollen cloth.

London for long wanted Hanseatic privileges abolished. They were very great: on the export of each broadcloth they paid 1s against an Englishman's 1s 2d and other foreigners' 2s 4d; and on general commodities, whether imported or exported, they paid nothing at all, against the 2s in the £ of other foreigners and 1s in the £ of Englishmen. Last year – against Hanse protests and after temporary concessions – the Council under Northumberland put them squarely on the same terms as other alien merchants. The Hanse demand the return of their centuries-old privileges – 'demand', although nowhere is their power what it was: there is now Netherlander and South German competition in the Baltic, and they can no longer intimidate Scandinavia nor, it seems, England. Northumberland has not yet allowed their delegation to land.[2]

iii

On the further side of the Steelyard is Dowgate Dock, where the Walbrook issues into the Thames. At Dowgate oxen are taken down for the filling of water butts for the breweries. Thames water makes good beer, and as the main drink at all meals, for both sexes of all ages and of all classes but the wealthiest, a great deal of beer is needed. A soldier receives as his ration 1½ gallons a day.

A little further along Thames Street and up Royal Street on the right is St Michael Paternoster, which was rebuilt by Richard Whittington, three times Lord Mayor of London, and where he is buried. The present Reformer incumbent, Thomas Mountayne, has dug up Dick Whittington in the hope of finding treasure: the lead was valuable but that was all he found.

A few yards more and Thames Street comes to the Vintry, the Three Cranes. The traditional quay of the vintners has indeed three cranes, and houses with enormous cellars, and a tavern or two. Out on the river are dozens and dozens of wherries, and lighters and barges. And of course scores and scores of swans, and from Bankside across the water comes the barking of dogs.

A vast amount of wine is imported, about 30,000 tuns a year. The tun is proving a difficult measure to standardize, but it seems to be settling down as 252 gallons. About 2½ million gallons a year.

Scheyfve, the Imperial ambassador, thinks the English do far too much tavern-haunting. By a new law of last March taverns are to be limited in number, in London to forty, in Westminster to three. They are pretty well always open, except on Sundays during morning service and evensong. They are altogether classier institutions than alehouses, of which there are far more, and rank with the better sort of inn. Perlin is impressed by their opulence and by the tavern-keepers with their enormous purses of money. They charge you about 4d a gallon for Rochelle wine, 8d for Gascon.

Perlin has been jotting down for his compatriots some useful drinking phrases. Your drinking companion says to you constantly, 'Drind iou!'; you reply, 'I plaigiu'. To thank him for your drink you say, 'God tangue artelay'. When the Englishman is drunk he swears to you blood and death you shall drink all you have in your cup. If you are French he calls you 'orson vilain'.

The English working man is complaining of the fall in his standard of living, but Perlin declares he sees artisans – hatters and carpenters – throw down their crowns and tuck into every kind of meat, especially rabbit – English rabbits are very plump, sweet and tender – and he has never seen this anywhere else. He says the workpeople here earn more in a week than Germans or Spaniards in a month.

The wine trade is controlled by the City through the Vintners' Company. Soon after the new wines arrive in the autumn the Company appoints searchers to visit all places where the old wine is kept. Any which they condemn is thrown into the ditch, and the tavern-keeper sent off to prison.

Most French wines are at their best three or four months after vintage, not more than a year at the latest, but the stronger wines of Italy improve up to five or six years or even longer. Almost a quarter of all wine imported is Spanish, and at the beginning of October there may be three score English ships away in Spanish ports. Some of the Spanish wines are the strongest and most lasting: if you can afford it you put some down when a son is born (first making sure it has not been doctored in the Netherlands en route), and drink it at his coming of age. And Malmsey from Candia is much liked: it does not come in so often nowadays, but when it comes it is as likely to be in an English ship as a Venetian.[3]

iv

At the Three Cranes you hire your wherry; you can hire at any of the stairs. If there is not one waiting (they are in shortish supply, like lightermen) you shout 'Oars!' and 'Westward ho!' until a (probably disgruntled) waterman brings up his boat. He may say that he is just going home and Whitehall is not on the way, or it would be against wind and tide and you really need two men and he has only a boy today, but he will oblige.

The boat is 20 feet or so long, 4 or 5 broad amidships; it is narrow in the bottom and very shallow-built so it can get to stairs at low tide. Chronically unsafe in bad weather or with a bad waterman. But it has embroidered cushions to sit on and lean against, and a canopy for the rain or, on a hot July day, the sun. Very pleasant.

From the cushioned seat, Paul's stands up enormous. The tower is 280 feet, and the spire – wood covered with lead – is a further 200 feet or so. On the spire there is a steel ball, and on the ball a cross 15 feet high, and on the cross a copper-gilt weathercock 4 feet long. The ball no longer contains the relics, one assumes, which used to protect the spire from lightning – a piece of the True Cross, a stone from the Holy Sepulchre, some bones of St Ursula's

11,000 virgins. Relics are officially superstitious, but the spire was struck only twice while under their protection. What effective alternative is there in 1553?

Due west up this wherry-streaked swan-spotted reach of the Thames, three-quarters of a mile away, the river has a right-angle bend from the south. First though, on the north bank for ¼ mile, there are more wharves and city buildings down to the edge; and then, for ½ mile, walled lawns leading down to the water from great and noble buildings. And at the bend, facing the reach, is Whitehall Palace, amorphous but impressive.

On the south bank, Bankside is below high-tide mark, behind an embankment, so there are few buildings. The bear-cages and eternally barking kennels of John Allen's bear garden are a little towards the west. His mastiffs are so heavy they are said to wear shoes if they walk any distance. On Sunday, the most popular day, 200 or 300 people pay their 2d or 3d to see a programme of baitings, a desecration of the Sabbath deplored by both Protestants and Catholics.

Further along west are the Stewponds for fattening pike and tench, and taking away their muddy taste. Then Paris Garden Stairs, and some houses where a few years ago by royal proclamation the brothel-keepers and women were required to cease operations. Even Reformed Religion cannot de-strumpet by trumpet, but prostitution in London is not excessive compared with other great cities.

Eastward on the south bank, towards the Bridge, is a big stone mansion with large wharf and landing place, and its hall parallel to the river. That is Winchester House, the London house of the bishops of Winchester until Bishop Gardiner was put in the Tower. For seventeen years he had cherished like a bachelor its great quadrangle of buildings and its park. Now it is in the hands of Catherine Parr's brother, the Earl of Northampton, important ally of Northumberland. Northampton is making his own improvements, which must trouble Gardiner, who is not a tranquil man and hopes one day to have Winchester House back.

The Bear Garden and the Stews and the Stewponds were all under Gardiner's jursidiction, and he used a damp little prison, called the Clink, which is underneath the lesser buildings of Winchester House which fringe the embankment.

The big church beyond Winchester House, almost at the foot of the Bridge, is St Saviour's, formerly St Mary Overy ('over the water'), big enough to be a cathedral. The Augustinian priory of St Mary Overy was bought by a good Catholic, Sir Anthony Browne, who sold the church to the parishioners as their parish church, replaced the cloisters by a public bowling alley, and himself occupied the other priory buildings, the garden and orchard. As does now his heir, who is also Sir Anthony Browne and a good Catholic.

Afternoon sun, when it shines, shines very handsomely on the west side of the Bridge. Now, as the wherry rows upstream, cease for a moment smiling at the swans and look again at the north bank. You see the two slight hills of London, Paul's on the western, Leadenhall on the eastern. And notice how central the Steelyard was in the old days when sea-going ships came up to Queenhithe; and how commanding it still is. Queenhithe is still an important quay. The tide which carries up a ship from Gravesend to Billingsgate helps barges from Queenhithe as far as Twickenham on their way to Buckinghamshire, Berkshire, Oxfordshire.

Then breweries; and the wharf where salt is unloaded, measured, and sold; the wharf for timber and boards; and then, under the majestic mass of the cathedral, Paul's Wharf. For a short cut up to Newgate and Smithfield one can go up Paul's Wharf Hill to Paul's Chain, which is the gatehouse in the south wall of the cathedral precinct, and then into the cathedral and across the nave and out the other side. It is a short cut which appeals to porters with heavy loads, water-carriers with 3-gallon 'tankards' strapped to the back, market women with prodigious baskets of produce, and horse-dealers with a horse or two.

Another of Northumberland's most important allies has as his London house the powerful-looking Baynard's Castle, which rises sheer from the river bank. The Earl of Pembroke, William Herbert, is a strong, bony, reddish-faced man with a sharp eye. He can sign his name in capitals but cannot write or read much beyond that. Brave soldier – in his youth a quite mad fighting fellow. He is allowed to keep 100 armed men in his livery: some are no doubt down at Wilton, where he has built himself a huge mansion to replace the dissolved monastery, but some overflow into London streets from Baynard's Castle. Arms are common, and liveries are common, but a private troop of armed and liveried men is not a popular sight.

Down in Wiltshire the gentry look on Pembroke as an upstart. The springboard for his rise to wealth and rank was his first marriage, to a sister of Catherine Parr. His son has just married a sister of the devised next sovereign.

Then, still another brewery, and Puddle Wharf, and the splendid old Dominican priory of Blackfriars.[4]

v

Blackfriars is now an exclusive residential area. The old walls still surround its 5 acres, and there are four gates, and a porter to shut them at night. At the dissolution the priory buildings were divided between a number of noblemen and gentlemen, Sir Thomas Cawarden getting the largest share.

Cawarden is Master of the Revels and Keeper of the King's Tents, Hales and Toyles, and most of his gear is stored at Blackfriars. 'Hales' are temporary wooden sheds used as stables, and the like; 'toyles' are enclosures for driving game into, and are also used as barriers in tournaments. Like the tents, they are used in war as well as in Court entertainments. Properties and clothes for Court pageants, masques and plays are kept here too, and kept in good condition. They can be borrowed for private festivities, but they are efficiently got back again.

Cawarden has pulled down the friars' church, which, like all friars' churches, was very large and, like all monastic churches, had to be pulled down by the new owner unless it was to be used as the parish church; and he has also pulled down the parish church of St Anne which was in the precinct, ostensibly in order to built a store for the King's gear but actually to make himself a tennis court. He has had to provide the parishioners with a room in its place.

The remaining buildings are very fine: pillared and painted cloisters, chapter house with fine ceiling, splendid arches, gold paint. It was in Blackfriars that Charles V stayed when he visited Henry VIII thirty-one years ago, and it was in the upper frater of the priory that twenty-four years ago there was a public trial to decide whether the previous marriage of Mary's mother, Catherine of Aragon, to Henry's brother, Prince Arthur, had been consummated.

Like several other precincts, Blackfriars is outside the jurisdiction of the City. It is not bound by City regulations; it is not subject to the City watch; it is exempt from levies of men and money imposed by the City. The occupiers see to the paving and lighting, and appoint their own officials.

Blackfriars is in the south-west corner of the walled city, and the Fleet River issues insalubriously into the Thames by its side. On the other side of the Fleet is Bridewell Palace (three courtyards stretching from Fleet Bridge down to the Thames), which was specially built for Charles's staff when he was at Blackfriars, and the little bridge between the two was also put up for Charles's convenience.

It was in Bridewell that the annulment proceedings against Queen Catherine were heard. Mary was thirteen years old and had already judged between her English father and Spanish mother. Where is Mary now – and what is she like?

A few days ago, she was on her way to London, to see the King and, presumably, since she is aware that by Henry's devise she is heir to the throne, to put her foot down on Edward's devise, but she has turned back to

Norfolk. She is short, thin, reddish-haired, round-faced, with red-and-white complexion, wrinkled. Her eyes look piercing but are in fact short-sighted, and she has to hold writing very close. Her voice is rough and loud, almost like a man's, so that when she speaks she is heard a long way off. She has lost a lot of teeth. She suffers from indigestion and from her heart, and has headaches, and has often to take medicine and be blooded. She is no longer young, and without beauty. But she looks and is a nice woman, kind and generous. This in spite of having been rejected by her English father, and forcibly kept from her Spanish mother; in spite of having been required to honour her mother's supplanter and the supplanter's daughter, and to give up her own title of Princess; and having been pressurized for twenty years by kings and councillors to repudiate her religion, and niggarded by having her household constantly tampered with and pared down.

She is fairly well read in Italian literature, speaks Latin, French and Spanish, and understands Italian. She plays the lute and spinet, and has taught several of her young ladies. She loves clothes and jewels, and dresses with more colour and gorgeousness than is common in these Reformed days.

Her devotion to her religion and her Pope is total. Her experiences have made her trust no Englishman. Almost none: she trusts Cardinal Pole, who disapproved of Henry's divorce of her mother, but Pole lives in Italy and Mary has not seen him since she was a child. She trusts Charles above all men, but he lives in the Netherlands and she has not seen him either since she was a child.

She is conscious of her own royalty and is intensely loyal to it. But she has not been brought up to rule, knows little of affairs, has no reliable adviser, and has built up no body of supporters. It is right for Scheyfve to advise her to lie low: she must not be tempted into rash action by that obstinate faith and courage which have enabled her to hold to daily celebration of the Mass.

Henry quickly gave up use of Bridewell as a palace: it was not attractive, the Fleet smelled and plague recurrently threatened from London. It has been used since to house French ambassadors, and later Imperial ambassadors. Scheyfve is there now, and Renard and his colleagues will join him there. They are unlikely to be in Bridewell long, because ten days ago King Edward signed it over to the City to be a place where the unemployed of both sexes will be trained for useful employment. Edward, with much pleasure to himself and the City, has been very helpful to the City's plans for social welfare.

Many people besides Scheyfve live in Bridewell. Until the week before last it was conveniently outside the City's jurisdiction, being a royal precinct. Still outside is the former Carmelite precinct next door: Whitefriars is favoured by debtors and by students from the Temple, but quiet Sir John Cheke also lives there.

Then, very handsome, the gardens and buildings of the Inner and Outer Temple, leading up to Fleet Street at the Temple bar, and thence by Chancery Lane to Gray's Inn and the other inns of court. With the buying and selling of monastic property there has been a boom in conveyancing and litigation, which has brought a boom in legal education: partly because gentlemen need legal knowledge for their own protection, partly because the law has become so promising a career. Besides, the King's service is no longer the preserve of the Church, and gentlemen can become diplomats, treasurers, royal dogsbodies, if they are educated.

So gentlemen's sons are going to Oxford and Cambridge in increasing numbers and then, or alternatively, they come here to the inns of court. Secretary Cecil, Sir Thomas Gresham, and the attorney of the Court of Wards, Sir Nicholas Bacon, are all of both Cambridge and Gray's Inn. Of every five students in the inns of court, four are gentlemen; at the universities, only two out of five. To study here gives you social cachet, and as well a temporary reputation for wildness. There are no arrangements for supervision of students' conduct, so you are free of the city to your east and the Court to your west. And there is no tutorial system, although the Common Law is so formless and detailed a subject of study; so you try to read the textbooks printed by Richard Tottel in Fleet Street (he has the monopoly) and published and sold in the Fleet Street bookshops – they are mostly in English nowadays instead of Latin or Norman French. And in term time you attend the courts at Westminster, and the readings and exercises in your inn. But it is not term now, so the lodgings of the Fleet Street area are empty of students.[5]

vi

From here all along the riverside as far as the bend are the houses of noblemen, the fronts of their quadrangles looking down over walled gardens to the Thames, each with its stairs and barge. The backs and stables face northwards to the Strand. These were all once the houses of great ecclesiastics, who were at the same time the King's ministers and councillors.

First, Arundel House, which used to be the London house of the bishops of Bath and Wells. It was extensively rebuilt by Somerset's brother, Lord Thomas Seymour. After Seymour's execution it came to Henry Fitzalan, the twelfth Earl of Arundel, compared with whom the other leading noblemen on the Council have scarcely ceased to be commoners. Northumberland, Pembroke, Paulet, Paget and Northampton are all first generation noblemen.

Arundel is in his early forties, a strong healthy man, plain and sound, of few words but those spoken so fast that it is difficult to catch them. He does not like new-fangled words. He can speak French but refuses to: 'I like to speak in that language in which I can utter my mind and not mistake.' A man of dignity who does not particularly count any cost to himself. Able. When he was in charge of Calais he greatly strengthened it. He was Marshal of the Field at the taking of Boulogne. When he was Lord Chamberlain to Henry he laid down comprehensive and detailed instructions for the staff of the Household. During the rural troubles of 1549 he tranquillized Sussex without taking up arms: he told everyone to go home, except anyone with a just complaint, who should come to Arundel Castle and he would be heard. They trusted him, came, and were well fed. He amended some enclosures and put some complainants in the stocks, and that was that.

He supported Northumberland, Northampton and Pembroke in removing Somerset from the Council, but then he came up against them himself and was fined and imprisoned, and his eldest boy was dismissed from among Edward's friends. He was then accused of being in Somerset's suspected plot to assassinate them all in Paget's house, which is next door to Arundel House. So he was in the Tower again. But he was let out last December with a fine, was discharged of the fine last Sunday, and has been readmitted to the Council. He signed the letters patent, witnessing the King's statement of his desires, but he did not swear the bond to carry out those desires. However, he has not been sent back to the Tower.

Now Paget House, which used to belong to the bishops of Exeter, and now to William Paget, the first Baron Paget. He is a man of ordinary London birth, who was supported at Cambridge by the Boleyns, and was then in the household of Stephen Gardiner. He became one of Henry's Secretaries and was much relied on by him. He was on Edward's Council in the earlier part of the reign and worked for some years closely with Northumberland, but he was put in the Tower for the plot (trumped up? – No one knows) to murder Northumberland and friends in his house. Later he was accused of having made large sums improperly when he was Chancellor of the Duchy of Lancaster. Last year he was readmitted to the Council, but he was deprived of his Garter on the ground that his blood was ignoble. He was replaced in the Order by Northumberland's eldest son. He is an able civil servant of few convictions, who cannot be supposed to love Northumberland. He has a special hostility, too, to his old patron Stephen Gardiner, whom he was active in getting put in the Tower.

Now the great house which the Duke of Somerset left unfinished last year. It looks from the river just a mixture of old Norman and modern Tudor; it is the other side, facing the Strand, which has a marvellous sophisticated face of a kind quite new to London. Presumably the whole was to have been re-made to match. For the site Somerset took a churchyard, a church, an inn of chancery, a tenement and three bishops' houses, and he spent £10,000 in less than three years on building works. Somerset House has now been allotted to Princess Elizabeth but it is not the house she wants: it would cost a good deal to finish, and both the Princess and Cecil, who is her Surveyor, have an eye for thrift. She is not there at the moment.

Somerset House is one of the very new sights of London, while the Savoy next door has been a sight for forty years: a very large and beautiful building, standing right up to the Thames, by the same architect as Henry VII's chapel at Westminster and King's College chapel at Cambridge. Henry VII founded it, on the ruins of John of Gaunt's old palace, as a hospital to give nightly lodging to 100 poor folk. The main part of the building, where the beds are, is like a chapel, longer than King's but narrower, with great windows by the same glaziers. All very splendid. According to the rules, an hour before sunset the poor folk were to be admitted, and cleaned up in hot baths, and their clothes deloused. They were to be given a bed with blankets and clean sheets, and a tapestry coverlet in the Tudor colours, and matching white-and-green curtains to pull round it. And they were to be seen off, prayed over but not fed, by seven in summer, eight in winter. But it degenerated into a miserable and scandalous doss, and within the last few days the King has closed the hospital and handed over to the City all the lands it was endowed with, and all the beds, bedding and furniture, to help maintain the future Bridewell and also St Thomas's Hospital in Southwark. The City will give pensions to the dishonest staff.

Next comes the house which used to belong to the bishops of Carlisle and now belongs to the Earl of Bedford, the Lord Privy Seal; a very honest decent man, of moderate Protestant views, he is blind in one eye from an old arrow wound. For what it is worth, Scheyfve says Bedford opposed the devise. But Bedford signed up as witness to the letters patent, like Paget and Arundel. And he swore the bond to see the devise carried out, like Paget.[6]

vii

And now Durham House, which belonged to the bishops of Durham until Henry pushed the excellent Tunstall into Coldharbour; and on Henry's death it belonged to Elizabeth until early this year Northumberland pushed the excellent Princess into Somerset House. For the head of government Durham House is more convenient than Ely Place up in Holborn where Northumberland had been living some few years. It is an old Norman building rising straight out of the Thames, with a small tower at its east end;

the chapel and hall are just behind, and there is a court, with stables and so on reaching up to the Strand, and there is a garden on the east side stretching the whole depth of the site.

The Northumberlands have been married thirty years and had thirteen children, of whom five sons and two daughters are living. Jane Northumberland is a literate, capable woman, and her children have been well educated. Brilliant twenty-five-year-old John Dee has just written a treatise on tides at her request, and has taught both parents and children some mathematics and cosmography.

All five sons and Northumberland's brother Ambrose Dudley actively work with him, and are men of courage. And both daughters have married men of ability and integrity: Mary has married Henry Sidney, and Catherine has married Henry Hastings, the Protestant elder son of the Catholic Earl of Huntingdon. The family has an air of being competent, decently cultivated, and more than commonly stable and loving. But it is large. Anyone even slightly hostile to Northumberland must feel that wherever he goes he stumbles into a Dudley son, Dudley daughter-in-law, Dudley brother, Dudley daughter, or Dudley son-in-law. Their mere existence suggests that titles, lands, jobs are being found for them. Was not the first Baron Paget pushed out of the Order of the Garter, and Northumberland's John, Earl of Warwick, pushed in?

But he has not got them great estates. Maybe he has not needed to because he has got them for himself? It is true that in the early stages of rebuilding his family fortunes he fought hard for his own and his wife's property rights and quasi-rights; there was no great sin in that. Under Henry he became Viscount Lisle and Earl of Warwick, with grants of land to match, as proper reward for military services. Under Edward he has become Duke of Northumberland, with grants of land to match, as proper reward for military services and for being head of the government. His lands are worth about £4,300 p.a., a good deal less than were Somerset's, but he is one of the wealthiest nobles. His income is about the same as was Tunstall's when Bishop of Durham and President of the Council of the North, or Gardiner's when Bishop of Winchester.

He certainly has not spent the country's wealth on new buildings for himself. He has put up no mansion in London or the country; at Ely Place and Syon and here at Durham House he has simply done routine repairs.

Edward noted a few months ago how anxious he was to have most of the Bishop of Durham's estates taken over by the Crown, and to have the management of them in his own hands. Was this avarice? Management is not ownership, but it is profitable. Or was it sense? The north of England has lagged in the religious revolution, and in economic development, and it is open to invasion from Scotland and therefore France. Those estates need to be under the control of an efficient, loyal, Protestant subject. Who more efficient, loyal, Protestant than himself?

It was here at Durham House that Jane Grey and Guildford Dudley were married last Whitsunday, 21 May, by the rites of the new Prayer Book. A marriage cannot be easy which binds a highly strung, opinionated blue stocking to a well-built, vigorous young man without intellectual or religious pretensions, and is unlikely to be eased by the news that the bride is to be Queen. Jane was soon in something of a state and, disobeying Jane Northumberland, went home to mother, to Suffolk House which is the next (and ex-episcopal) house along. Jane has now left Suffolk House and gone into the country, to Chelsea.

At the river bend here, beyond Durham House, are breweries and back entrances and then Scotland. Scotland is where kings of Scotland used to put up when they came to London: the grandmother of Mary Queen of Scots, Henry's elder sister Margaret, stayed here when she was the widow of James IV of Scotland.

And then Whitehall Palace, which Henry enlarged after he took it from Wolsey. An assemblage of courtyards, halls, chambers, and galleries with windows on both sides. From the outside it looks unplanned, but inside it is comfortable, and very handsome indeed, with much gilding and carving and many painted ceilings, and the many times repeated face and figure of Henry of immortal memory, and tapestries, tapestries, tapestries. While the Court is at Greenwich there is only a caretaking staff at Whitehall, and all the tapestries are put away.

On the further side of the palace, King Street runs down from Charing Cross to Westminster with, on its west side, the Tiltyard and Tennis Court and St James's Park, and beyond, in the fields, St James's Palace. From Whitehall Palace's main buildings one can reach the Park and the Tiltyard by crossing over King Street through the upper parts of a fine gateway, named after the late Hans Holbein, which serves as a bridge.

The wherry might well now turn back towards London, say to Blackfriars.[7]

viii

The waterman will presently, if he has not already done so, give his opinion on the subject of fares: they are too low; they have been the same for years. He is right. They are governed by a law of 1514 which made compulsory the fares which even then had been compulsory 'time out of mind'. The rich men in the City government, he says, prevent them from being raised; and everyone knows prices have trebled – the other rich men in the Duke of Northumberland's government have seen to that, making themselves richer and everyone else poorer. Who made everyone's silver sixpence worth fourpence? Who put a ragged staff on the King's coins? It is true that, a while ago, a few coins did look as if the three leopards had been replaced by Northumberland's emblem if you were determined to see them that way; but it was simply that a mould at the Mint had cracked.

What should he be paid for the round trip? A fare of 2d would be reasonable. The waterman can be fined if he overcharges and, as usual with fines, half would go to the King and half to the informer. But anyone who informs against a waterman is a fool. A stranger would be advised to pay a little more than a Londoner, say 2½d, and go in peace.

For a drink or supper in the Blackfriars neighbourhood one could do worse than walk straight through the precinct, turn left through Ludgate, then down Ludgate Hill, and into the St John's Head. Two questions for meditation or discussion there.

First: the majority of London businessmen are Protestants. Have they ganged up against the Catholic minority either in everyday business or in the Companies? No. Then do English businessmen keep religion in second place? No, but it is not allowed to affect business. And vice versa.

Second: the Council. This group of high-powered heterogeneous noblemen have been held together for four years – since Somerset's fall in 1549 – by a man who has neither royal blood nor even prestigious birth, and who has had neither legal nor military power over them. How has Northumberland done it? He has kept them working hard, especially at the country's finances; that has probably helped. And perhaps he has done the civilian equivalent of making them kiss one another's sword, and reminded them of their duty to their king. And perhaps, as in battle, they have reminded themselves that united effort brings success, and success brings profit.[8]

3

Aldgate to Cheapside and Guildhall

i

The eastern boundary of the City is 'the bars', 300 yards east of Aldgate. It is on a wide cobbled road which comes from Mile End and Whitechapel, with a few good houses on the north side, a few tenements on the south, and common fields on both. The lane just within the bars, Hog Lane, going to the north-west, should be avoided: all summer it smells terribly, full of infection, and all winter it is filthy in deep mud. Hogs can be kept outside the walls as here, but by regulation not inside.

As the road approaches Aldgate there are good inns for travellers from East Anglia, and then St Botolph's with a large churchyard; a paved street, Houndsditch, runs north-west by the church, separated by a mud wall from the city ditch.

The alterations in Houndsditch exemplify this age of rapid change. Twenty years ago it was lined with little two-storeyed houses for the bedridden poor: devout Londoners walked this way of a Friday, and through the low windows looked at the poor folk in their beds and gave them food or money. At that time, beyond the houses to the east, there was a field where you could walk, belonging to the priory of Holy Trinity Christchurch. Then the field became market gardens, where you could not walk but which you could at least see. Within the last few months it has been divided into garden plots for rich men to build themselves summerhouses and put up brick walls all the way round. And Houndsditch has no more little houses tempting one to charity: only dealers, mostly in old clothes, and gunfounders. Houndsditch makes good ordnance, but not handguns, which are imported from Germany.

St Botolph Aldgate is a fairly typical London parish church. It still has its bells, but there has been parish argument as to whether they should be sold. Bell-ringing, other than simple tolling, is Popish, but Londoners love their bells, just as bells. The organ is still in the church but it is not played. However there is music, because the English like to sing, and the congregation sings a great deal. Cranmer has instructed that as far as possible there should be only one note to a syllable, and all the words should be clearly audible; as a result the present compositions of Tye, Tallis and Shepherd are strong and easily singable, very different from the magnificent polyphonic elaborations which used, popishly, to hide the verbal meaning.

It is the meaning, the simple literal meaning, of Scripture and Reformed Religion which has burst like a sun on so many Londoners. Compared to it music, vestments, rich plate are nothing – worse than nothing, idolatrous interpositions. There is a Bible in St Botolph's, as in all other churches, in English, *in English*; and Erasmus's paraphrase of the New Testament, *in English*. The entire history and meaning of life, God's words of guidance and comfort, for men to read for themselves – after centuries of the Bible being hugged out of reach by priests and the Pope, who confused innocent Englishmen with Latin mumbo-jumbo and bamboozled them with superstition.

The high altar of St Botolph's has been taken down. Instead there is a table east-and-west, and the minister stands on the north side for Morning and Evening Prayer. For Communion, communicants sit round the table, usually one from each family. Instead of the congregation receiving only half the sacrament, the bread, as in the Mass, while the other half is reserved for the priest, the congregation receive both bread and wine. At first the families used to take turns in supplying a loaf of the bread they used at home and some wine, but now, more conveniently, they take turns in giving the clerk 2d after Matins.

Since 1549 there has been an English *Book of Common Prayer,* in plain English. To outlandish people like Cornishmen English prayers are probably as unintelligible as Latin, and to many they were at first almost blasphemous. The common people took to arms against them down in Cornwall and Devon, and even here at St Botolph's the conservative curate had to be got rid of; but, on the whole, London was happy enough, and is happier still now. The complaint of radicals was that the reform was timid: the status of the bread and wine was left ambiguous. Cranmer has now put that right, encouraged by continental Protestants like Bucer and Bullinger. There is no ambiguity in the new prayer book published last November. The bread remains bread; there is no magical change of its substance into the substance of Christ's body, and its taste, smell, mass, its accidents, do not hang alone in the air without any bread-substance to inhere in. The Mass, or rather the Communion, is now specifically an act of remembrance; there is no True Presence: 'Take, eat this remembrance that Christ died for thee and feed on him in thy heart by faith with thanksgiving.' It is received on the knees, but not in adoration of the bread and wine.

The old Catholic service books have been sold off. At St Botolph's the buyer managed to remain anonymous. The paraphernalia of idolatry have been destroyed at St Botolph's as everywhere else: rood screens have been broken up, images smashed (only of saints, not of noblemen or businessmen), and the walls have had texts written over the whitewashed wall-paintings, with the arms of the head of the Church. Honest plainness is agreed to be essential, so churches have obeyed pretty well the instructions received a couple of months ago to send any gold- or silver-embroidered vestments or copes to the Master of the King's Wardrobe, and to sell any others and send the money to the King's Treasurer. Chalices and other plate have been sent to the Master of the King's Jewels in the Tower, and just one plain cup reserved for use (large, instead of the small chalice for priest only). After all, what more is needed?

St Botolph's held their sale in May, providing beer and ale as is customary. The plate fetched about £30, and twelve copes of velvet with gold embroidery about £2 each. Most of the lots fell to Robert Dunkin, a tailor of Cornhill, and some to Humphrey Allen, a tailor of Houndsditch. The parish would have liked to spend the money on dwellings for the curate and clerk, but commissioners arrived from the Lord Mayor to take it all for the King. Or for the Council, or Northumberland – who can say?

Has no one been appalled by the desecration of images and the transmogrification of the Mass? Is no one angered by the blasphemous questionings of Reforming activists? How does the whole Christ become a piece of bread? Is a tiny homunculus hidden in each crumb? Or does just a part of Christ become bread? Which part? Are any parts left out?

The explicit opposition has been less than one would have expected. Common people have rebelled in other parts of the country for a variety of reasons of which religion has been one, but not in London. In the whole country there have been only two martyrs for religion, two in the last six years since the Mass was destroyed, and they were not Catholics but Anabaptists.

The punishment for attending other forms of worship is laid down as six months imprisonment for the first offence, twelve months for the second, life for the third.

Perhaps Edward's Council has acted with forbearance because Reformed Religion has not been fully codified? It is pretty well codified now. Last year there was Cranmer's second Prayer Book; last month the Forty-two Articles, and the Catechism of John Ponet, Bishop of Winchester in succession to Gardiner; and Cranmer's revision of the canon law, defining with precision the many criminal varieties of heresy and idolatry, has been ready a good while for Parliamentary approval. When Jane is Queen it is unlikely she will forbear with dissenters: no monarch tolerates religious dissent.

People of the Reformed Religion, prompted maybe by hearing and reading God's Word in English, have a developing feeling that the English are God's Chosen People. There is attachment to the legend that, in one of God's special operations, Joseph of Arimathea and some of the Apostles evangelized Britain. And Constantine was born in Britain. So England never owed anything to Rome. Nor to Germany. The German Luther has spoken out these thirty years, and the Swiss Zwingli these twenty, but England's John Wycliffe preached the truth 150 years ago, there have been Englishmen ever since who have suffered for it, and now England is the only nation, only real nation, to adopt true religion.

Every Sunday at St Botolph's and in every other church the congregation prays:

Priest:	O Lord, save the King.
Answer:	And mercifully hear us when we call upon thee.
Priest:	Endue thy Ministers with righteousness.
Answer:	And make thy chosen people joyful.
Priest:	O Lord, save thy people.
Answer:	And bless thine inheritance.
Priest:	Give peace in our time, O Lord.
Answer:	Because there is none other that fighteth for us but only thou, O God.

This last answer is literally true: the heretic English have no useful allies.

Further, English divines such as Latimer, enamoured of the splendid Protestantism of Edward, and not averse to out-Poping the Pope, have been stressing afresh St Paul's doctrine of the divine nature of kings. A king is God's chosen viceroy, not always wise and good, but incontrovertibly chosen by God to rule, to be obeyed whether you think him right or wrong, in religion as well as in secular matters.[1]

ii

Aldgate is a heavy, thick, Norman-style gatehouse. Like the other gates, it is normally allotted by the City as a residence to one of its retired servants, who is then responsible for it, employing citizens for the actual opening and closing at dawn and dusk. The guard is doubled at the present time.

The night watch has also been doubled, but not the other constables who relieve them at dawn. Aldgate Ward normally has six constables all told, under the control of its alderman, Thomas Offley. He also has nine scavengers. The day-to-day supervision of the ward's affairs is done by his deputy and a beadle. Householders act as constable, scavenger and so on in rotation, but often pay someone to deputize, that is to say they 'pay scot' rather than 'bear lot'.

Just inside the gate, at the beginning of Aldgate Street, there are a well and a pump where early in the morning water-carriers, servants and poor men's wives fill their buckets or barrels. A few apprentices too, although it is not proper work for an apprentice. The water-carriers barge their way through the streets with their broad-bottomed 3-gallon tankards strapped to their backs, and are a menace. And at seven, morning and evening, the ward scavengers draw water for street cleaning.

In a house overlooking Aldgate Pump, only recently set up in business, is a young Merchant Taylor, John Stow. What distinguishes Stow is that he collects relics and records of London's past. If he had his way, this age, which has destroyed so much of the past, would also be the first to try to preserve it.

Further along Aldgate Street lives one of London's two sheriffs for the year – a bald, clean-shaven chap with a pucker in his right cheek as if he were a joker – John Maynard. Maynard, like Stow, casts some backward looks. Last month he put on, at his own expense, a carnival procession from his house here, just to give the citizens some nostalgic merriment: morris dancers, giants, hobby horses, minstrels, men in armour, trumpeters, standard-bearers, his retainers in velvet and with gold chains, and a devil and a puppet show. An expensive affair, but London merchants are prosperous. There are a dozen or score of them worth £50,000 or more.

Both wealthy Maynard and modest Stow probably breakfasted in much the same way at six or seven this morning: herrings, salted or pickled, and/or cold meat, and bread and cheese, and ale.

A typical merchant's house has glass windows nowadays, and not only for the living quarters, but for the shop and workshop. The Companies insist on goods being both made and sold by daylight.

Another sign that the English, in spite of the European picture of them, may indeed be the Chosen People, is that they make their houses smell sweet with strewn herbs, and are apt to have flowers in their windows, and even in their workshops.

On the north side of Aldgate Street is what used to be the priory of Holy Trinity Christchurch, one of the richest in London. Sir Thomas Offley acquired it and offered the big Norman church free to anyone who would take it away, but he had finally to knock it down himself and sell the stones at 6d or 7d a cartload, and he built the roofless nave and choir into his new mansion.

St Catherine's Christchurch, in the cemetery of the priory, still remains as the parish church. The curate likes to preach from an elm tree, and for a Communion table he uses a tombstone and faces north, whereas the orthodox heretic faces south.

Follow Aldgate Street along. There are good merchants' houses all along here. Very soon on the north side is St Andrew Undershaft, which was rebuilt on a larger scale twenty or thirty years ago when a good many parish churches became too small. The increase in population was due presumably to the Tudor peace of the previous forty or fifty years, and to recovery, slow but at last achieved, from the Black Death of the fourteenth century. However, pressure on church space has declined: first the old religion became unpopular with some, and now the new religion is unpopular with others.

St Andrew's is called 'Undershaft' because there used to be a maypole in front, taller than the church tower. Just before the rebuilding, the maypole was taken down and hung along the houses over the front doors. It stayed there until four years ago, when the curate of St Catherine's Christchurch preached a sermon at Paul's Cross attacking the idolatrous names of the days of the week, and the idolatrous names of many churches, including St Andrew Undershaft. That same afternoon the householders got the pole down and cut it in pieces, each keeping his share as perquisite.

The rector of St Andrew Undershaft is John Standish, who is also archdeacon of Colchester in Essex, vicar of Northill in Bedfordshire, and rector of Wigan in Lancashire. About half the beneficed clergy in London are pluralists like Standish, employing curates. About half are, like him, married. The marriage of clergy was authorized by Convocation and then by Parliament five years ago. Northumberland says many of the new divines are 'so sotted with their wives and children that they forget both their poor neighbours and all other things which to their calling appertaineth'. There would be a great untying of conjugal knots if Mary were to accede.[2]

iii

Aldgate Street now becomes Cornhill Street, always crowded, with fine merchants' houses-cum-shops particularly on the south side, and the famous, useful old Leadenhall, which belongs to the City, also on the south side. It is a large stone building around a very large square courtyard.

Leadenhall is the great wool market (raw wool and wool yarn, not cloth), with the largest wool warehouse in the kingdom, and on the east side of the gate it has the beam on which export wool is weighed for customs duty. Wool comes to London from all directions by road, and some of it by sea from the south and east coasts; and then it is carried west and north to the cloth-making areas, by the same wagons which have brought up their cloth, which is sold not in Leadenhall but at Blackwell Hall. Bales of cloth and wool all have clipped to them for identification a little lead tag carrying the merchant's initials or heraldic device. Wool prices are low this year after three years when they were very high. The wool merchants sell wool for export here as well as at Calais. Their Company, the Staplers, rents rooms in Leadenhall from the City and sublets them to its members.

Leadenhall also has, on the west side of the gate, the beam for grain. And the courtyard is a market, particularly for 'foreigners' bringing victuals into London. It is well known for fresh fish, and 'foreign' butchers are here on Wednesdays and Saturdays between nine and twelve. Nowadays there is a certain demand for prime mutton: hitherto the commercial value of sheep has been almost entirely in wool and dung. Leadenhall is also the storehouse and workshop for the City's gear for pageants and processions.

In the middle of the crossroads outside Leadenhall there is a castellated conduit, with similar water-collecting activities as at Aldgate Pump, and a few yards west there are some stocks. It is a very busy part of the city. Porterage and cartage are constant between the carriers' termini in innyards and the markets and the merchants' stores and the beams and the wharves.

From here Cornhill slopes down. On both sides there are big houses, and on the left two parish churches almost side by side. St Peter Cornhill, which has a famous preacher, John Pullen, is the church of the Fishmongers. Last Thursday, which was St Peter's Day, the Company attended service here in new liveries, as on every 29 June. By the Fishmongers' rules the members must have a new livery every two years but not give any livery away to an apprentice or anyone outside the fraternity: with the exception that, as token of friendship, eight Fishmongers must every year exchange newly made liveries with eight Goldsmiths. The two Companies are so near in status that if they were not friends they would be mortal enemies and so loosen the City's nexus of goodwill and discipline.

You are surprised that Fishmongers have the same status as Goldsmiths? Some of them are among the richest men in the city. There are over 100 freemen in the Company, rather more of them selling saltfish than stockfish. Fresh fish are only a small part of the trade. Saltfish are mostly herrings, cod, eels, whiting, mackerel from the east coast, the Netherlands and the Baltic. Stockfish are dried fish such as cod and haddock, mostly from Norway and Iceland.

St Michael Cornhill nearby is darkened by tenements the parish has just built on its little churchyard fronting Cornhill. It has, but does not use, the best ring of six bells in England. The sixth bell, named Rus after the alderman who donated it, is rung at eight every evening.

Before moving from St Michael's, note that it has a book (of paper, alas, not parchment), where every baptism, marriage and burial in the parish is registered. Throughout England (more or less) parish registers have been kept since Thomas Cromwell ordered it in 1538. He had seen the practice in the Netherlands, where it had been introduced by the Spaniards.

Every person living in London, whether a citizen or not, is a member of a parish, under the care of a parish church and vestry. It is through the parishes that many of the appeals to morality and charity are made by the City, the Crown, the Church.

The rector of St Michael Cornhill, John Willoughby, a quite noted physician, is another of the married clergy. It is a good living, worth £33 a year, but he is not keeping the rectory in good repair.

Leave St Michael's. On the other side of Cornhill, with tenements facing the street, is the Weigh House where merchandise from abroad has to be weighed on the Great Beam. There are porters, and a cart, and four horses to watch out for.

The houses are taller as you get to the bottom of the hill, past on the left the back gate of Sir Martin Bowes, goldsmith and sometime Lord Mayor. His front door is 75 yards south in Lombard Street, and there are two passages through to Lombard Street via the Pope's Head and the Cardinal's Hat, inns which have signs untouched by Reformed Religion.

Not only inns and taverns have signs, of course: fishmongers are apt to be at the sign of The Dolphin or The Salmon; shoemakers at the sign of The Boot, or The Cobbler's Last, or The Three Goats' Heads, the emblem of the Cordwainers. Sir Thomas Gresham's house and goldsmith's shop is at the sign of The Grasshopper.

Gresham keeps a 'running cash' at The Grasshopper: his clients can get cash at any time in exchange for a 'bill'. Business dealings as a whole are on credit, with specific dates for payment, and the 'bills' are enforceable in the courts. Interest is illegal, so it is charged by inflating the principal.

Merchants are apt to congregate around here, in the passages through to Lombard Street, and in Lombard Street. Gresham's father used to say a long while ago that they ought to have a covered meeting place, an 'exchange', like merchants in Antwerp, and there has been talk of using part of Leadenhall, but nothing has come of it.[3]

iv

Now, the heart of the city. At the bottom of Cornhill is the Stocks Market, which is a rectangular area containing a covered market and the churches of St Mary Woolnoth and St Stephen Walbrook. The market has eighteen meat stalls and twenty-five fish, with rooms over. Living in one of the houses facing the Stocks Market, on its east side, is the weightier of this year's sheriffs, William Garrard. Enterprising, grave and a very great merchant, with heavy jowl, close-cropped hair, he is friend of Sir William Petre, the senior Secretary.

On the other side of the Stocks, the Poultry slopes gently up, with the shops and houses of grocers, haberdashers, upholsterers, and several inns. The poulterers used to be here (they scalded their birds in Scalding Alley), but they have moved now to Gracechurch Street. Four doors beyond Scalding Alley a long passage leads to one of the two Counters, the prisons used by the sheriffs.

Then there is The Red Cock, the haberdashery shop of homely, cheerful Hobson, who makes everyone laugh. It is Hobson who is supposed to have written an epitaph on an undistinguished friend: 'He was begotten, born, and cried. He lived a long time, fell sick, and died.' Hobson flourishes. When the chapel of Corpus Christi next door was dissolved four years ago he bought it for a warehouse and shops, which he has called The Golden Cock. He is always complaining that the moment his back is turned his apprentices slip out to a tavern or to eat pies across the road at the Dagger. On Sundays they follow him obediently to church but at the door disappear to find a drink.

Apprentices are recognized by their blue smocks and white breeches. They serve seven years, living in, and during that time they are supposed not to haunt taverns or gamble, and to be celibate. An apprentice is also supposed not to 'absent himself from his master's service by day or night unlawfully', so he is constantly at beck. Nevertheless there are always plenty propping up walls, and making ribald comments on passers-by.

Then Conihope Lane leading up to Grocers' Hall, and Old Jewry, and a rich church, St Mary Cole, where Thomas Becket was baptized, London's patron un-saint. The parish of St Mary Cole sold their plate, vestments, altar cloth and pall two years before the Council's instructions and raised £70 for parish uses. Next to St Mary Cole is a famous tavern, the Mitre, over four shops, and in the middle of the street is the Great Conduit, which is a lead cistern of water castellated around with stone, much used by water-carriers. The water is piped from the Tyburn two or three miles west. The turning on the left, going backwards south-east is Bucklersbury, mostly grocers and apothecaries.

Here at the Great Conduit is the beginning of West Cheap, Cheap, or Cheapside. It is wide, but the market stalls down the middle clog it somewhat. On the left is the wonder of visitors: the window displays of gold plate and medals in Goldsmiths' Row. What are the gilded sculptures on the face of the houses? They are woodmen, because a Mr Wood built Goldsmiths' Row sixty years ago when he was sheriff, and he gave it all – four storeys, ten houses, fourteen shops – to the Goldsmiths' Company, together with money to be lent out to set up young men in the shops. The Goldsmiths' Company stamps with its assay mark both gold and silver. There is more gold and silver on the market now, with Spanish imports from America and the melting down of church plate. The Goldsmiths also own the Eagle tavern nearby.

The next group of fine houses and shops on the left are owned mostly by mercers, selling not only silks but velvets and rich cloths in general, and on the right-hand side of Cheap is Mercers' Hall. Underneath their hall, at street level, are shops. Behind are courtyards and cloisters used by the Company as offices, dwellings, storerooms; and there is an armoury, since Companies are responsible for arming a number of their members. All these premises were part of the Hospital of St Thomas Acon (not a medical hospital), dissolved fifteen years ago. The Mercers bought the lot. In the chapel there are still some of the old monuments but most have been defaced in the last four or five years. The Mercers have reopened the free grammar school which used to be run by the Hospital.

In all the streets along here off the south side of Cheap, such as Bread Street, there are good houses for merchants, and inns for travellers and carriers. The Mermaid in Bread Street is famous for fish dinners. Also in Bread Street is the second and larger of the sheriffs' counters; both are open all night for the reception of anyone arrested by the watch. They are intended specifically for offenders against City laws, and anyone else who finds himself in a counter is transferred to another prison as soon as possible. The keeper of the Bread Street counter is an undisciplined, cruel man but the City cannot get rid of him: a man's job, after all, is his property – especially if he has paid good money for it.

Now, up Ironmonger Lane off the north side of Cheap, and across Catt Street and Lothbury with its brass foundries and their rasping and banging: the first building on the left in Basinghall Street is one of the most important buildings in London, Blackwell Hall, where the national market for woollen cloth is held every Wednesday, Thursday and Friday, opening at nine and closing at noon.

Cloth can be sold freely in the shops of liverymen of the Drapers' Company and the Merchant Taylors', but 'foreigners', including all cloth-makers and cloth-dealers of the Cotswolds, the Midlands, Wales, the North and East Anglia, cannot sell in London except here at Blackwell Hall. And only freemen of London can buy here. The Hanse used to have the privilege but not this last two years, so they and London-based Italian and Flemish merchants have to buy either at up-country markets or from the shops of Drapers or Merchant Taylors.

Cloth is mostly semi-finished when it is for export, and some of it comes back again for sale in London after dying and finis' ing in Antwerp. Broadcloth goes mostly to the Netherlands and German the kerseys, the lighter cloths, go through Italian hands in Antwerp (the .talians dominate business in Antwerp) and thence to Italy by land. Carriers between Antwerp and Italy are faster, more regular and more secure than ships which have to brave Barbarossa's pirates in the western Mediterranean. From Italy, English kerseys go east to the Levant, and west to Spain and the New World. There have been complaints about English broadcloths and kerseys: short length, poor quality. Merchant Taylors and Merchant Adventurers do not, as sellers, admit there can be anything wrong with English cloth; but as buyers they complain much, and are echoed by the London Clothworkers – there is too much get-rich-quick production by country clothiers. The old trouble: outside London, according to London, not enough training, not enough supervision.

There may be another trouble. English pastures have improved (with enclosing), so fleeces are heavier than they used to be, and the wool has a longer fibre. With the best will in the world it does not make as good broadcloth, although excellent for the lighter cloths. Wools nowadays need more sophisticated sorting and grading, and are only slowly getting it. The people to do it are the wool-broggers who go around buying raw wool. Unfortunately an axiom of the day is that middlemen are one of the sources of economic trouble, so last year wool-broggers were, legally, abolished.

To 'field' a piece of cloth in Blackwell Hall costs 1d, and a further ½d a week for the time it remains there. There are the clerks and porters to be maintained but the City makes about £1,000 a year profit.[4]

v

Just west of Blackwell Hall, along Catt Street, is Guildhall Gate, giving entrance to the yard of Guildhall. The Great Hall of the City's Guildhall is very large, two-thirds as long and wide as the King's huge Westminster Hall. Wherever the eye falls – on stone walls, purbeck marble floors, stained glass windows, timber roof, tapestries – it is on the effects of corporate strength: of the civic loyalty and generosity of both Companies and individual citizens, and of their decent affluence and steady solvency. The Companies built it, but the individual Richard Whittington is here in the floor and windows as he is in so many places in the city: in the stone wall round the pool outside Cripplegate, in the rebuilding of Newgate, in the foundation of (now dissolved) Whittington College, the repair of St Bartholomew's Hospital, and in the library of Guildhall (unfortunately destroyed by Somerset). Every generation of City magnates has had care for civic works, contrasting with the nobility who have spent on houses and chantries for their own present display and future comfort.

The governing body of London, the Common Council, is elected annually by the whole body of freemen, ward by ward, and it meets in the Great Hall half a dozen times a year. The city is protected against mere democracy by the Council being weighted with aldermen, and by its being large and therefore a bore to attend: the real work is done by the Court of Aldermen.

There is an alderman for each ward, selected by the Court of Aldermen itself from four nominees put forward by the freemen of the ward. He is likely to be a successful practical man, eminent in his trade, eminent on his parish council, eminent in his ward-mote, and eminent in his Company. If he is not already a member of a major Company he must immediately become one. Sir John Ayliffe, alderman for Bridge Ward Without (which is Southwark), had to leave the Barber-Surgeons and get himself accepted by the Grocers.

The City is structured for the production of capable conservative governors, and as a result is sound and strong. Which is not to say there are no conflicts of interest within the organism. Mutual recrimination between cloth-merchants and cloth-makers is eternal, and is paralleled in every area of trade: between Leathersellers and Glovers, Cordwainers and Curriers, Haberdashers and Feltmakers. But the City, with unceasing ceremonies and banquets and committees, holds everyone pretty well on speaking terms.

And is not afraid to discipline important citizens. When Thomas White, Merchant Taylor, refused to serve as Cornhill alderman he was fined; he still refused; he was put in prison and his shop windows were boarded up; he gave way. The Lord Mayor and the sheriffs are elected from the aldermen: last year two aldermen were fined for refusing the post of second sheriff, which was ultimately filled by Maynard.

The Court of Aldermen meets two or three times a week. At its meeting on the morning of Thursday, 6 July there is nothing unusual on the rough hew or, as some people call it, 'agenda'. The Court will deal with Edward Hobson, Tiler, who has forged a 'bill', and will probably put him in the stocks in Cheap. It has to see that a recent Act of the Common Council for the pulling down of unlawful penthouses is put into force: the first action will be to have it proclaimed in the streets. It will note that Sir William Chester, alderman for Farringdon Ward Without, has granted his car-room to John Richard, Armourer. It will more or less automatically confer the freedom of the city on David Evans and John Bryden, who have become Clothworkers 'by redemption', that is to say they have not served apprenticeships and so have to pay fines of £6 13s 4d; and on John Morse, who has to pay £10 to become a Leatherseller. It has to authorize the City Chamberlain to pay somebody at the Exchequer 40s for supplying copies of certain records. And, as so often, it has some orphanage cases: when a freeman dies his widow, or someone else, has to bring sureties for the maintenance of his children.

The Court of Aldermen fixes prices, from bread to tallow candles, and also the price the chandler, who is usually poor but a citizen, shall pay the butcher for tallow. It settles a squabble between the parson of St Peter Cornhill and one of his tenants. It cares for the city's beer and wine. It punishes selling coal underweight, burying the filth of a jakes (cesspit) within the city, fornication, and reporting that the King is dead.

The administration of the City is fairly tight. In each ward the alderman is expected not only to maintain order and cleanliness, but to keep a roll of the name, dwelling and trade of every inhabitant. And within each ward each parish council normally knows every individual in its area with some intimacy. The Londoner likes to think he is freer than the inhabitant of almost any foreign city you can name, but he is also more closely (efficiently) organized for his welfare and protection, and more closely (efficiently) known to authority.

Just as the aldermen are a long-serving stable body, so are the permanent officials. Robert Smart has been Swordbearer (in charge of the mayoral household) for fifteen years, John Green Common Crier and Serjeant-at-Arms for thirteen. One can start low in the career structure among the meal weighers or the thirty or forty serjeants and yeomen, and finish up as swordbearer.

The serjeants and yeomen see that the streets are kept clear of rubbish and ill-placed scaffolding, and that people are fined who throw water out of windows, put excreta in the street, or pile rubbish in front of a neighbour's house. Others see that victuals and fuel brought by water, chiefly to Billingsgate, are sold at the prices fixed by the City. The Water Bailiff sees there is no fishing out of season, or with the wrong sort of net, or by the erection of unlawful weirs. The Common Hunt looks after the City's hawks and hounds: the hounds are for hunting hares and otters, and are kept in a dog house in Moorfields. And the Lord Mayor himself is expected to go out into the streets and check now and again that regulations, especially of prices and weight, are in fact being observed.

For its justice the City has its own courts, held here in Guildhall and manned by practising business men – the Lord Mayor, sheriffs and aldermen – helped by the Recorder. The City courts have a good reputation for their judgments, and for being quicker and cheaper than the King's courts at Westminster. On the dais of the Great Hall the Court of Husting is in session every Tuesday, and has a number of conveniences. To mention three: an absent defendant causes little delay because he can be rapidly outlawed; wills can be proved speedily, just by two witnesses; it has a system of land registration by which titles can be securely and quickly transferred. The Sheriffs' Court carries the overflow from the Court of Husting, and is used a good deal for debt. The Lord Mayor's Court meets every day and is much used for disputes between merchants; the Recorder usually presides instead of the Mayor. The Chamberlain, the City treasurer, also has a court which deals with disputes involving apprentices.

For its defence, the City organizes and trains a proportion of the able-bodied freemen, and every master has to equip his journeymen with a bow and four arrows. The trained bands of London are dressed in whites (unfinished broadcloths), with the arms of the City embroidered in front and behind. No apprentices, no 'foreigners'. They are better trained and equipped than any other militia in England. They are called out, not by the King, but by the Lord Mayor and Common Council.

When Edward dies, can Northumberland, President of a King's Council which will no longer have a status, get the London trained bands to support Jane's accession? Freemen of London are exempt from impressment in the armed forces of the Crown and cannot be compelled to go to war outside the city. The City refused troops to both the Council and Somerset when they were first in conflict, but in the end lent 15,000 men and 300 gentlemen to the Council under Northumberland. The Council and Northumberland can raise the Londoners if London itself is in obvious and immediate danger, for example from an invading Charles or an invading Henri or from rebels likely to sack London. Otherwise they have no certainty whatever. Everyone knows this, except perhaps the Imperial and French ambassadors.

The City leaders will play the crisis by ear, in accordance with their motto. *Domine dirige nos.* Matters of the succession are not, they consider, for them, but for Parliament and Council and Crown. The City minds its own business. Its needs from central government are few: peace, non-interference, low taxes, no fiddling with the currency; the simple wants of businessmen. Peace, but war maybe against trade rivals. Non-interference, but suppression of unfair competition, and preferential treatment. Low taxes, but prompt

47

payment of Crown debts. No fiddling with the currency, but a low exchange rate for selling and a high for buying.[6]

vi

A little further along in the middle of Cheap is the Standard, a stone structure with a much used pillory. On the south side of the street, opposite, there is a big stand made of stone, known as the King's Head. In the old days it was used by the Court to watch jousts in Cheap.

The King's Head keeps the light out of St Mary-le-Bow just behind. St Mary's is called 'le-Bow' ('the Arch') because of its four arches on the top of the tower, surmounted by a fifth. Or, some people say, because of the arches in the crypt where the Court of Arches sits, the Archbishop of Canterbury's highest ecclesiastical court. There used to be a grammar school in the churchyard here, but it ran to seed. Bow Bells are not rung nowadays except for the Great Bell, the fifth of the ring, which is rung every night at nine by order of the Common Council. Anyone out after that is put in a counter by the Watch and brought before the alderman or his deputy in the morning.

A little further up the same side of Cheap is another famous Mermaid, and in the middle of the street and surrounded by market stalls stands the Great Cross of Cheap, one of Edward I's crosses marking the rests of his Spanish Eleanor's funeral, remade fifty years ago. The cross is wood covered with lead; below there are stone images of the Resurrection, the Virgin Mary, Edward the Confessor, and so on. These have not been defaced: it is only those in churches which by law have to be defaced, but it is surprising that no enthusiast has knocked off a head or two.

If one is ready for a sit-down and a drink, at the cross one might turn down Friday Street for the Saracen's Head. It is a tavern much used by carriers bringing up cloth from the west. With the double ale one should have a warm saffron-and-raisin bun, which brings out the flavour.[6]

vii

Ponder London. It is strong. But 'strong' is the word, not 'enterprising', and enterprise is needed if that strength is not to depend too heavily on one commodity, woollen cloth, and one market, Antwerp. At Antwerp, Protestant merchants cannot expect for ever to be physically secure. The Emperor has not yet let the Inquisition run wild in Antwerp, lest it upset trade, but in the Netherlands as a whole the number of heretics burned, beheaded, hanged or buried alive in the last thirty years is estimated at 100,000. Be conservative: say 50,000. These last three years the Inquisition has been particularly active.

What is being done to find new markets? There have been half a dozen voyages by English ships to the Moroccan coast in the last two years. The Portuguese have tried to keep them away and have shot at them, but all the voyages have been profitable. Morocco is not an outlet for woollens but for linens, and for trifles like coral, amber and jet. Moroccan sugar sells well in London, and there is always a sale for almonds and dates. William Garrard, Sir John York and Sir Thomas Wroth are big in the Moroccan trade, and Michael Lock, one of the score of children of the late Sir William Lock, has based himself in Lisbon for it.

The Guinea coast is also being tested. There are three little ships out there now (including a warship lent by Northumberland's government), under Thomas Wyndham, with a renegade Portuguese navigator, Antonio Pinteado. The Portuguese have forts there and regard it as their own, and it is unhealthy, but there is plenty of gold, ivory and red pepper. William Garrard, Sir John York and the Lord Mayor, Sir George Barne, have all backed the venture.

A few Englishmen have got to the American lands across the Atlantic, going on Spanish ships, but nothing can be done against the Spanish monopoly.

The Mediterranean has been virtually closed to the English these last twenty years, because the Turks in the east and the Barbary pirates in the west are in league with each other and the whoreson French. And Italian competition is fierce. A few ships try to get to Candia for the Malmsey, but it is risky, and not only from pirates: this spring a ship lent by the government was on the way to Candia when it was seized by the Spaniards at Cadiz. For several years the English have been chased away from the Levant by the Turks, but Anthony Jenkinson is in Syria negotiating with them for trading rights to Baghdad, the Persian Gulf, the Far East.

Then there are Sir Hugh Willoughby's three ships making for the Far East via the Arctic. That is London's wildest speculation but the risk is well spread, Merchant Adventurers and courtiers alike subscribing £25 a share.

London's attempts on new markets are late in the day and small. Nothing, nothing is allowed to jeopardize London's solvency and strength. And that is one reason why Northumberland, in the last resort if not the first, should be able to rely on City support against Mary: not against Mary the bastard but against Mary the sometime-affianced cousin of Emperor Charles, with his Inquisition and his concern for the interests of London's trade rivals.[7]

4

The Saracen's Head to St Paul's, Christ's Hospital and Newgate

i

Return to Cheap. A few yards to the west, in the middle of the road, there is the Little Conduit, and on the south side the Little Gate. Through Little Gate enter the precinct of St Paul's, by age and magnificence and constant use London's most familiar and loved building.

In front of you is the north wall of the choir, on your right the north transept, and in the angle between them the open-air preaching place called Paul's Cross. The pulpit is a lofty octagonal affair with a roof surmounted by a cross. The Sunday morning sermon, with a prayer before and after, is attended by the Lord Mayor and the aldermen and a large crowd. They stand, or stroll and talk. The hour glass is expected to be turned once, but not twice. There used to be an awful burial-ground smell at the sermon, but the Charnel House at the north end of the transept was cleared away a few years ago and a Netherlander has built some shops in its place. The stones of the Charnel House went into the building of Somerset House, and the bones (500 tons, it is said) into making a little hill in Moorfields. 'Bunhill' they call it now.

The sermon often indicates turns in government policy. Last Sunday, 2 July, there were not the usual prayers for the two Princesses.

On the left, against the wall of the precinct, is St Paul's School, where 153 poor boys (the same number as the miraculous draught of fishes) study Latin, and other subjects through Latin, as in all grammar schools, and are also taught Greek. When Dean Colet founded the school, before the religious rumpuses, instead of putting it in the hands of the Church he gave it into the government of the Mercers' Company, reliable administrators.

Between the school and the east end of the cathedral is the spired bell tower (St Paul at the top) belonging to the sometime Jesus Chapel at this end of the crypt. The four Jesus bells in the tower were lost by the gamester head of the English Church, but the tower remains.

There is a crowd of bookstalls against the walls of the precinct and between the buttresses of the cathedral. What books sell best? Religion. Then romance. Then cheap stuff – jest books, children's ABCs, ballads, *How to Look at a Horse,* and that sort of thing. For a *New Testament* there is a 1553 quarto edition for 1s 10d unbound, or an octavo for 1s. A complete Bible is 10s unbound, 12s or more bound. The 1552 *Book of Common Prayer* is 2s 6d unbound, 3s or 4s bound. They can all be got from a bright young bookseller called William Norton: his sign is a tun with NOR written on it, and a sprig of sweet william. Ponet's *Catechism,* which came out in June, is printed by John Day who has a shop, at the sign of the Holy Ghost, just outside the precinct by the Little Conduit.

A good piece of religious controversy is *A Preservative, or Triacle, Agaynst the Poyson of Pelagius* by William Turner, Dean of Wells, which is printed by Richard Jugge here in the Churchyard at the sign of the Pelican and published by Andrew Hester at the White Horse. For a more material taste the same writer has *A New Herbal,* published in 1551. It is worth inquiring for: part one of the first systematic study of English plants, with their uses and virtues, and it is in English.

What strikes an Englishman is the increasing (slowly increasing) number of books in English. Take medical science: in the last eight years there have been three reasonably informative works on anatomy for the general public, and there is a gynaecological work, *The Birth of Mankind,* which the printer Thomas Raynolde keeps bringing out in larger and better editions. For professional medical men there is no English translation of the great 1543 work on anatomy *De humani corporis fabrica* by Andreas Vesalius, but the engraved illustrations have been published here this year (copied inaccurately), attached to an English text (monstrously outdated). And there is an English version of Joannes de Vigo's work on surgery.

On physiology there is nothing that is not based simply on the ancients, because medical science – although physicians would deny it – really has only three branches: herbalism, surgery and astronomy. There are several good books on astrology and astronomy in English, but they concentrate less on the medical aspects than the basic geometry, which is also relevant to surveying and navigation. Dr Robert Recorde's *The Pathway to Knowledge* (1551) was the first of these. It estimates the circumference of the earth as 21,600 miles. Anthony Ascham's *A Little Treatise of Astronomy* calculates the exact length of the year and says what adjustment is needed to the Julian calendar. Prognostications, prophesying the year's events and saying which days will be good for medicine-taking, are of a lower order and sell for 1d.

How many people can read? When it was a question of reading Latin, very few, only those who had been to grammar school or had comparable home tuition; now that there are books in English which people really want to read, especially the Bible, reading the vernacular turns out to be a very simple thing. Perhaps half the male population read English. When Cuthbert Tunstall, ex-Bishop of Durham, wrote a very useful book on arithmetic thirty years ago, because he thought the accounts brought to him hid false arithmetic, it was the first published in England. But it was in Latin and did not sell well. Now Dr Recorde has done an arithmetic in English, *The Ground of Artes*, which sells very well indeed.

Are there books about the newly discovered lands? Yes: Richard Eden, who is Secretary Cecil's secretary, has translated the relevant section of Sebastian Münster's *Cosmographia universalis*, and dedicated it to Northumberland.

English history? Yes, Polydore Vergil's, in Latin. Vergil is a prebendary of St Paul's. In English, there are several chronicles covering events almost up to 1553: Hall's, Grafton's, Cooper's.

English literature? Chaucer, Langland, Lydgate, Gower.

Classical literature? Gradually more and more is being translated but the Continent is much better off for translations, and even better off for editions in the original languages. The man who has the monopoly of printing Latin, Greek and Hebrew is Rayner Wolfe, the Netherlander who built his shop (The Brazen Serpent) and several others on the site of the Charnel House. Others besides Wolfe can publish and sell the classical languages but he alone can print. It is not a very profitable monopoly since continental versions can be imported so easily, but Wolfe has flourished. He has taken out papers of denization, and become a freeman of the Stationers' Company.

The Stationers' Company controls the trade, but to trade as a bookseller or stationer you need not be a freeman of the Stationers' as long as you are a freeman of some Company, like John Wight, bookseller at the sign of The Rose, who is a Draper. This is general in London: as long as you are a freeman of a Company you are a freemen of London and can follow any trade you wish, subject to regulation by the appropriate Company. But you cannot influence a Company's policy unless you are one of its freemen.

Now, leave books and go into Paul's – which cannot be done from this part of the Churchyard. Go out of Little Gate and turn sharp left along Paternoster Row (still more books), which follows the wall of the precinct.[1]

ii

One could turn out of Paternoster Row through a postern in the precinct wall to Canon Alley; this leads towards the north transept, and has on its left Wolfe's shops, and on its right the college of minor canons. But don't take Canon Alley. Instead, continue 30 or 40 yards west along Paternoster Row and enter a gatehouse in the wall which leads to Paul's Alley.

On the right of Paul's Alley is one of the walls of the Bishop of London's palace, separating you from his garden and chapel. On the left, between Paul's Alley and the north transept, is where Somerset pulled down the chapel and cloister of Pardon Church Haugh, with the famous wall-paintings of a Dance of Death. The stones went into Somerset House.

Paul's Alley leads to a door in the north side of the nave. This is the *Si quis* door where notices are put up by clergy in search of a benefice and by serving men in search of a job. And this door is the north end of the short cut through the nave from Paul's Chain and Paul's Wharf.

Enter. Norman nave, many-shafted pillars. Early English clerestory, high vaulted roof. This is the sixth bay from the west end. It is a vast nave, but without chairs or pews because the congregation stand or bring a stool. Every city needs its covered place where men can stroll, show themselves, gossip, do a little business: Paul's nave, 'Paul's Walk', is ideal and usually crowded. Be ready for pickpockets, and for choirboys who, if you are swashbuckling enough to wear spurs, will demand spur money. At the west end are a dozen scribes at small tables, who write letters and legal documents. Here in the north aisle clergy are apt to foregather and talk benefices; the south aisle is the place to borrow money. The place to pay it back is the font. At one of the pillars serving men habitually hang around for a job, as distinct from advertising for it at the *Si quis* door. At other pillars legal gentlemen receive their clients.

The choir and beyond, up to the east wall with its rose window, is late thirteenth century, and the vaults continue the vaults of the nave. The stone screen which divides nave from choir, led up to by wide, shallow steps, used to have a rood over it, but Christ crucified, with Mary and John, went six years ago, and soon after all the remaining images went by Order in Council. There had been casualties before that: it is fifteen years since the famous crucifix which hung aloft in the north transept was taken down and burned. A pity, because it was carved by Joseph of Arimathea.

The special pride of St Paul's used to be, from about 675, the miracle-working shrine of St Erkenwald, which is up beyond where the high altar once was. It was magnificent, with many images and jewels and precious metals given in the course of the centuries, but it was stripped quite a long while ago, in 1540. More recently, all tombs which were in any way shrines, and all holy images, have come in for a battering, but John of Gaunt's tomb, made by Yevele, with its alabaster effigies and Gaunt's helmet, spear and targe, is still undamaged. Bishop Ridley ordered the destruction of all the thirty-odd altars in Paul's last October.

So there has been a very clean sweep, under pressure from Ridley, and from the dean William May, the precentor Edmund Grindal, and three Reformist prebends appointed by Ridley: John Bradford, John Rogers, Edmund West. Of the rest of the prebends on the chapter, five are strongly Catholic (two relatives of the imprisoned ex-Bishop of London Edmund Bonner, and three of his chaplains), and a score conform without joy. It is not a happy or united staff.

But it is a distinguished staff, if not always present. A prebendary is supposed to be a resident canon, but Polydore Vergil lives now in Italy; John Warner is Professor of Medicine at Oxford and Warden of All Soul's; Henry Cole was Warden of New College, Oxford, until two years ago; the Dean, William May, is President of Queen's College, Cambridge; John Palsgrave spends his time in Northamptonshire studying French grammar; Peter Vannes is the King's envoy to the Doge and Senate of Venice; and there are several eminent practising lawyers.

The junior canons have fewer duties and smaller incomes than when they used to sing Masses in the chantry chapels. There were thirty-five chantries at the time they were abolished, compared with seventy a century before. Their passing has been little regretted except by the junior canons. It is true that some chantry priests in England kept small schools as a sideline, and the Council, while confiscating endowments, has tried to keep any educational activities going by fixed and regular stipends, but the Paul's chantries had no educational activities.

To the recent call-in of jewels, plate and embroideries Paul's contributed a good deal, and many bargains were picked up at the sales. Some of the altar hangings will soon be seen, it is said, in Valencia; the Adam and Eve cope will be in Saragossa; some images in Istanbul. The linen was burned at street corners until hospitals petitioned to have it for bandages.

The organ has not been played since last September, nor the bells pealed, nor on certain festivals does the choir any longer chant and sing on the tower at the foot of the steeple. However, you can still pay to go up the tower to look at the view, and to shout and hoot and carve your initials.

Now, if one goes out by the west door, the gatehouse of the Bishop's palace is on the right, leading into his courtyard, with Ridley's private apartments on the left and his hall on the right. He has had as prisoner-guest these last two years Nicholas Heath, the ex-Bishop of Worcester, who had refused to take down altars and set up tables instead.

Turn round and look again at the cathedral. There are two towers flanking the west front: the one on the left is part of the palace, the other is the Bishop's prison, known as the Lollards' Tower. There is a church, the parish church of St Gregory-by-Paul, adjoining the Lollards' Tower and the nave. Beyond it, in the corner between the south wall of the cathedral nave and the south transept, there used to be the handsome cloisters and chapter house, until Somerset House needed the stone. In the crypt at the west end there is another parish church, St Faith, and much of the rest is let out to stationers and others.

The buildings to the south and west in the precinct are a brewhouse, a bakehouse, and the dwellings of the canons actually in residence, including little John Rogers and his Netherlandish wife and their ten children. The Rogers' house is on the west side, the one next to the Bishop's palace.

Exit by the Western Gate. Turn right immediately up Ave Maria Lane, then right into Paternoster Row, to issue once more at the Little Conduit in Cheap.[2]

iii

West along West Cheap, and on the right is another of the areas outside the jurisdiction of the City. The old Hospital of St Martin-le-Grand has been rebuilt as tenements and a very large tavern. The tenements fetch good rents from thieves and whores who are safe here from arrest; and good rents from Germans, Flemings, Frenchmen and others, who operate as shoemakers, tailors, felt-hat-makers, pouchmakers, button-makers, stationers and silk-weavers, largely outside the supervision of the Companies. Continental refugees are not popular, in spite of their Protestant religion: not only are they foreign but they have skills which give them unfair advantage over English artisans.

St Martin-le-Grand is so packed with people that it is a parish in itself, and also forms a part of two other parishes. Beyond it, away to the north under the walls, there is a noisy concentration of chicken farmers.

West Cheap veers north at St Martin's to become Bladder Street, which widens into Newgate Street, with its market. This is the summit of London's western hill.

Newgate Market is a conglomeration. First, there is the Shambles, or Flesh Market, which used to be just a row of sheds in the middle of the street, but little by little the butchers and tripe-sellers have managed to turn them into houses. Behind are slaughter houses and drinking shops. Then there is the Meal Market, only a few years old, a good strong timber-framed building roofed with lead. In the courtyard are countrywomen selling provisions. Until a couple of months ago they used to obstruct the open street and be themselves plagued by carts, horses and cattle, but the Court of Aldermen decided they should go into the courtyard. They do not like it.

Newgate Street now slopes slightly downwards with, on the right, the huge Christchurch, 100 yards long, which used to be the preaching place of the Greyfriars, the Franciscans of Christ's Hospital, and full of fine monuments. You can walk from Newgate Street straight through the church and out of the north door into the Great Cloister of Christ's Hospital. Over on the left are the main buildings of the old Greyfriars priory which opened last November as a foundling hospital and orphanage, the City's joy and boast. Gifts from citizens met the cost of getting the place ready – about £2,500 – and citizens are finding a regular £250 a month for its maintenance. The 200 or 300 boys and girls saved from the devil were put each in a blue coat over a yellow kersey, with a red hat, and were soon being educated.

Who are they? Elizabeth Catlin, seven-year-old illegitimate daughter of Alice Catlin by William Widnall. A three-year-old girl who was born in Bedlam. An eight-year-old boy, Matthew Thomas, who is about to be taken as his own by one John Sewell on condition that the Hospital takes the six-month-old girl who was found on his stall in St Sepulchre's parish. Besides the children in the school there are 100 or more sucklings who are put out to nurse.

The petties, the four to eights, are taught to read and write English, and then will be put out to service, unless they are bright. In that case they will be kept in the grammar school, to study Latin, and through Latin to read poetry, drama, history, biography, moral essays and orations, in the usual grammar school syllabus. A boy will then, at about sixteen, become an apprentice, or he may go on to a university.

The getting-up bell in the morning is at six; school starts at seven and ends at eleven; after dinner there is more school and then play. Holy days are half-holidays, and they get a few days without work after the half-yearly examinations, but they do not officially go out of the premises except to attend the St Paul's Cross sermon and on special occasions. At Christmas they memorably lined the streets for the Lord Mayor's procession to and from Paul's Cross. They were not then in blue but in russet cottons, which sound like a cold two hours' of standing, but 'cottons' are rather coarse woollen cloths made in Lancashire, and they wore kerseys underneath them, and they had stockings and caps.

The week before last, on 26 June, Edward signed a charter for Christ's

Hospital. It is true that some of the children 'being taken from the dunghill, when they came to sweet and clean keeping and to a pure diet died downright', and some have run away, but the institution is settling down into a success.

The City, in tackling the problems of the poor and sick systematically, has been inspired by the writings of Luther and the Spanish humanist Ludovicus Vives, and by what has been done in Flanders, but it is fair to say that this inspiration did not lead to practical action until Bishop Ridley preached before the King about the plight of London's poor, whereupon Edward summoned the Lord Mayor. The young King's determined goodness was the final cause of the City's pulling itself together. Last year in every ward the numbers in need were assessed:

i	Fatherless children	300
ii	Sore and sick persons	200
iii	Idle vagabonds	200
iv	Poor men overburdened with their children	350
v	Aged persons	400
vi	Decayed householders	650
	Total [according to the Treasurer's addition]	2,160

The fatherless children are now well cared for. The sore and sick persons are dealt with by St Thomas's Hospital (the maintenance of which is also met by the £250 a month given by citizens). The idle vagabonds will be dealt with as soon as Bridewell gets going. The fourth, fifth and sixth groups need more help; about £40 a month is given them, obviously not enough.

The lazar houses outside the city wall receive £5 a month between them in exchange for stopping the lepers from begging within three miles of the bars. The precincts and the suburbs are quite outside this first attempt at systematic social welfare.

The governors in charge of the scheme on behalf of the City are able and conscientious men: Sir Andrew Judd, Skinner, ex-Lord Mayor; William Chester, Master of the Drapers, alderman; Thomas Lodge, Grocer, alderman; John Calthrop, Draper; Rowland Hayward, Clothworker; Sir Rowland Hill, Mercer, MP, ex-Lord Mayor; Richard Grafton, Grocer, who is Treasurer to the hospitals.

This last, Richard Grafton, is in his professional life the King's Printer. He has his press here in Christ's Hospital and has the monopoly of printing *The Book of Common Prayer*. It was he who, with Edward Whitchurch, printed the Great Bible which Henry caused to be put in all churches, and he has just finished printing a new smaller (quarto) Bible. He is at the moment setting up a wholly English work on book-keeping: the first. At present the best on the market is one he himself printed, an English translation of a French translation of a Flemish translation of an Italian book.[3]

iv

And so to Newgate itself, rebuilt under the will of Richard Whittington, the most handsome of the city's gatehouses and containing the most disliked of its prisons.

Newgate prison is principally for felons. They will appear at the next London or Middlesex assizes and be whipped or hanged. You can be hanged for rape, for abduction of a woman or girl; for stealing hawks' eggs, stealing cattle, stealing deer by night; letting out a pond; buggery; desertion of the army in the field; coining, coin-clipping; cutting a purse, robbing on the highway or on the sea; embezzling goods from your master worth more than 40s, stealing from your dead master; conjuring, sorcery, witchcraft. A woman who poisons her husband is burned alive, other poisoners are boiled in water or lead. Killing is punished by various forms of death: kill your master and you are hanged, drawn and quartered. If you refuse to plead, so that your property will remain with your family and not be confiscated, you are pressed to death. This is sometimes mercifully speeded by a sharp stone being placed under the prisoner's back. Several men are pressed each year in the pressing yard here at Newgate. Foreigners are shocked that the English quite often kill a man for the theft of a few shillings; on the other hand a felon is not normally tortured to betray his confederates, as he might be abroad. Three or four hundred common thieves, and many others, go to the gallows each year. A stay in Newgate is not comfortable. If you have any money it is extracted from you by the keeper for fees – on entry, on discharge, for a bed (shared), for exemption from fetters, etc – by fellow-prisoners ('garnish') and for food. If you have none, you are dependent on charity for food and are dumped in the Hole (packed, stinking, both sexes).

Go through Newgate. Which way now? A turn to the left, southward, along the Old Bailey beneath the city walls, would bring one out in Ludgate Hill near the St John's Head. Not south. Straight ahead, due west, would take one down Snow Hill to Turnmill Brook, which is the Fleet Ditch under another name, and up Holborn Hill into Holborn. Further along Holborn, on the north side, is the very large Ely Place which used to belong to the Bishops of Ely (100 servants, and 200 poor fed at the gates) and which Northumberland occupied for a few years. A little further there are some inns of court (on the left Furnivall's, Barnard's, Staple Inn; on the right Gray's Inn), and then the bars, and two miles further Tyburn gallows where it is the custom to cut out the heart of a living traitor and fling it in his face. Not west.

Turn right, northward along Giltspur Street, with John Rogers's St Sepulchre on the left, and come into the wider Pye Corner. Halfway along Pye Corner, again on the left, is the Hand and Shears. For some Malmsey, or Spanish. And a ponder.

Forget the punitive excesses of Newgate and Tyburn, so plainly barbarous, and ponder the civic zeal of Londoners in Christ's Hospital, so plainly civilized. And consider what else some Londoners have done and are planning to do in the field of education. Thomas White, the reluctant alderman of Cornhill, is preparing to found a college at Oxford, which he will dedicate to his Company's saint, St John. His Company, the Merchant Taylors', are planning to found a school in London. Sir William Laxton, Grocer, is going to endow a school at Oundle. Sir Thomas Gresham is meditating a sort of London college of business studies. His uncle, Sir John Gresham, has founded a school at Holt in Norfolk and put it in the hands of the Fishmongers. Sir Andrew Judd, Skinner, has this year founded a school at Tonbridge and put it in the hands of his Company. William Harper, Merchant Taylor, is planning to found a school at Bedford. Sir Rowland Hill, Mercer, has endowed a school at Drayton in Shropshire, and exhibitions at both universities.

Why this passion for education? Because it gives access to God's testaments in languages nearer the originals; because it opens up the new sixteenth-century world; because it is an engine which, with wealth and land, will lift a man in the social scale; because knowledge itself is a lovely thing.

The decline in effective grammar-school education through the Dissolution has been negligible, if there has been any at all, because many of the schools which went were decayed or did not answer to modern secular needs. Besides, those founded or reconstituted under Edward VI are better distributed geographically. But the population has increased, and also the demand per head has increased.

Neither Crown nor Church has the money or the urge to found more schools. Commerce has the money, and London magnates, having managed successfully their businesses and Companies, want to try their hands at managing schools, and other institutions in need of better administration, such as hospitals. Hence this burst of foundations. Which are not all by Protestants – Thomas White is a sound Catholic.[4]

5

The Hand and Shears to Smithfield, the windmills, Bedlam and Bishopsgate

i

Turn left out of the Hand and Shears into Smithfield. It is properly West Smithfield: East Smithfield is out east beyond the Tower.

A large area of bare earth, except where it is dung. Markets on various days of the week for horses, cattle, sheep and, on Thursdays, hay. Good houses on the west side of the square. In the north-west corner, sheep pens, as well as Smithfield Pond which is no longer a pond, and the Elms which are no longer elms but gallows. The north-east corner is all tenements, taverns and brewhouses. The east side is the impressive side, with what used to be the Benedictine priory of St Bartholomew, and its hospital.

Bartholomew Fair is held here for three days around the day of the saint, 24 August. It is a fair for cloth, horses, cattle, leather, dairy produce, but more famous for its fairground amusements: freaks, performing animals, puppets, fortune-tellers, balladmongers, quacks, gingerbread women, and sellers of rattles, toy drums, toy halberds, Bartholomew babies (which are dolls), and especially of roast pig. Pigs' heads stare at one from stall after stall.

It is a great time for pickpockets, coiners, and tricksters with false dice (which, for those interested, are made especially well in the Marshalsea and King's Bench prisons in Southwark). Rapid justice during the Fair is dealt out by a Court of Pie Powder held in the Hand and Shears. Pillory and whipping post are conveniently near.

And it is a great time for beggars. Begging is legal only if you have a licence. The City gives you a licence if you are physically impotent, or have lost your all by fire or shipwreck, or if you have been whipped as a vagabond and sent to beg your way home elsewhere. The vice-chancellor of your university may give you a licence if you are a poor student, and you are allowed to beg if you are a graduate of Bedlam. You can also beg on behalf of a leper or a hospital, or of a Christian who has been captured by Barbary pirates and needs to be ransomed.

The City is responsible for all the Fair which is inside Smithfield itself, but not for the cloth fair from which the whole thing started, and which is still held on a narrow strip of land within the grounds of the priory. The cloth stalls pay their rents to Sir Richard Rich, who bought the priory for a bit over £1,000. Rich, who is a member of the Council and until eighteen months ago was Lord Chancellor, has worked well with Northumberland although he is a strong Catholic. As Henry's Solicitor-General he out-lawyered to death fellow lawyer Sir Thomas More, and he handled with the greatest competence the financial side of monastery-dissolution. He uses the prior's house as his winter residence, and Sir Walter Mildmay and other respectable people rent houses from him in the precinct. Rich was required to demolish the nave of the church of St Bartholomew the Great, but the magnificent Norman choir is now the parish church. The lady chapel has been incorporated in his residential developments.

St Bartholomew the Less, on the south-east of the square, is the church of a very small parish, just the precinct of St Bartholomew's Hospital. Would one with confidence enter St Bartholomew's Hospital as a patient? Well, hospitals are for the poor.

ii

The gate of the hospital is by the side of the church. Beyond the church, on the left is the Great Cloister, with rooms over, and a smaller cloister; on the right the Great Hall. Beyond, courts containing the wards, and burial grounds, and miscellaneous houses and gardens. Numbers of people unconnected with the hospital live in the precinct, including one of the King's physicians, John Kaye, several times President of the College of Physicians.

Why should the distinguished Dr Caius (Kaye Latinizes himself, as do most international scholars) be unconnected with the hospital? Because physicians are expensive. For the 100 patients there are a matron; twelve sisters to make beds, wash linen with wood ashes, attend on patients, and in spare time spin flax for sheets; a hospitaller to visit patients and handle admissions and other administrative matters; a steward, a butler, beadles . . . . And three surgeons at £20 a year each. But no physician.

The order of precedence in the medical profession is: physician; surgeon; apothecary; barber. A physician is a university graduate, and may have studied abroad (Dr Caius studied in Padua and Florence) and he has to be licensed by the College of Physicians. He is responsible for internal medicine: he has you purged, dosed with drugs, blooded. A surgeon is for external medicine: he deals with wounds, dislocations, fractures, skin diseases including syphilis, and childbirth; he cuts for stone, he amputates, and he especially (as directed by a physician) lets blood. He has had a grammar-school education to gain some Latin, has served an apprenticeship to a surgeon, and has been passed as qualified by the surgeon section of the Company of Barber-Surgeons. An apothecary buys and sells drugs and dispenses prescriptions, and is usually a member of the Grocers' Company. A barber cuts hair, shaves, and draws teeth, and is a member of the barber section of the Company of Barber-Surgeons.

How good or bad are English surgeons? Five or six years ago, when Jane Northumberland had a bad leg, Northumberland was terrified that, if the Bordeaux surgeon was not brought to her, some London surgeon would incontinently cut it off.

An assiduous governor of Bart's, Thomas Vicary, three times Master of the Barber-Surgeons, has written a book on anatomy, in English. So clearly the hospital's surgery must be forward-looking? No. Vicary's book is an unacknowledged abridgment of works written 200 years ago.

The Barber-Surgeons are allowed four felon-corpses a year, and they arrange a dissection every quarter at their hall, which all surgeon members have to attend. But can they see the dissection? No. Because they see with the eyes of their lecturer, and the white-aproned lecturer pointing at the exposed anatomy with a long white wand is Dr Caius. Caius is a fine scholar, but the eyes he sees with are not those of today's Andreas Vesalius but of Galen. Galen in the second century saw more than the fourteenth-century authors plagiarized by Vicary, but nine times out of ten Galen had been looking at an animal dissection, not a human.

Does out-of-dateness really matter? Patients might sometimes think so. English surgeons use boiling oil to clean gunshot wounds, although Ambroise Paré in France wrote a book about his successful mild dressings twelve years ago. And Bart's surgeons use a red-hot iron to stop bleeding, although Paré stops it by tying up an artery. But English surgeons cannot be blamed for not knowing Paré's methods: the whoreson fellow wrote his books in French.

Physicians, with their university education, write to one another and publish in Latin. Does physicians' knowledge therefore spread more rapidly? Yes, as rapidly as their ignorance. Physicians sniff at every fashion wafted to them on international Latin. A succession of elixirs and essences sweep into English medical practice from the Continent, useful, useless, and dangerous. A physician is an old fogey if he does not give ruthless doses of mercury, antimony and their compounds. Thank heavens for out-of-date Dr Caius, whose Galenist herbs are safer.

Not always much safer. Greek herbs are easily misidentified in un-Aegean England. But henceforth misidentification in herbalism and human anatomy should slowly become rarer, because copper-plate engravings can be so much more precise than the old woodcuts. The engravings illustrating Vesalius's *De humani corporis fabrica* were swiftly pirated in London by a Fleming, Thomas Geminus, working in Blackfriars, to the great benefit of English surgeons. The benefit would have been greater if they had been copied accurately; and if for the accompanying text a translation of Vesalius had been used: instead the publisher printed the fourteenth-century manuscript which had been the basis of Vicary's book.

You may deduce from all this that English doctors are unreliable, but their patients have faith in them. Bart's is usually full, and most of its patients recover (the hospital admits, rightly, only those it believes it can cure). At the end of their treatment, before being sent off with money and a passport for their journey home, they come to Little St Bartholomew's and thank God for having moved the governors and surgeons to cure them.

After the dissolution of the old Bart's in the late 1530s, the City took over management, with a board of governors like that of Christ's Hospital, competent and humane. They have treated staff rows with understanding, and administered the estates with decency, waiving rents and debts where need be, and usually granting a tenant's request for a chimney.

The old Bart's was in debt and bad repair. The City has guaranteed an adequate income by giving the hospital the profits from the Beams, and by taxing all the Companies, from £24 a year from the Mercers down to 13s 4d from the Brown Bakers, Turners, Long Bowstring Makers, and the like. That is to say, every single London citizen contributes a mite annually through his Company, and the money is collected with certainty and little labour: as a method of financing a social institution, surely a pregnant innovation.

And another is the publication of a book, *The Order of the Hospital of St Bartholomew in West Smithfield in London*. It gives the citizens full descriptions of their hospital's work and its administration, from the charge given to its governors to the charge given a matron or beadle, from the money it spends on candles to the money it receives from Brewers and Stationers. A great organ of government is exposing to its citizens the workings of one of its services.

So . . . if a London physician's prescription of antimony gives you some discomfort, and a London surgeon cuts off your leg before you can say 'Knife!', you can rejoice that both are members of properly qualified and organized professions. And if, reduced to poverty, you die in a Bart's bed, in the smell of your own burned or boiled flesh, you can lie afterwards in a Bart's burial ground happy in the excellence of the City's administration.[1]

iii

Go north across Smithfield to the bars. Turn round and note the area of what used to be surrounding religious foundations, five of them. St Bartholomew's is contiguous, by a postern in the city wall, with Greyfriars; and eastward from the bars is a lane into the third dissolved foundation, the Charterhouse. Lord North has done much pulling down and building in the Carthusians' old priory but the handsome court remains. The French ambassador thinks his lodgings in the Charterhouse the finest in London. When the last Carthusian prior and seventeen of his monks refused to accept Henry as head of the English Church, they were efficiently prosecuted by Catholic Sir Richard Rich, and executed. The great mass of priors and monks in England accepted Henry.

Up John Street and at once, on the left, is the fourth religious foundation, the old priory of the Knights Hospitallers of St John of Jerusalem. Northumberland paid Henry £1,000 for it. The nave of the church had to be blown up (Somerset had the stone for his house), but it is a pity that the bell tower was also: it was carved, gilded, enamelled, very pretty.

Northumberland paid thirty-three times the annual value, a good deal more than the going rate. Henry gave little away and sold priories usually at fourteen to twenty-one times their annual value. Henry, of course, marvellously liberated the market in land, but let what could have been another happy result of the Dissolution, the solvency of the Crown, drain away in splendour and war.

Next door to St John's is the fifth of the group, Clerkenwell Priory, which used to house Benedictine nuns and is now Sir John Pope's. Pope, who also has Bermondsey Priory, occupies the prioress's house. The church has become the parish church, and the remainder residences and tenements.

There has been some recent building in John Street but one is quickly in the fields. It is in these fields by Skinners' Well and Clerks' Well (which are no longer wells), just north of Clerkenwell Priory, that at Bartholomew-tide the Lord Mayor and aldermen watch the City sergeants and yeomen wrestle the men of the suburbs.

Further north, past some very decent new houses and through half a mile of pastures and market gardens, there is the salubrious little town of Islington. Go thither if the fame of Islington's custards and curds-and-whey tarts is irresistible, but otherwise turn back to Smithfield, and take the road at its north-east corner, Long Lane.

After 300 or 400 yards of Long Lane, cross Aldersgate Street into Barbican. On the left side of Barbican there is a curious house which has a chapel on top, Garter House, which belongs to one of the Heralds, Charles Wriothesley; and next to it is Barbican House, the owner of which is a notable thirty-three-year-old widow, Catherine, Dowager Duchess of Suffolk, Baroness Willoughby de Eresby, equally notable for her nobility, Protestant-ism, wit and beauty. When she was sixteen she married Henry VIII's friend Charles Brandon, who was then Duke of Suffolk. Recently she became a widow no longer, marrying a common-sensible Protestant commoner named Richard Bertie. Her two sons by Brandon died while they were undergraduates at Cambridge, died within twenty-four hours of each other, of the sweating sickness. Irrepressible and attractive (but not unopinionated), she once mortally teased the imprisoned Stephen Gardiner. She has a saying, 'God is a remarkable man'. A good saying.

Over Whitecross Street and in another 300 or 400 yards Finsbury Court, with a moat and some pavement, abuts the road up from Moorgate. Ahead are Finsbury Fields, and to the north Bunhill Fields (with the hill of charnel bones) and the three windmills which have been built on hills of refuse and are turned to catch the wind. They grind flour mostly. One of them belongs to the Lord Mayor, Sir George Barne.

Here and in all the fields up to Islington one must walk with discretion: arrows. There are between 100 and 200 3-foot marks between here and Islington, and Londoners spend happy hours shooting from one to another. If a bowman calls out 'Fast!' he takes it that he has given warning enough. Heads of households have to see that their males from the age of nine are equipped for archery; and there are shooting matches here at every Bartholomew-tide, for prizes of gold crowns and golden arrows and the like (maximum value 13s 4d). Standards of archery are said not to be as high as they were, but any self-respecting English bowman can shoot more accurately at 150 or 200 yards than an arquebusier at 100, and he can aim twelve or eighteen shots while the arquebusier bangs off two.

The English do use other weapons besides the bow, but the Act which stipulates what every Englishman must provide himself with was passed in 1285, 100 years before firearms came on the scene. So bows and halberds are the English weapons still, while the Continent theorizes around calivers and pikes (the caliver is a light form of arquebus which can be fired without a rest). One wonders that there are not more murders, ambushes and petty insurrections in England than there are, the bow being so admirable for all three.

South of Finsbury Fields, and up to the wall, is Moorfield, where the hazards are less from archers than from washerwomen, who defend their drying linen to the death.

From the windmills there is a road to the east which leads into Bishopsgate Street close by a cross and a well. Bishopsgate Street runs due south. On the left are good class houses with handsome gardens, which have replaced the old priory of St Mary Spital and its hospital with 180 beds. About all that remains of the priory are the pulpit and cross in the churchyard where at the Spital sermons last Easter Week the Lord Mayor and aldermen were joined by the Christ's Hospital children.

Further down Bishopsgate Street, behind the houses, besides gardens with summerhouses there are tenter grounds where woollen cloths are pegged out after being cleaned and thickened at the fullers. On the left is Bearwards Lane, which leads to a brick-walled field, Teazle Close. This is where Londoners, a relatively small number, practise with their handguns, and the Tower gunners come here every Thursday practising, and testing out new cannon.

Back in Bishopsgate Street, and on the right is the entrance to Bedlam, the old hospital of St Mary of Bethelehem. It is dirty and smelly, because a fair number of the lunatics have to be kept chained and so get very filthy. Shock treatment, in the form of whipping, is recommended by the experts and is sometimes beneficial. Walking patients are allowed to exercise in the yard and the corridor, and in wintertime to warm themselves at the fire in the kitchen if the keeper's wife, Mrs Allen, allows. After a year the patients are either cured or incurable, and are therefore returned to their relations or put on the roads with a licence to beg.[2]

iv

Continue down Bishopsgate Street. On the left is Fisher's Folly, the large house and pleasure garden of Jasper Fisher, Chancery clerk (larger than his station and wealth justify), and then an inn, and Houndsditch running up from outside Aldgate. On the right are an inn and a church, and then come the city wall, and Bishopsgate which, like all the other gates, has on poles the parboiled heads of persons a sovereign has had condemned as traitors.

Bishopsgate Street holds many prosperous merchants' houses, but only one or two buildings of interest. On the left are the large courtyard of St Helen's and the slightly smaller one of Little St Helen's, which used to be a Benedictine nunnery but is now the hall of the Leathersellers. Further down is the fine stone-and-timber house, Crosby Place, which was the tallest house in London when it was built 100 years ago. It was once Sir Thomas More's and afterwards belonged to a great Italian merchant, Antonio Bonvisi.

If one went straight on one would cross Cornhill and ultimately walk straight over the Bridge into Southwark, but instead take the right fork, Three Needle Street. At the fork itself there is a well which disposes some to philosophize: when one bucket rises, the other falls. On the right in Three Needle Street is St Anthony's Church, given over to French refugees, and St Anthony's School, which has a good reputation. On Bartholomew Eve in the churchyard of St Bartholomew the Great all the grammar schools compete in Latin disputations, and St Anthony's is apt to be the winner.

A few steps further, Broad Street joins Three Needle Street from the north, coming from Lord Treasurer Paulet's very great house, which used to be the priory of the Augustine friars. The nave of the priory church is used now by Protestant refugees from the Netherlands, with their Polish supervisor John à Lasco. When Paulet goes down to Westminster he rides this way, attended. Walk by the same route to the river, through the Stocks and along Walbrook, and at Walbrook's crossing with Candlewick Street spare a thought for the sometime inhabitant of the fifteen-room house on the left, Henry VII's servant, Edmund Dudley. How effective and vigorous Northumberland's father was! He argued in a book he wrote for Henry VIII (who did not need to read it) that Nobility, Church and Commons are all self-seeking and will only combine for the common good if the Crown is dominant. A most loyal servant, but Paulet would shake his head over him: Edmund Dudley was too loyal, too effective, too vigorous to survive.

And so, into Thames Street and down to the Three Cranes. London river on a July day! Enter a famous old inn, the Crane in Vintry. Dinner, and a sorting of impressions.

Far from being unstable, the English have carried through their Protestant revolution, digested and developed a mass of confiscated Church property, endured inflation, survived a bankrupt Treasury and the reign of a child monarch, all with grumbling near-equanimity. Insurrection has been quelled, and discontents of commoners and jealousies of nobles have been contained. The English have been so little stirred up by local and world events that most of their habits and practices are still deep in the past: crafts and trades rigid in old monopoly and regulation; customs duties assessed by fifty-year-old values; bread prices, and even the arming of the militia, fixed by 300-year-old formulas.

London itself is the epitome of stability: its self-government orderly, its business unenterprisingly sound. There is no sign that London is about to plunge into riot or civil war. The Catholics of London have given Edward's Protestant government little anxiety, even less than they gave Henry. Catholic and Protestant work together, City and Crown work together. No vested interest – neither the nobility, the gentry, nor the City – has reason to oppose Jane. On the contrary, the vested interest of property-owners is wholly on her side. So, no civil war.

As for foreign invasion, neither Charles nor Henri would stir unless he had certainty of rapid, total and profitable victory: that is to say, unless invited by either Mary or Northumberland, with a sizeable supporting English party and little opposition. But in that case, there would be no need for the invitation to be offered. So, no invasion, no civil war.

6

The Crane in Vintry
to Westminster and Syon

i

No, the devise will not go through like that. The argument is logical but this is England. Against sense the Protestant revolution is at risk, and there may be bloodshed.

Meanwhile, a longer river trip, a pleasant trip to Syon, Northumberland's place, stopping off for a few minutes at Westminster. The wherry should have two watermen. Set off among the swans and wherries and barges, past Bridewell, where Renard and party are due, past the Temple and the Savoy and the noblemen's houses, with the Northumberlands' Durham House, and round the corner southwards past Whitehall Palace with all the portraits of Henry. Henry's immortal omnipresence is the real snag in the devise.

Land at Westminster public stairs (known as Westminster Bridge) projecting well into the river below low-tide mark. The stairs lead into New Palace Court with, on the left, the entrance to Westminster Hall. The clock tower in the court has a bell which strikes the hours and can be heard, usefully, in the law courts in Westminster Hall, and even in London on a calm day. The north side of New Palace Court, on your right towards the orchard of Whitehall Palace, is Canon Row, where Second Secretary Cecil has a convenient *pied-à-terre* he has bought from Paget.

Another resident of Westminster, humbler but well known, is a cobbler, Richard Castle. Every morning, winter and summer, he can be heard at his work before four. Industrious and thrifty, he has given nobly to Christ's Hospital.

Enter Westminster Hall, the largest hall in the kingdom. It was part of the New Palace built about 500 years ago by William II. Beyond it are parts of the Old Palace, built a little earlier by Edward the Confessor. The Palace of Westminster has not been used as a royal residence since a fire early in the 1500s, but it houses the King's law and revenue courts and his parliament.

Westminster Hall is empty now, but in term-time it is crowded. There are hucksters' stalls up this northern end by the entrance. Then halfway up the hall, on the right, is the Court of Common Pleas; at the far end, on the right is the Court of Chancery and on the left the King's Bench. The law officers, who professionally fussed about the devise, professionally did what they were told: all witnessed the King's patent and swore the bond, all except one, Justice Hales of the Common Pleas.

Up the shallow stairs at the end, and turn left to the chapel of the palace, St Stephen's, which has been fitted out with four rows of seats all round, in tiers. For the last three or four years the House of Commons has met here. The Speaker's Chair is at the east end, in the middle of the front row. In front of the Speaker, who is elected afresh for each session, the Clerk John Seymour sits at a small table. Seymour has been keeping a journal of the House's doings (recording is a fashion of the age): it is very brief, with no details of who says what, but it is something. The City gives him and the Speaker a few pounds each session for their lawful favour.

To what extent was Northumberland able to pack the last Parliament, and how far could he pack a new one in September? Hardly at all. A royal and ruthless Henry could frighten the House but he could not much pack it. The Crown always has in the House a fair number of Councillors, Household officials and other servants of the Crown who have been returned as MPs, and they sit all together close to the Speaker's right ear, but most of the 377 members are independent gentlemen whose independence has been mightily nourished in the last twenty years by possession of new land. Further, a fair number of MPs have some intellectual and legal assurance through being practising lawyers, or at least having attended the Inns of Court. The House is not complaisant these days, except to a royal Henry.

Retrace your steps out of the Chamber and through the Lobby, the old antechapel; then turn left, away from the Hall. In front now are the White Hall, given over to the Court of Requests, and the Painted Chamber and the House of Lords; on the right is the Court of Wards, where orphaned children of the rich are sold to the highest bidder.[1]

ii

Now pass back along the length of Westminster Hall towards the entrance, where there are stairs to left and right. Those on the east lead to the Exchequer of Receipt, those on the west to the Exchequer of Account, and to the west also is the Court of Augmentations, which looks after ex-Church property. Here the money comes and goes, grossly inadequate to the Crown's needs.

Edward's normal income – from the rents of Crown lands, from Customs, and from various fees and exactments – has been less than his normal expenditure by about £60,000 a year. If Parliament has voted him a 'fifteenth and tenth', this has amounted to about £29,000 in any one year. A fifteenth was originally a fifteenth of the movable property of persons outside the royal demesne; and a tenth was a tenth of the moveable property of persons living on the royal demesne or in cities or boroughs. But after a couple of centuries it is no such thing: it has become a very low fixed tax on land. Tradition is such that while occasionally assessments are reduced or dropped altogether, none is increased. 200 years ago the tax brought in £38,000–£39,000; by 1553 it brings in theoretically £32,000, but actually £29,000, although taxpayers' real wealth has increased, and the value of money has declined.

If Edward is involved in war, Parliament votes him a subsidy, which in the old days raised £120,000 but now £90,000, and he gets £35,000 from the Church. But wars have become expensive. In Edward's first five years war cost £1,300,000, while for the whole of his reign so far the income from Parliamentary grants – fifteenths and tenths and subsidies all put together – has amounted to less than £300,000.

Has the Crown always been so bankrupt? No. When Henry VIII came to the throne there was money in the Treasury; by its end he was making ends meet by debasing the currency, selling away his great bonus of monastic lands, forcing gifts and loans from his subjects, and borrowing abroad.

Henry was a king and could get by. Can a Lord President of the Council?

What Northumberland did first was identify and use the four ablest financial administrators the Crown could command. William Paulet, Marquis of Winchester, Great Master of the Household, he made Lord Treasurer, a post which had been a sinecure, but Paulet was to be active in general financial matters and at the Exchequer. He made Sir Thomas Gresham the King's Agent at Antwerp. The third, Sir William Cecil, he made second Secretary of State. The fourth, Sir Walter Mildmay, Surveyor-General of Augmentations, he used on commissions to bring in money owing to the King, and to investigate the sources of revenue, and to examine the revenue departments. This last commission reported fraud, theft, corruption, arrears, careless book-keeping, dilatoriness, waste, sinecures, unauthorized increases of salary, and indiscriminate payment of claims for postage and travel; and it recommended that the revenue departments should be united.

Then he tried to keep out of war, and succeeded. He tried to keep free of rebellion, and succeeded.

He sold Boulogne back to the French, for £130,000. He reduced the garrisons at Calais and Berwick, disbanded mercenaries, reduced the fleet (after somehow gathering enough money to pay the men their arrears). He reduced (a little) the expenses of the Household, for example by cutting down the postal service. He debased the currency for one last time, making £160,000, and then took the first clumsy and confusion-causing steps to restore it. He took, from the Church, estates of the remaining excessive episcopates, and the plate and vestments which right-thinking persons regarded as superstitious and idolatrous. And he went at last to Parliament, in March, and asked for a subsidy: £90,000. This was unprecedented – it was not a time of war. He hoped Parliament would not retort that the Crown would not be so short if so much had not been given away to Councillors (how else does one keep such great men happy when there is no adult king to touch them with grace and fear?). Parliament discussed the subsidy for two days, and voted it, but the money is not yet in.

In the summer of last year the Treasury had nothing, nothing at all. The departments of government, the King's Household itself, suspended payments, ostensibly because the King was on progress. They owed £135,000.

In this extraordinary and worrying time, Thomas Gresham has so acted on the Antwerp money market that the exchange rate of the £ has been higher than for years: he is repaying the King's foreign debts at £1 = 22 Flemish shillings, and they have been reduced to £61,000. The King's credit in Antwerp has never been higher.

This particular piece of magic has been done by juggling with the Merchant Adventurers' consignments to Antwerp, and taking over their foreign currency. The government has had to stretch the goodwill of London merchants, but it has compensated them by not revising upwards the rate book for customs, by reducing the privileges of the Hanse, and by giving help to the expeditions to Morocco, Guinea and Cathay.

So, a reason for thinness of naval and military preparation, as for discontent-causing delays in payment of government bills, salaries and pensions, is shortage of money. And the reason for that shortage is the unwillingness of the English Parliament to vote themselves into paying adequate taxation. Henry VIII could make Parliament vote white black and black white, but he could not make it pay for the full costs of government and war. If a full-blooded king could not, how could Lord Protector Somerset, or Lord President of the Council Northumberland?[2]

iii

Beyond the Palace of Westminster is the walled precinct of the dissolved Abbey, with its church of St Peter. Henry VII's Chapel is new and gleaming.

Inside St Peter's there has been the usual spoliation. Edward the Confessor's shrine has lost its jewels and gold to the King, but his bodily remains were spirited away by angels.

Many of the priory buildings have been sold off, but the grammar school remains, and so does the Sanctuary. The dozen or score of Sanctuary men (mostly debtors, a few thieves, one or two homicides) can be recognized by the crossed keys of St Peter on their garments. They are not confined to the Sanctuary building (a central tower, with two wings) but are allowed to wander freely in the precinct, as long as they do not hawk foodstuffs without a licence.

St Peter's is now a cathedral, but its diocese is combined with that of St Paul's. The Dean, Hugh Weston, is a famous preacher but he has a peccant private life, and his clergy are disorderly.

A little further along, on the east bank of the south-to-north stretch of the Thames, is Lambeth, its parish church right against the gate of Archbishop Cranmer's palace. Nearby is the house which was the Duke of Norfolk's suburban residence until he was attainted, and is now Northampton's, like Winchester House.

Cranmer was the only important churchman who was not pushed by Henry into an exchange of his house for one remoter from Court – except Gardiner, whose Winchester House was already remote. The greater part of Cranmer's work on the Prayer Books of 1549 and 1552 and his revision of the canon law was done at Lambeth. His study is in a small square tower at a corner of the chapel, on the first floor up a spiral staircase. He prays and studies there every morning from five till nine, and then does his official work, breaking it when possible by study or writing, which he does standing up at a tall desk. He likes chess in the afternoon, and walking in his park after supper. Northumberland crushed his hope that the March Parliament would confirm his new canon law – having doubts, perhaps, about confirming the legal powers of opinionated bishops, or simply thinking there were enough troubles to deal with already.

In this age of galloping Protestant radicalism Northumberland is only an averagely religious man, exasperated often by the over-weaningness of religious professionals. He has tried to move with his age, but he speaks the current religious language a little stiffly, like a military man, and his conscientious hobnobbings with John Knox have been without pleasure: 'I love not men which be neither grateful nor pleasable.'

Cranmer, one may be sure, took Northumberland's suppression of his Bill hard, but he witnessed the King's devise and swore the bond. A churchman of the Reformed Religion obeys his monarch, the head of his Church, right or wrong.[3]

iv

Round a bend in the river, and due west again, past market gardens, past the fringe of Tothill Fields, and then of Neat Park which stretches down from Knightsbridge, one of Henry's hunting grounds, and into the country.

Chelsea, on the north bank on a low gravel hill, is pleasant to escape to from the Court or the city. There are four fine brick houses here. First, the Manor House which Henry gave Catherine Parr. It was here that, later, Catherine's next husband, Tom Seymour, rumpled Princess Elizabeth. It now belongs to Northumberland, and daughter-in-law Jane, née Grey, is very fond of it. She has removed herself there these last few days but the peace of the country has not tranquillized her. She has a stomach complaint and believes Northumberland has poisoned her.

What is she like? Very short, very slim. Hair nearly red, and eyebrows rather darker than her hair. Lively hazel eyes. Freckles.

Next, a house belonging to the Earl of Shrewsbury; then the Old Manor House; then Chelsea Church, red-brick and stone; and finally the house which used to be Sir Thomas More's and now belongs to Lord Treasurer Paulet. Paulet has added a covered gallery which looks down over the grass to the Thames and the Surrey woods beyond.

Now on the south bank is Putney church and, two or three miles inland, Wimbledon. For the last three years the Old Rectory at Wimbledon has been Secretary Thomas Cecil's home, with classically educated wife Mildred, son Thomas, and five relations and wards regarded as family. And twenty-five staff and servants, the servants in livery embroidered with his badge, and twenty-nine horses. He keeps meticulous accounts, in Roman numerals like everyone else: present income *MD libri*, a large income, but not as large as that of a major London merchant.

His friends are normally of the Reformed Religion, but he is not especially religious himself. He keeps Cicero's *De officiis* in his pocket, not a book of Christian meditation. He was sick earlier this year, but back at the Council table in time for signing the letters patent. He swore the bond also. He is aware of the risks in the devise and would like to run away: there might so easily be conflict in which one found oneself on the wrong side and therefore guilty of treason. He has made some night-time visits to London by boat, collecting money, plate, papers, weapons. Cheke has told him to read Plato again: Socrates did not flee.

On the north bank opposite Putney church is Fulham church and a footpath along the riverbank to the Bishop of London's moated country house, Fulham Palace, with its 30 acres.

Then round the bend at Chiswick, where Sir Henry Sidney has a house. In a wicked world Sidney is a man to rely on, and his wife Mary, Northumberland's elder daughter, a female counterpart.

Then, on the south bank, Mortlake, Kew and Sheen. Sheen now belongs to the Duke of Suffolk, and Lady Jane Grey has spent much time there since he came into possession. A lovely part of the river. Sheen used to be an opulent Carthusian monastery. There is a long Gothic gallery from end to end of the abbot's house. Very fine. Somerset got it first, and then Jane's father when Somerset was attainted.

Most of the monks died in prison, but eleven are still receiving state pensions of between £6 and £8 a year. The Crown is burdened with pensions of many hundreds of monks, while the capital value of their monasteries has long since been spent.

Opposite is Syon, which was also Somerset's from 1547 until his execution last year. It had belonged to the Bridgettines, an order founded in the fourteenth century by St Bridget, the Swedish mystic who had eight children. Syon was one of the richest monasteries in England, with an income of £1,750 from estates scattered all over the south, and with a reputation for asceticism and for the learning and preaching of the fathers. There was an abbess and about sixty nuns in the inner court, and thirty religious men in the outer. Somerset began to rebuild it as soon as he had it but had not time to finish. Northumberland has had it since, and has used it a good deal, but he has done nothing to finish it. Three storeys round a courtyard, with square towers at the corners, faced with stone, and topped with balustrades. Handsome.

It is unlikely that Northumberland is at Syon on Thursday 6 July if Edward is truly dying. He must be at Greenwich.

If one went further up-river one would come, after bearing left, to one of the most imposing of the King's palaces, Richmond. And if further still, to the town of Kingston, which has the first bridge across the Thames above London Bridge. And then the King's palace of Hampton Court. And then to the King's Castle at Windsor. Plenty of palaces, but no money for a few mercenaries.[4]

II

God Save the English

7

'O Lord God, save thy chosen people of England'

i

Greenwich Palace, Thursday evening. Edward's two doctors are with him: George Owen and Thomas Wendy, as good physicians as are to be found in England; and in addition his old and competent nurse, Mrs Sybil Penn. Three other doctors have been brought into consultation on his urine and excrement but have now been banished, as has a woman healer brought in as a last resort. Good intentions, pain, distraction.

Also present are two Gentlemen of the Privy Chamber, Sir Thomas Wrothe and Sir Henry Sidney, and a groom who has been Edward's personal attendant throughout his reign, Christopher Salmon. They hear him praying.

'O Lord God, deliver me out of this miserable and wretched life, and take me among thy chosen. Howbeit, not my will but thy will be done.

'O Lord, I commit my spirit to thee.

'O Lord, thou knowest how happy it were for me to be with thee, yet for thy chosen's sake send me life and health that I may truly serve thee.

'O my Lord God, bless thy people, and save thine inheritance.

'O Lord God, save thy chosen people of England!

'O my Lord God, defend this realm from papistry, and maintain thy true religion, that I and my people may praise thy holy name.

'For thy son Jesus Christ's sake.'

Then he notices them. 'Are ye so nigh? I thought ye had been further off.'

Dr Owen says: 'We heard you speak to yourself, but what you said we know not.'

He says, smilingly as is his way: 'I was praying to God.'

At about eight o'clock: 'I am faint. Lord have mercy upon me, and take my spirit!'

He dies at about nine.[1]

79

ii

One might add a prayer of one's own: 'When, O God, thy chosen people of England are in a right mess, and you decide to save them, remember kindly, O Lord God, those who *ex officio* are your instruments for the saving – on this occasion a Papist Princess, spinster, unprepared, unsupported; and a Protestant Lord President of the Council, family man, soldier, uneasy statesman.'

III

Crisis Resolved

8

In time of miraculous revolution

i

On Saturday morning, 8 July, the Lord Mayor's barge arrives at Greenwich, along with some others. Northumberland announces to the Lord Mayor, Sheriff William Garrard, six Aldermen, six Merchants of the Staple, and six Merchant Adventurers, the death of King Edward VI and the arrangements for the succession. They all sign the patent and swear the bond. No problems from the City.

On Sunday, Bishop Ridley preaches at Paul's Cross that Mary and Elizabeth are both bastards. Neither cheers nor protests. Jane goes up to Syon, and so do members of the Council. She is told formally that she is to be Queen.

On Monday morning Jane comes back by water to Whitehall Palace, where she picks up queenly clothes. Then she dines at Durham House. In the afternoon, in green velvet stamped with gold, with Guildford in white and gold, she is brought in the royal barge, in splendid sunshine, attended by City barges and by music and noise, to the usual temporary residence of a new monarch, the Tower.

At the Cross in Cheap she is proclaimed. Not a great deal of enthusiasm. In fact one Gilbert Potter, drawer at the St John's Head in Ludgate Hill, shouts out that Mary has a better title. How could there be much enthusiasm? The Princesses are Mary and Elizabeth – Jane is none. On the other hand there is no disorder. The English simply withdraw into themselves.

Gilbert Potter is put in the pillory with his ears nailed, and then has them cut off: punishment by Justice of the Peace. But his employer, who informed on him, a part-time gunner at the Tower as well as a Vintner, is drowned when shooting the Bridge: punishment by God or waterman.

In the Tower the Council sends letters to lords lieutenant of counties

83

proclaiming Jane and denouncing as bastards Mary and Elizabeth. Jane has been asked to name Guildford King-Consort, but she says she will just make him a duke. And she has made him sit at a lower table than his Queen. She is wrought up: the skin peels off her back.

News comes that Mary has had herself proclaimed and some lords and gentlemen are going to her at Kenninghall in Norfolk. A letter comes from her claiming the Council's allegiance. A letter is sent to her, saying she must submit to Queen Jane. The Dudley young men – sent with inadequate force and too late – have failed to bring her in, and it is decided that Jane's ineffective father, the Duke of Suffolk, shall collect some troops and fetch her.

Strange. If Northumberland were one-tenth as ambitious, ruthless, crafty and all-powerful as hostile alien ambassadors make out, or simply one-tenth as efficient as in past military operations, Mary would have been in his hands a fortnight ago, and steps would have been taken to introduce Jane to her people beforehand and ensure her acclamation. What has been the matter?

It is as if he is as unconfident in political and state matters as in years past. Consider. An important draft of Secretary Cecil's for the March Parliament (making the case for a subsidy) was passed to Northumberland for approval; he disagreed seriously with its approach, but all he did was apologetically make some suggestions and put them in the margin so they could be ignored if other Councillors disagreed.

He wants everyone's agreement and approval. So that all could go forward together he has brought back to the Council Catholic Arundel and untrustworthy Paget. He is at least as naive as he is crafty, as conscientious as ambitious. And certainly not ruthless. What is his tally of political executions? One, Somerset's – which was unavoidable, and was only after, in desperate endeavour for collaboration, he had married his heir, John, to Somerset's daughter.

His health, which has been bad for several years, seems in the last six or twelve months to have broken: he was away from Court for some months at the end of last year and at the beginning of this, he has taken cures, complained of fever, dieted, said he is sick of government.

Has he health and devil enough to impose the devise?[1]

ii

It would be good if we could hear what the Councillors are saying to one another in the Tower.

Journal of unidentified person in the Tower (how fortunate there is such a journal; how unfortunate some of it smells less of a journal than of supposititious journalism)

By night of the same day the said voyage of the Duke of Suffolk was clean dissolved by the special means of the Lady Jane his daughter, who, taking the matter heavily, with weeping tears made request to the whole Council that her father might tarry at home in her company. Whereupon the Council persuaded with the Duke of Northumberland to take that voyage upon him, saying that no man was so fit therefor, because that he had achieved the victory in Norfolk once already [*in suppressing Kett in 1549*], and was therefore so feared that none durst once lift up their weapons against him. Besides that he was the best man of war in the realm; as well for the ordering of his camps and soldiers both in battles and in their tents, as also by experience, knowledge and wisdom he could animate his army with witty persuasions, and also pacify and allay his enemy's pride with his stout courage, or else to dissuade them if need were from their enterprise.

'Well', quoth the Duke then, 'since ye think it good, I and mine will go, not doubting of your fidelity to the Queen's Majesty, which I leave in your custody.'

So that night he sent for both lords, knights and other that should go with him, and caused all things to be prepared accordingly.

The morrow following, great preparation was made. The Duke early in the morning called for all his own harness, and saw it made ready. At Durham Place he appointed all the retinue to meet. The same day carts were laden with munition, and artillery and field pieces prepared for the purpose. The same forenoon he moved eftsoons the Council to send their powers after him, as it was before determined, which should have met him at Newmarket, and they promised him they would.

Could no one else go? There was Northampton, although he failed against Kett, and Pembroke was a good soldier. Perhaps the biddable Duke went to be a soldier again with relief.

The journal:

Therewithal the first course for the Lords came up. Then the Duke did knit up his talk with these words:

'I have not spoken to you on this sort upon any distrust I have of your truths, of the which always I have hitherto conceived a trusty confidence; but I have put in remembrance thereof, what chance of variance soever might grow amongst you in mine absence; and this I pray you, wish me no worse speed in this journey than ye would have to yourselves.'

'My Lord,' saith one of them, 'if ye mistrust any of us in this matter, your Grace is far deceived thereof. And if we should shrink from you as one that were culpable, which of us can excuse himself as guiltless? Therefore herein your doubt is too far cast.'

'I pray God it be so,' quoth the Duke. 'Let us go to dinner.'

And so they sat down.

After the dinner the Duke went into the Queen, where his commission was by that time sealed for his lieutenantship of the army, and there he took his leave of her; and so did certain other lords also.

Then, as the Duke came through the Council Chamber he took his leave of the Earl of Arundel, who prayed God be with his Grace, saying he was very sorry it was not his chance to go with him and bear him company, in whose presence he could find in his heart to spend blood, even at his foot.

Then my Lord of Arundel took also my Lord's boy, Thomas Lovell, by the hand, and said, 'Farewell, gentle Thomas, with all my heart.'

Then the Duke came down, and the Lord Marquis [*of Northampton*], my Lord Grey [*brother of Suffolk*], with divers other, and went out of the Tower and took their boat and went to Durham Place or Whitehall, where that night they mustered their company in harness.[2]

iii

On Thursday morning, 13 July, Northumberland marches about 600 men out through Bishopsgate, past Bedlam on his left, towards Shoreditch and Epping on his way to Newmarket. It is being said that Mary has been proclaimed in several places outside London, that quite a number of lords and gentlemen have gone and are going to her, and that quite considerable forces, of some few thousands, are now available to her. It is a week since Edward's death, and Northumberland has only 600 men. He says to someone riding with him: 'The people press to see us, but not one saith God speed us.'

The hydra-headed people of London have become, in silence, of one single mind about the crown of England: Henry's loins have the monopoly. They ignore the old marriage annulments, which were nonsense anyway. They shut their eyes to the perils of Papistry. It must be the eldest of Henry's progeny, Mary.

London remains quiet. No rioting. Quiet.

On Sunday the sixteenth the preacher at Paul's Cross is small John Rogers, the prebendary of Paul's who edited the Great Bible and supplied it with a Protestant apparatus. He preaches an ordinary sermon on the text of the day, without abuse of Mary or Elizabeth.

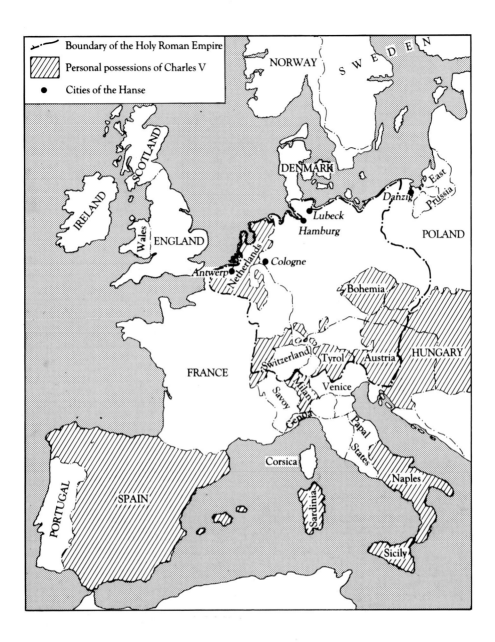

Map of the Holy Roman Empire, with the
shaded areas representing the personal
possessions of Emperor Charles V.

ABOVE Greenwich Palace from the north: detail from Wyngaerde's Panorama drawn for Philip II of Spain. (*The Sutherland Collection, Ashmolean Museum, Oxford*)

BELOW The coronation procession of Edward VI from the Tower of London to Westminster. (*Museum of London*)

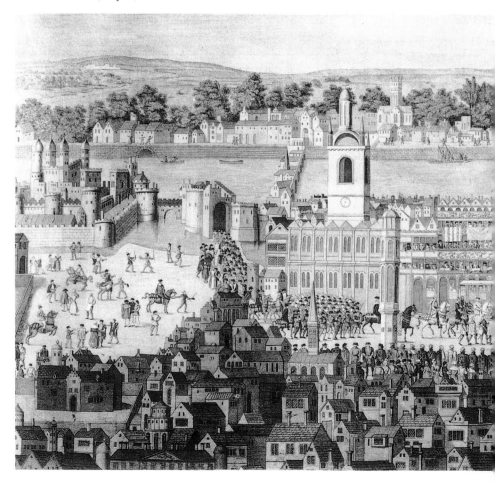

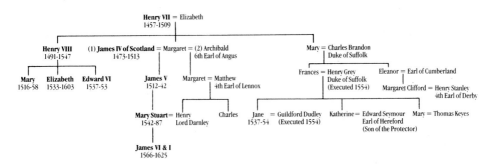

The family of Henry VII:

Henry VII = Elizabeth
1457-1509

Henry VIII
1491-1547

(1) James IV of Scotland = Margaret = (2) Archibald
1473-1513   6th Earl of Angus

Mary = Charles Brandon
       Duke of Suffolk

Mary   Elizabeth   Edward VI
1516-58   1533-1603   1537-53

James V
1512-42

Margaret = Matthew
           4th Earl of Lennox

Frances = Henry Grey
          Duke of Suffolk
          (Executed 1554)

Eleanor = Earl of Cumberland

Margaret Clifford = Henry Stanley
                    4th Earl of Derby

Mary Stuart = Henry
1542-87   Lord Darnley

Charles

Jane = Guildford Dudley
1537-54 (Executed 1554)

Katherine = Edward Seymour
            Earl of Hereford
            (Son of the Protector)

Mary = Thomas Keyes

James VI & I
1566-1625

ABOVE   The family of Henry VII, showing
the line of succession.

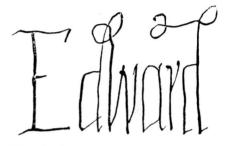

My devise for the succession...

OPPOSITE   Edward VI, at the age of 14 years. A portrait at Hampton Court. (*H.M. The Queen*)

ABOVE   Edward's 'devise' for his succession. This first named 'Lady Jane's heirs male' but was changed to read 'Lady Jane *and her* heirs male'. The devise was ratified by a bond signed by Council.

BELOW   Edward VI and the Pope. On one side sits Henry VIII, on the other side sits Edward Seymour, Duke of Somerset, John Dudley, Duke of Northumberland, and Archbishop Cranmer. (*National Portrait Gallery, London*)

Edward's signature.

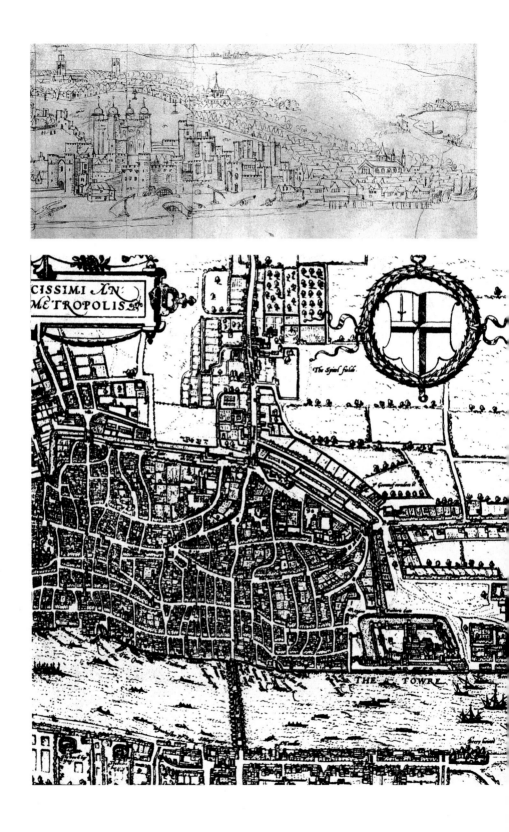

OPPOSITE The Tower of London.
Wyngaerde Panorama. (*The Sutherland Collection, Ashmolean Museum, Oxford*)

BELOW The Braun and Hogenberg Map of London. *Londinum Feracissimi Angliae Regni Metropolis*, by Frans Hogenberg, was published in 1572 but shows a London that is pre-1561.

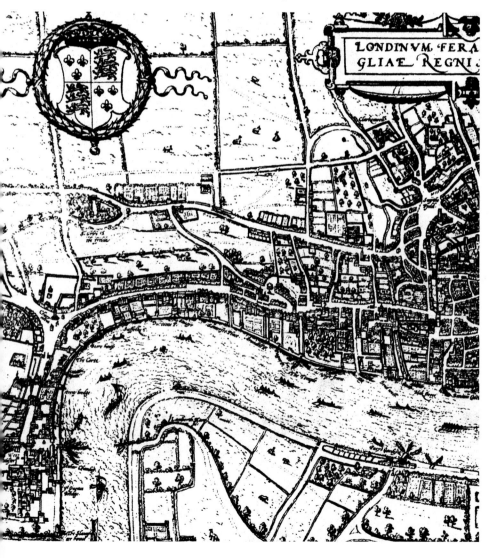

The Duke of Northumberland, John Dudley,
father-in-law of Lady Jane Grey. Engraving
from the original at Knowle. (*The Hulton-
Deutsch Collection*)

It is said that the ships sent to lie off the East Anglian coast have gone over to Mary, with their artillery. And specifically that Mary has been proclaimed in Oxfordshire and Buckinghamshire.

No reinforcements have been sent to Northumberland although he must certainly need them, and Councillors could have provided them from their own followers. The Councillors are remaining in the Tower, except for Paulet who, during the course of Sunday, goes to his house near Bishopsgate. However, he is brought back, and Jane personally, it is said, takes charge of the Tower keys, as if to hold the Council her prisoners.

On Wednesday the nineteenth the Councillors, led by Arundel and Pembroke, contrive to leave the Tower and go to Pembroke's Baynard's Castle. Soon the Lord Mayor and some aldermen and City officials ride down to join them. They all together ride up from Thames Street to the Cross in Cheap. With a herald.

Mary is proclaimed. Cheers and shouts. Great, great rejoicing. Caps and money thrown in the air. Bonfires are lit in the streets and lanes; tables are brought out for feasting and drinking. In Thames Street outside the Steelyard there is free wine provided by the Hanse, and other foreign merchants do likewise elsewhere. Arundel and Paget ride through the bonfires to post to Mary at Framlingham, whither she has removed from Kenninghall. Mary's proclamation comes out in print, printed by Richard Grafton on his press at Christ's Hospital, like Jane's nine days ago.

Stories circulate. A Gentleman Pensioner, Edward Underhill, was having his infant son christened Guildford at Allhallows Barking, close to the Tower. As godmother, Jane Northumberland was standing proxy for Queen Jane. By the time she returned to the Tower she found Jane's cloth of state being taken down. By the time Jane's father returned to the Tower after proclaiming Mary on Tower Hill, he found Jane quite unattended. She asked: 'May I go home now?'

The bells go on ringing till ten at night. St Michael Cornhill has to spend 4d on men to ring them; St Martin-in-the-Fields has to buy two new bell ropes. Once again true father-to-offspring succession, an adult Tudor sovereign, a rest from government by dukes.

The following Tuesday Northumberland enters through Bishopsgate. Arundel has him and three of his sons under heavy guard. From Shoreditch onwards the Londoners have been shouting 'Traitor!', 'Heretic!'. They tell Northumberland to take off his hat. He does so. Men of the trained bands stand at every door. He keeps his hat off all the way down Bishopsgate Street, past Leadenhall, down Gracechurch Street and Fenchurch Street. People go on shouting 'Traitor!', although there are some attempts to stop them.

Northumberland heard that the Council had proclaimed Mary the same night it was done. Next morning, last Thursday, he proclaimed Mary in Cambridge market place, throwing his hat in the air. If the country's decision is for Mary, so be it.

As he enters the Tower an old woman thrusts under his nose a cloth which last year she soaked in Somerset's blood.

It is doubtful whether a shot has been fired, on either Jane's side or Mary's. Northumberland and Mary have between them brought peace and relative unity out of a situation where there was no course of action which would have united support. The Duke, inefficiently but courageously performing his duty to Edward VI, tried to carry out the plan to which he was personally sworn, so giving the English something they could unitedly reject. Mary, against the Imperial ambassador's expert advice, naively but courageously performing her duty to her Tudor birth, had herself proclaimed Queen, so giving the English an immediate alternative to Northumberland's Jane.

God has saved his people. Not from Papistry, but first things first. He has saved England from indecision and civil war.[3]

iv

All around there is relief, and action. The Lord Mayor, Sir George Barne, with the doyen of the Goldsmiths, Sir Martin Bowes, ride off to Mary with the City's plea for forgiveness, and 1,000 half-sovereigns. The Court of Aldermen has 'Jana' deleted from recent minute-headings, and 'Maria' substituted. The Council has managed to have no minutes extant from 16 June onwards.

All and sundry send self-exculpatory letters to Framlingham. Cecil writes that he refused to swear the bond (this is a lie – his signature is on the document). He says he avoided drafting Jane's proclamation: Sir Nicholas Throgmorton did it. He says he avoided drafting the letters to lords lieutenant declaring Mary a bastard: Northumberland did it. He says he avoided drafting the letter to Mary telling her to acknowledge Jane: Cheke did it. And he says he sabotaged his own raising of reinforcements for Northumberland (he did).

Chief Justice Sir Edward Montague writes that he would not have put the devise into legal form if he had not been forced: Northumberland looked as if he was going to hit him. So easily was a Chief Justice intimidated.

Jane, in the custody of the Lieutenant of the Tower, writes that she had not heard of the plan to make her Queen until after Edward died; and that when at Syon the Lords of the Council promised 'even to shed their blood, exposing their lives to death' in defence of her title, she wept bitterly and fell to the ground. Mary believes her.

Some are trying to improve their standing less directly. A tract is published in the form of a letter to the new hero Gilbert Potter, the drawer who shouted for Mary. It gives mention, bare mention, to a number of noblemen who behaved worthily in the crisis, but mention less bare to Arundel; and for the loyal behaviour of the much less eminent Sir Edmund Peckham it really spreads itself.

Mary has put the London end of her government in the hands of Arundel and Paget. She pardons some of Northumberland's commanders (Clinton, Sidney, Lord Grey), tells Pembroke to stay inside Baynard's Castle, and sends Northampton and Huntingdon to the Tower. She also sends Suffolk to the Tower but pardons him after his wife, her friend, tells her everything was the fault of Northumberland – the horrid man even tried to poison her husband. She has Jane Northumberland released, but refuses to see her when she comes to Framlingham to plead for her sons. Cecil remains free, Cheke goes to the Tower. One man who has not had to plead forgiveness for supporting the devise is Sir James Hales, Justice of the Common Pleas, the only man who refused to sign. Had Northumberland hit him? No.

Still in the Tower, but probably not a prisoner for much longer, is Stephen Gardiner. He is believed to have sent to Northampton's wife to get out of Winchester House at once; and to Pembroke to give back some property to the see of Winchester. Is it starting already? Are Church lands which have come lawfully into the hands of laymen to be taken from them?

In the middle of the week after Northumberland was brought in prisoner, Princess Elizabeth, after staying at the Somerset House she does not want, rides into the city attended by some hundreds of gentlemen, in through Ludgate and out through Aldgate. She has gone to meet Mary, who is now well on her way to London, and has so far risen to every occasion. Mary kisses not only Elizabeth but all her women.

Mary has had a visit from Renard. He advises her to dissemble her intention to restore Catholicism (unnecessary advice: she has been dissembling admirably; in spite of which people point at heretics, and at priests and bishops who have wives, as if they knew her intentions). She has told Renard, on the question of marriage, that she requests the Emperor's advice (as if Charles could be prevented from giving it).

And so, on Thursday, 3 August, four weeks after Edward's death, crowds wait at Aldgate for their new Queen. In the highway, holes where paving stones are missing have been filled with gravel.

Queen Mary is on a palfrey solid as a circus horse, which is led by Sir Anthony Browne, the Catholic owner of the priory of St Mary Overy. She is dressed in purple velvet, with her train over Browne's shoulder. She greets the Lord Mayor. The Christ's Hospital children, drawn up outside Aldgate in blue, with red caps, have twelve-year-old Edmund Campion to speak their Latin welcome. She looks at them but does not speak: Christ's Hospital will have to be given back to the Franciscans.

She enters Aldgate with the procession, while the Tower guns boom as never before, bells ring as never before (St Michael Cornhill spends three times as much as when she was proclaimed), and people weep at the miracle and the blessing. The procession forks left at Aldgate Pump; along Fenchurch Street, down Mart Lane, and left again past Allhallows Barking, and into the Tower by the Barbican Gate. On the Green she is welcomed by Sir John Gage, the Constable, who presents some kneeling prisoners, including rheumatic dyspeptic old Norfolk ('I have never read the Scripture nor ever will read it'); swarthy Bishop Gardiner with the fleshy well-shaven cheeks, whom she has never been able to like; unexposed young Courtenay, who presumably will be a candidate for her hand.

Paget, conversing with Renard, says it would be an excellent thing if the Queen married the Emperor's son, Philip.

Mary retires to the Queen's Lodgings.[4]

v

The time for miracles is over. The unfledged monarch must have a Chief Minister and a Council, men who will restore the Mass for her, free England from heresy, make a celibate and trained priesthood, return England to the Papacy, and give back to the Church all that was taken from it. Run through the members of her chosen Council, who will be regularly gathering in the White Tower. First the assured Catholics:

Stephen Gardiner: inevitably her Chief Minister by his energy and competence, but under Henry he was active in the divorce, and he willingly renounced Rome; aged seventy, he has been five years in the Tower.

Thomas Howard, third Duke of Norfolk: experienced, but eighty and has been longer in the Tower than Gardiner; vengeful, and half the Council were party to his imprisonment.

Cuthbert Tunstall, ex-Bishop of Durham: almost eighty; will have to be brought out of the Queen's Bench Prison.

Sir John Gage: not quite so old at seventy-four.

Sir Edward Hastings: too young, in his early thirties and inexperienced;

and his father the Earl of Huntingdon is in the Tower as one of Northumberland's chief allies.

Sir Richard Southwell: close with Norfolk and the Howards, and wealthy, but no backbone.

Sir Richard Rich: first-rate administrator, but indissolubly connected with the execution of More and Fisher and the Dissolution; in bad health.

Sir Thomas Pope: undistinguished; has altogether too much Church property.

The Earl of Bath: joined Mary before she was proclaimed, but otherwise not significant.

Sir Francis Englefield: trusted officer of her former small househould; untried in national affairs.

Sir Edmund Peckham: reliable; a suitable Master of the Mint, but no more.

Arundel: thank goodness for Arundel.

All the others, as much Protestant as Catholic:

Paget: experienced and competent but of little integrity; he and Gardiner are totally antipathetic – he was active in getting Gardiner imprisoned.

Pembroke and Paulet: leaders in Northumberland's Council and Mary trusts neither; she may have to have them on her council but cannot yet bring herself to do so.

Sussex: was in charge of her forces in Norfolk, but he has a great deal of monastic property which will have to be restored.

Bedford: the one-eyed and moderate; but his son and heir, Francis, Lord Russell, is a committed heretic.

Sir John Mason: useful administrator and diplomat ('none seeth further than Sir John Mason'); but his wife is related to Jane Northumberland, and by a previous marriage she has Cheke for son-in-law.

Mary must have Petre continue as first Secretary: he is sober, experienced, and at least as Catholic as Protestant, but he was actively involved in dissolution. As second Secretary she will not have Cecil or Cheke, neither of whom she trusts; she will have to have Sir John Bourne, Catholic but mediocre.

She has chosen her Council as well as it can be done, certainly without narrow-mindedness, but as a revolutionary government it is unimpressive. She has always turned to Charles V when in trouble, and she is now taking great comfort in his Renard, although she cannot discreetly see him as much as she would like. She complains to him that her Council do not seem to know what to do. Which may be true but is not what a monarch says to a foreign ambassador. She is a half-Spanish housewife complaining to a visiting Spaniard of the native servants.

Is it bad that the Council do not know what to do? A know-all united vigorous Council would tear England in two.

vi

The Council knows one thing it can do: it can try to suppress heretic street ballads. One, written by that Underhill whose infant was being christened Guildford at the moment Mary was being proclaimed, comes into the hands of Secretary Bourne on Friday 4 August, the day after Mary's entry into London. In the evening Underhill is arrested in his house in Limehurst (he is in bed) and brought to London. Early next morning two guards with halberds take him to the Tower. After waiting all morning outside the Council Chamber in the White Tower along with other culprits, he has dinner at an alehouse with his guards, and returns to the White Tower.

Edward Underhill's story:

Immediately as [the Council] had dined Secretary Bourne came to the door, looking as a wolf doth for a lamb; unto who my two keepers delivered me standing next unto the door, for there were more behind me. He took me greedily and shut the door; leaving me at the nether end of the Chamber he went unto the Council showing of me, and then beckoned me to come near.

Then they began the table and sat them down. The Earl of Bedford sat as chief, uppermost upon the bench. Then next unto him the Earl of Sussex; next him Sir Richard Southwell. On the side next me sat the Earl of Arundel; next him the Lord Paget. By them stood Sir John Gage, then Constable of the Tower; the Earl of Bath, and master [Sir John] Mason. At the board's end stood Serjeant Morgan and Secretary Bourne. The Lord Wentworth stood in the bay window talking with one, all the while of my examination, whom I knew not.

The great mercy of God provided for me that master Hastings was not at my examination [*Underhill once wrangled with Hastings about the Real Presence, perhaps excessively*].

My Lord of Bedford, being my very friend (for that my chance was to be at the recovering of his son, my Lord Russell, when he was cast into the Thames against the Limehurst, whom I carried to my house and got him to bed; who was in great peril of his life, the weather being very cold), would not seem to be familiar with me, nor called me not by my name but said, 'Come hither, sirrah! did not you set forth a ballad of late, in print?'

I kneeled down saying, 'Yes, truly my Lord. Is that the cause I am called before your Honours?'

'Ay, marry,' said Secretary Bourne, 'you have one of them about you, I am sure.'

'Nay, truly, have I not,' said I.

Then he took one out of his bosom and read it over distinctly, the Council giving diligent ear.

When he had ended, 'I trust, my Lord,' said I, 'I have not offended the Queen's Majesty in this ballad, nor spoken against her title but maintained it.'

'You have, sir,' said Morgan, 'yes, I can divide your ballad and make a distinction on it, and so prove at the least sedition in it.'

'Ay, sir,' said I, 'you men of law will make of a matter what ye list.'

'Lo,' said Sir Richard Southwell, 'how he can give a taunt! You maintain the Queen's title with the help of an arrant heretic, Tyndale.'

'You speak of Papist there, sir,' said master Mason, 'I pray you, how define you a Papist?'

I look upon him, turning towards him for he stood on the side of me. 'Why, sir,' said I, 'it is not long since you could define a Papist better than I!' With that some of them secretly smiled, as the Lords of Bedford, Arundel, Sussex and Paget.

In great haste Sir John Gage took the matter in hand. 'Thou callest men Papists there,' said he, 'who be they that thou judgest to be Papists?'

'Sir,' said I, 'I think if you look among the priests in Paul's, ye shall find some old mumpsimuses there.'

'Mumpsimuses, knave!' said he, 'Mumpsimuses! Thou art an heretic knave, by God's birth!'

'Ay, by the Mass!' says the Earl of Bath, 'I warrant him an heretic knave indeed!'

'I beseech your Honours,' said I, speaking to the Lords that sat at table, for those other stood by, 'be my good Lords! I have offended no laws, and I have served the Queen's Majesty's father and brother a long time. And for my part, I went not forth against her Majesty notwithstanding that I was commanded, nor liked those doings.'

'No, but with your writings you would set us together by the ears!' said the Earl of Arundel.

With that came Sir Edward Hastings from the Queen in great haste, saying, 'My Lords, you must set all things apart, and come forthwith to the Queen.'

Then said the Earl of Sussex, 'Have this gentleman unto the Fleet until we may talk further with him.'

'To the Fleet!' said master Southwell, 'have him to the Marshalsea!'

'Have the gentleman to Newgate!' saith master Gage again, 'call a couple of the guard here.'

'Ay,' saith Bourne, 'and there shall be a letter sent to the keeper how he shall use him, for we have other manner of matters to him than these.'

'So had ye need,' said I, 'for else I care not for you.'

'Deliver him to master Garrard the Sheriff,' said he, 'and bid him send him to Newgate.'

[The Council usually commits to the Fleet or the Marshalsea. The Fleet is the less uncomfortable of the two if you have money: for example, for a fee you can use a bowling green. At either of these you may be kept a longer or shorter time and then released, but at Newgate you will be charged at the next Assizes with a specific crime.]

'My Lord,' said I unto my Lord of Arundel, for he was next to me, as they were rising, 'I trust you will not see me thus used, to be sent to Newgate. I am neither thief nor traitor.'

'You are a naughty fellow,' said he, 'you were always turning in the Duke of Northumberland's ear, that you were!'

So went I forth with my two fellows of the guard, who were glad they had the leading of me for they were great Papists.

'Where is that knave the printer?' said master Gage.

'I know not,' said I.[5]

vii

As well as a heretic's-eye view of the new Council at work, Underhill gives a heretic-gentleman-prisoner's-eye view of the walk to Newgate.

Edward Underhill's story:

When we came to the Tower gate, where Sir John Brydges had the charge, with his brother master Thomas with whom I was well acquainted (but not with Sir John) who, seeing the two of the guard leading me without their halberds, rebuked them; and stayed me while they went for their halberds.

His brother said unto me, 'I am sorry you should be an offender, master Underhill.'

'I am none, sir,' said I, 'nor went against the Queen.'

'I am glad of that,' said he.

And so forth we went at the gate, where was a great throng of people to hear and see what prisoners were committed, and amongst whom stood my friend master Ive, the High Constable, my next neighbour.

One of the guard went forth at the wicket before me to take me by the arm, the other held me by the other arm, fearing belike I would have shifted from them amongst the people.

When my friend, who had watched at the gate all the forenoon, saw me thus led, he followed afar off as Peter did Christ, to see what should become of me. Many also followed, some that knew me, some to learn who I was for that I was in a gown of satin.

Thus passed we through the streets, well accompanied, unto master Garrard the Sheriff's house in the Stocks Market. My friend master Ive tarried at the gate.

These two of the guard declared unto master Sheriff that they were commanded by the Council to deliver me unto him, and he to send me unto Newgate, saying, 'Sir, if it please you, we will carry him thither.'

With that I stepped unto master Sheriff and, taking him a little aside, requested him that forasmuch as their commission was but to deliver me unto him, and he to send me into Newgate, that he would send me by his officers, for the request was of mere malice.

'With a good will,' said master Sheriff.

'Masters,' said he, 'you may depart. I will send my officers with this gentleman anon, when they be come in.'

'We will see him carried, sir,' said they, 'for our discharge.'

Then the Sheriff said sharply unto them, 'What! do you think that I will not do the Council's commandment? You are discharged by delivering unto me.'

With that, they departed.

My friend, master Ive, seeing them depart and leave me behind, was very glad thereof and tarried still at the gate to see further.

All this talk in the Sheriff's hall did my Lord Russell, son and heir to the Earl of Bedford, hear and see; who was at commandment in the Sheriff's house, and his chamber joining into the hall wherein he might look: who was very sorry for me, for that I had been familiar with him in matters of religion as well as on the other side the seas as at home. [*Russell in due course sends Underhill 20s every week he is in Newgate.*]

When these two companions of the guard were gone, the Sheriff sent two of his officers with me, who took no bills with them, nor led me but followed a pretty way behind me.

When I came into the street my friend master Ive, seeing me have such liberty and such distance betwixt me and the officers, he stepped before them and so went talking with me through Cheapside, so that it was not well perceived that I was apprehended, but by the great company that followed.

The officers delivered me unto the keeper of Newgate as they were commanded, who unlocked the door and willed me to go up the stairs into the hall. My friend Ive went up with me, where we found three or four prisoners that had the liberty of the house.

After a little talk with my friend I required him not to let my wife know that I was sent to Newgate but to the Counter, until such time that she were near her churching. And that she should send me my nightgown, my Bible, and my lute. And so he departed.

In a while after it was supper time. The board was covered in the hall. The keeper and his wife came to supper, and half a dozen prisoners that were there for felonies.[6]

viii

It is a muddling time for everyone. The law cannot catch up with Mary's will for several months, and meanwhile some people think they are still free to act the Protestant, and others that they are already free to act the Catholic.

On Sunday John Rogers preaches again at Paul's Cross. Not an innocuous sermon like his last. He expounds the Reformed faith and exhorts to beware of pestilent Popery, idolatry and superstition. Brave man.

During the week he is summoned before the Council. He says that he was preaching the religion established by law. They let him return to his house in Paul's precinct.

Gardiner leaves the Tower and visits his old house; then goes up-river for dinner with Arundel, and so back to Winchester House to settle in.

Tunstall is brought out of the Queen's Bench prison in Southwark, and reinstated as Bishop of Durham. Nicholas Heath, released from Ridley's palace, is reinstated as Bishop of Worcester.

Edmund Bonner, a boorish man for a bishop so quick-witted and able, is brought out of the Marshalsea and conducted by bishops and prebendaries to the Bishop of London's palace at Paul's, lately vacated by Ridley. While it is being got ready for him he lives at the Deanery: the married Dean May has resigned. Stout, red-faced, eloquent Feckenham is brought out of the Tower and reinstated as Bonner's chaplain.

Bonner goes down to his country palace at Fulham where, while he was in prison, his mother was allowed by Ridley to remain. But he does not let Ridley's sister remain in quarters for which Ridley gave her a lease. So notes Reformer John Foxe.

This John Foxe has been tutoring the grandsons of the Duke of Norfolk. The moment Norfolk is out of the Tower he sacks Foxe and puts the elder boy, Thomas, his heir, into Gardiner's household at Winchester House.

Edward must have a funeral, for which his embalmed body has waited a month. He is brought up-river from Greenwich to Whitehall by Cranmer, who was his godfather and loved him. The official ceremonies are going to be Protestant, not because they are the only legal ones but because a heretic cannot receive Catholic rites. He is to be buried in Westminster Cathedral (ex-Abbey) under an altar by Torrigiano.

He will be much mourned. In the procession from Whitehall Palace there is a mighty display of black velvet (Reformed funerals are as black as Catholic), but no crosses or candles. Mary is not present: she is attending a requiem Mass of her own. Funeral ballads are on sale.

> Adieu pleasure!
> Gone is our treasure,
> Mourning may be our mirth:
> For Edward our King,
> That rose and spring,
> Is faded and lyeth in earth.
>
> Gone is our joy,
> Our sport and our play,
> Our comfort is turned to care:
> To England's great cost,
> This jewel we have lost,
> That with all Christendom might compare.
>
> In his tender age
> So grave and so sage,
> So well learned and witty:
> And now, that sweet flower
> Hath builded his bower
> In the earth – the more is the pity.
>
> Out of Greenwich is he gone,
> And lieth under a stone,
> That loved both house and park:
> Thou shalt see him no more,
> That set by thee such store,
> For death has pierced his heart.

97

Gone is our King,
That would run at the ring,
And oftentimes ride on Blackheath:
  Ye noble men of chivalry,
  And ye men of artillery,
May all lament his death.

Farewell, diamond heart!
Farewell, crystal clear!
Farewell, the flower of chivalry!
  The Lord hath taken him,
  And for his people's sin;
A just plague for our iniquity.

But now, ye noble peers,
Mark well your years,
For you do not know your day:
  And this you may be bold,
  Both young and old,
You shall die, and hence away . . .

. . . our royal King,
The noblest living,
No longer with us may tarry:
  But his soul we commend
  Unto the Lord's hand,
Who preserve our noble Queen Mary.

Long with us to endure,
With mirth, joy and pleasure,
To rule her realms aright:
  All her enemies to withstand
  By sea and by land,
Lord preserve her both day and night!

Cranmer is still undisturbed in his see. He went one day to Court but Mary would not see him. He noticed Cecil there but did not speak to him, knowing Cecil wanted to be inconspicuous (as physically Thomas Cecil has always been: he has just weighed himself at the Thames Street house of his brother-in-law Nicholas Bacon: 9 stone 5 pounds).

There has been little religious disorder. A priest who said Mass in St Bartholomew the Great was pulled down by some of the congregation, but that is about all. Mary is being very discreet. She wants the true religion restored instantly: in ceremonial, in obedience to the Papacy, in re-establishment of the dissolved institutions (why be Queen of England if you cannot make a kettle of incense?), but Emperor Charles says she must wait for Parliament or all will be lost.

Sunday, 13 August, Paul's Cross again. The sermon is by Gilbert Bourne, one of the prebendaries of Paul's and nephew of Bourne the second Secretary. Avenging Rogers's sermon of last week Bourne abuses some of the Reformed proceedings under Edward, and there are shouts of 'Thou liest!'. In spite of the Lord Mayor and aldermen being present, and also Courtenay, a dagger is thrown at Bourne and there are shouts of 'Kill him! Kill him!' Two other prebendaries, Protestants, spare and auburn-haired John Bradford and dark little John Rogers, pacify the crowd and hustle Bourne into St Paul's School.

No doubt Mary and the Council will take it very seriously, but only a month ago the majority of Londoners were Protestants, and their conversion cannot be instantaneous.

The City is ordered to prevent such incidents. Bradford is sent to the Tower, and Rogers is confined to his house and ordered to speak to no one but his immediate household.

The following Friday there is a proclamation that the Queen personally would like everyone to follow the old religion – and the Latin Mass can from henceforth be used – but each man must live after the religion he thinks best until Parliament takes order in the matter. Meanwhile no one is to call anyone else either heretic or Papist.

This same Friday, 18 August, Mary's Councillors have an appointment at Westminster Hall with Northumberland, his eldest boy John Dudley, Earl of Warwick, and the Earl of Northampton.[7]

9

Truth on Tower Hill,
truth on Paul's door

i

In Westminster Hall a stage has been erected at the south end and hung with
tapestries, and a great canopy put up in the middle of it. Under the canopy
sits the Duke of Norfolk, Earl Marshal of England, holding a long white
wand of office. On his right and left sit the commissioners for the trial: six
lords of the Council on his right, including Lord Treasurer Paulet and
Arundel, and six on his left, including Bedford, Shrewsbury and Paget.
Below them are four London aldermen, and four judges in scarlet with small
white caps, and to the left and right of these other government officers. There
is a large attendance.

One of the four heralds cries 'Silence!' The commission of the court is read
out in Latin, and the Lieutenant of the Tower commanded to bring forth the
person of the Duke.

Northumberland comes in, under escort and preceded by a guard carrying
the Axe of Justice. He makes three low reverences and comes to the bar 'with
a good and intrepid countenance, full of humility and gravity' – as described
by Antonio de Guaras, a Portuguese onlooker. The Duke of Norfolk and the
commissioners look at him severely, but one or two slightly touch their cap.

He is accused of three things. He was in the field with an armed levy
against the Queen's Majesty, her Highness having been proclaimed Queen
the same day in London and throughout the kingdom. Second, he caused
himself to be proclaimed Captain-General of the Kingdom. Third, he
proclaimed Jane Queen and the Queen's Majesty a rebel and a bastard.

His confession is read out and he is asked if he maintains what he there
states so that judgement may be given according to custom.

He raises his hand in sign of taking the oath, and falls on his knees.

He protests his faith and allegiance to the Queen whom he confesses
grievously to have offended, and says that he means not anything in defence

of his fact, but requests to understand the opinions of the court on two points. First, may a man be charged with treason for an act done by authority of the Prince's Council, and by warrant of the Great Seal of England? Secondly, may persons who are equally culpable in that crime, and by whose letters and commandments he was directed in all his doings, be his judges?

The answer to the first is that the Great Seal was not the seal of the lawful queen of the realm but the seal of a usurper. The answer to the second is that as long as no attainder is brought against any of these persons they are able in law to judge in his trial.

Northumberland confesses the indictment.

Norfolk, without consulting the commissioners, pronounces sentence: The accused to be had to the place whence he came, and from thence to be drawn through London to Tyburn, and there to be hanged, his heart to be drawn from his body and flung against his face, and then to be cut down and his bowels burned and his head to be set on London Bridge.

Northumberland says: 'I beseech you, my Lords all, to be humble suitors to the Queen's Majesty to grant me four requests, which are these. First, that I may have that death which noblemen have had in times past, and not the other. Secondarily, that her Majesty will be gracious to my children, which may hereafter do her Grace good service, considering that they went by my commandment who am their father and not by their free wills. Thirdly, that I may have appointed to me some learned man for the instruction and quieting of my conscience. And fourth, that she will send two of the Council to commune with me, to whom I will declare such matters as shall be expedient for her and the commonwealth. And thus I beseech you all to pray for me.' He is led out, the edge of the axe toward him. The other two accused are similarly tried and condemned. An officer holds the white wand before the Duke of Norfolk, who breaks it.

Look up at that great hammerbeam roof, and ponder. Was the Councillors' betrayal of Northumberland evidence of the famous untrustworthiness and changeableness of the English? No. They acted correctly for the nation. The first qualification required of a professional man of politics and government is to be sensitive to society's will, and able accordingly, with speed and without fuss, to change policy, and if necessary desert a colleague of long standing. The Councillors cannot be blamed for not having read the nation's desires earlier because the desires were contradictory and inchoate. As soon as the desires took shape, the Councillors performed their somersault. In impeccable formation.[1]

ii

At eight o'clock on Monday morning, 21 August, a huge crowd are on Tower Hill, with the Lord Mayor and the Common Council. Standing with their halberds to make a lane from the Tower to the scaffold are the Sheriff's officers, the Guard, and men from the surrounding wards. The sand and straw are ready. The executioner is ready. Suddenly all are told to disperse, except the Lord Mayor and the Common Council who are to enter the Tower. Is Northumberland reprieved?

News is more than an hour in coming out, by the Common Councillors. They had been led across Tower Green, past the Lieutenant's Lodging (where Jane is) and the Beauchamp Tower (where Northumberland's five sons are), into the Tower church, St Peter-ad-Vincula. For what? At about nine the Constable, Sir John Gage, brought to the church Northumberland and four others who have been condemned: his brother Andrew Dudley, Northampton, Sir Harry Gates and Sir Thomas Palmer.

Northumberland had turned to the congregation and said they had all been seduced from the true religion these last sixteen years. Mass was then said as in the old days, with elevation of the host, the giving of the pax, the sign of the cross, and turning about and about. All the prisoners received the sacrament.

It is a shock for Reformers. They begin to explain that the traitor cannot ever have been a sincere Reformer. True – he had followed where his ruler, contemporary thought and political advantage had led. But now the country must unite behind their new ruler, and he must therefore adopt her religion, which is the religion of his childhood. Betrayed and defeated, he probably finds relief in re-entering it. And in any after-life his Catholic father and mother will be better company than John Knox.

Next morning at about eight 'all London' are on Tower Hill again. Northumberland is brought out by Gage and Garrard, after the Tower Constable and City Sheriff have signed for his delivery from one to the other. He has been given some coins, provided by the Council, so that he can tip the executioner.[2]

iii

He climbs the scaffold and takes off his cloak of grey damask. He tips the executioner, who is in white like a butcher and has a limp. He approaches the railing and begs to speak to the people as is the custom. There is profound silence.

'Sirs and friends, I have come to die as ye see, having been condemned by the law, and I declare and confess that I have grievously offended God, and I beseech you earnestly that ye would implore God for my soul, and if there be any here, or absent, whom I have offended, I crave their forgiveness.'

The crowd answer: 'May God forgive you.'

When there is silence again, he goes on: 'I have been condemned by the law to be drawn, hanged and quartered, but the Queen's Majesty, whom I have grievously offended, has shown this clemency that I should be beheaded, for which I thank her, and I pray her to pardon me, that God may.'

He makes so low a reverence that his knee touches the ground.

He goes on to say that, although it is true that he was chief in bringing these things to pass for which he has been condemned, it is also true that he did it by the instigation of many whom he would not name, and that he forgives them as he desires the forgiveness of God. And he begs the people not to take any kind of action against them.

'Brethren,' he says, 'ye are not ignorant in what troubles this realm has been and now continues, as well as in part of the reign of King Henry, as from then until this day, all of which are notorious: and I wot well that there is no one of you but knows what has befallen us for having departed from the true Catholic Church, and believed false prophets and preachers, who have persuaded us of their false doctrines, and have brought me as the chief offender in this and other things to the extremity which ye behold, as they have done to many others, as ye know. For which I ask God pardon, and declare to you that I die a true Catholic Christian, and confess and believe all that the Catholic Church believes.'

Some parts of the crowd object strongly to all this.

'And I warn you, friends and brothers, that none should believe that this great novelty and new conscience arises from being urged upon me by any, or that any have persuaded me in this: but I tell you what I feel at the bottom of my heart, and as ye see I am in no case to say aught but the truth.

'And thus I charge and enjoin you straitly that ye give no credit to the preachers of such false doctrine. And consider, brethren, what I say, and do not forget that I charge you to have no let or shame in returning to God, as ye see that I have not, and to consider what is written in the Apostles' Creed, "I believe in the Holy Ghost, the Holy Catholic Church, the Communion of Saints."'

Great offence is taken again.

'Think upon the miseries in which so great a multitude has lived and died in Germany: one against another, and that they have been trampled down for having forsaken the Catholic faith, wherefore God has forgotten them as he has forgotten us. And if this does not move you to feel as I have declared to you, let each one make his private reckoning and consider how it has fared with him in his own condition. And if he is not utterly blind, I am sure that he will come into this my true knowledge.

'And therefore I again charge you to embrace what the Catholic Church believes; which is what the Holy Spirit has revealed from generation to generation from the time of the Apostles until our days, and will continue until the end. And live peaceably, and be obedient to the Queen's Majesty and her laws, and do that which I have not done.'

An unpopular speech.

He withdraws from the rail and, kneeling in the middle of the scaffold, he reads aloud a prayer from a book handed him by his confessor, Nicholas Heath, Bishop of Worcester, and with devotion repeats the Creed in Latin. Then his outer garment is taken off and his eyes bandaged. Before he lies down on the beam where his head will be cut off, he makes the sign of the cross. Still more offence.

The bandage does not fit properly and he gets up again on his knees for it to be re-fitted. Then, with obvious self-control, he hits his hands together as if to say 'It has to be done', and lays himself down. The executioner strikes off his head at a blow, and holds it up. Children collect the blood, as usual, to sell or put in their collections. His head is carted with the body back to the Tower, to be buried in St Peter-ad-Vincula. So it will not be on London Bridge.

Instead of damaging Mary by trying to bring down half the Council with himself, he has accepted (pretty well accepted) the role of scapegoat. Instead of damaging Mary by giving the Protestants a martyr, he has annihilated his own reputation and shaken their confidence. As he would have wished, he has helped signally to unite the country behind its new sovereign.[3]

iv

Northumberland's speech is published in full. Good Catholic propaganda. Printed by the new Queen's Printer, John Cawood, in the crypt of St Paul's.

In Paul's and a few parish churches there are Masses again, and high altars and crucifixes are re-established, but in most London churches the Reformed services continue, with zeal of repentance, and communion in two kinds, and mourning for Edward but not Northumberland.

Mary has removed from divided and August-smelling London to Richmond. This is for two reasons: Renard can come to her less remarked (she did suggest he came to her in the Tower disguised but he raised objections); and Richmond is her pleasantest palace for the late summer.

So she has herself rowed up the silver Thames between the meadows and woods. Syon, which appears on her right, will be the Crown's to dispose of as soon as Northumberland has been attainted; Mary will be able to bring back the Bridgettines. From Syon the towers and pinnacles of Richmond Palace appear due south across the deer park, owing to the turnings of the river; the palace when finally reached is on the left, facing south-west.

It is very handsome, not in the Alberti fashion but in the English fashion of the Henry VII chapel at Westminster and the chapel of King's at Cambridge. It was Henry VII who built it, one of the few English palaces designed and built as a whole. The clustering stone towers which face the river are the royal apartments which extend back in a three-storeyed quadrangle. Behind that is a middle court, also of stone, with the lofty chapel and hall – each with tall windows like those of King's – facing each other east and west. North of that court there is a brick court which accommodates the Household, with kitchen quarters and the like further to the west, and recreational areas further to the east.

The chapel and hall contain a history lesson. There are portraits of English kings between the windows, of saintly kings in the chapel, of martial kings in the hall. By divine providence there are enough of each. The middle court has a fine fountain with dragons, lions, and other beasts, and the water pouring from red Tudor roses. But the fountain is even finer in substance than appearance, because the water is pure (brought from two springs, not from the Thames which, although silver, receives a large amount of sewage from the palace), and also because the water is piped into the palace for wash-basins and water-closets.

But what makes the palace such a delight is that its design takes account of English weather. In the worst storm it is possible to get from anywhere to anywhere without getting wet, and yet one can take advantage of the baking days: Henry VII was prodigal with open galleries as well as closed; with places for sport, and as well with convenient places for watching the sport, wet or fine. And the orchards and gardens have always been famous. Mary is no doubt enjoying them, and remembering her childhood enjoyment of them.

She has the Council meet at Richmond instead of in the Tower or at Westminster. She is entirely sure she cannot govern alone, and must marry. The Council want her to marry an Englishman. Gardiner's candidate is Edward Courtenay, who, although unable to ride a great horse in a tilt and still sowing Tower-procrastinated wild oats, has royal blood. As also has Cardinal Pole, who is technically eligible since he has not taken orders. But she is unimpressed by Courtenay. And she wants Reginald Pole to return from his exile in Italy and be her Archbishop of Canterbury. Besides, he is over fifty. Her salvation would be marriage to Philip. Every time Renard tempts her towards what she most desires, she cannot keep her lips from smiling. But there must be secrecy, above all from her principal minister.

Renard is also pressing her to destroy Jane and Pembroke and, if possible, Elizabeth. She has executed only Northumberland and two of his non-noble allies, Sir John Gates, who was Edward's Captain of the Guard, and Sir Thomas Palmer, who was a member of the Council. Exceptional moderation. She certainly will not execute Jane who, she believes, never wanted the crown.

Happy at Richmond, and overflowing with gratitude for her accession, she has a proclamation read in Cheapside on 4 September: she will not accept the desperately needed subsidy which was voted by the March Parliament. There is wild cheering.

Alas, foolish woman? Perhaps not.[4]

v

Far from God having saved his people from Papistry, he has handed them over to it. How quiet the Reformers are being! The effect of Northumberland's recantation has not yet been countered by any speaking out from senior Reformist churchmen. Some are in prison: in the Tower, Ridley and Bradford; in the Fleet, Hooper; in the Marshalsea, Cox. Some are due to appear before the Council: Latimer, Saunders, Coverdale. Rogers has to stay in his house.

Of Cranmer there are rumours that he offered to say Mass at Edward's funeral and at St Paul's, and that he has instructed Mass to be celebrated at Canterbury. This could be true: he believes he must obey the ruling monarch whether God's viceroy appears to be right or wrong, and he cannot therefore speak against Mary's policies.

But one day there is on sale in the street a printed statement by Cranmer. This is unexpected. He had felt finally that he had to defend himself against the rumours of his apostasy. But when he had drafted a statement what was he to do with it? If he stuck it on the doors of Paul's or had it printed, would he not in effect be disobedient to the Queen, although doing nothing against the law?

He was expecting from Oxford his friend Pietro Martiro Vermigli: he would discuss his problem with Peter Martyr. The draft remained on his study windowsill. But he had a call from John Scory, the just deprived Bishop of Chichester. Scory read it, liked it (he shouldn't have – it was not good), and asked if he could make a copy. Forthwith there was a copy on Paul's door, and copies were on sale.

Cranmer's statement:

As the devil, Christ's ancient adversary, is a liar and the father of lies, even so hath he stirred up his servants and members to persecute Christ and his true word and religion with lying: which he ceaseth not to do most earnestly at the present time.

For whereas the prince of famous memory King Henry the Eighth, seeing the great abuses of the Latin mass, reformed some things therein in his lifetime, and after, our late sovereign lord King Edward the Sixth took the same wholly away for the manifold and great errors and abuses of the same, and restored in the place thereof Christ's holy supper, according to Christ's own institution and as the Apostles used the same in the primitive Church; the devil goeth about now, by lying, to overthrow the Lord's supper again, and to restore his Latin satisfactory mass, a thing of his own invention and device.

And to bring the same more easily to pass, some have abused the name of me, Thomas Archbishop of Canterbury, bruiting abroad that I have set up the same at Canterbury, and that I offered to say mass at the burial of our late sovereign prince King Edward the Sixth, and that I offered to say mass before the Queen's Highness, and at Paul's church and I wot not where. And although I have been well exercised these twenty years to suffer and bear evil reports and lies, and have not been much grieved thereat, but have borne all things quietly: yet, when untrue reports and lies turn to the hindrance of God's truth, they are in no wise to be suffered.

Wherefore these be to signify unto the world that it was not I that set up the mass at Canterbury, but it was a false, flattering, lying and dissembling monk which caused mass to be set up there without mine advice or counsel. And as for offering myself to say mass before the Queen's Highness or in any other place I never did it, as her Grace knoweth.

But, if her Grace will give me leave, I shall be ready to prove against all that will say to the contrary that all that is contained in the Holy Communion, set out by the most innocent and godly prince King Edward the Sixth in his high court of Parliament, is conformable to that order which our Saviour Christ did both observe and command to be observed; and which his Apostles and the primitive Church used many years. Whereas the mass in many things not only hath no foundation in Christ, his Apostles, nor the primitive Church, but is manifestly contrary to the same and containeth many horrible abuses in it.

And although many, either unlearned or malicious, do report that master Peter Martyr is unlearned, yet if the Queen's Highness will grant thereunto I with the said Peter Martyr and other four or five, which I shall choose, will by God's grace take upon us to defend, not only the common prayers of the Church, the ministration of the sacraments and other rites and ceremonies, but also all the doctrines and religion set out by our sovereign lord King Edward the Sixth, to be more pure and according to God's word than any other that hath been used in England these one thousand years.

On 13 September Cranmer is summoned to the Council. He tells them he intended to enlarge the statement and have it affixed to church doors. The Council, which has just seen Latimer and put him in the Tower, does not also put Cranmer there but tells him to come back to them in the afternoon.

After dinner he tells Peter Martyr, who has at last arrived and approved of the statement and the challenge, that he had better get a passport or, if he cannot, leave the country secretly and as quickly as possible. Cranmer has sent his own wife, Margaret, and their two children to Germany, and has paid his creditors. He has been married to Margaret for twenty-one years, but for the first seventeen the marriage had to be kept secret.

In the afternoon he is at the Council again, and is imprisoned in the Tower chamber vacated by Northumberland. He has been told that his seditious 'bill' has revived his guilt of treason for supporting Jane. Simultaneously Cheke is released from the Tower, with £50 given him by the Council because he is penniless.

The streets are being got ready for the Coronation and London is beginning to fill up, not only for the Coronation but for Parliament, Convocation and the Law Term soon afterwards.

There are unhappy rumours that the Queen wants to marry Philip, Prince of Spain. They are fanned by the French embassy in the hope of causing opposition. And heretics are making trouble with scurrilous leaflets and prophecies that Mary will not reign a year. There are rumours of plots.

Londoners have a fair idea now that the Queen means to make them Catholic and to be herself the docile daughter-in-law of the Inquisition-loving Emperor. However miraculous her accession, it will be a greater miracle if the more fervid Protestants, the Edward Underhills, are not stirred to throw rudenesses or worse at her Coronation procession. The question is only, how violent will the protests be?[5]

IV

Sovereign Lady

10

'Yea, yea, yea!'

i

On Thursday, 28 September she goes from St James's to Whitehall and thence by barge to the Tower, with Elizabeth and other ladies and attended by the Lord Mayor and the aldermen and all the Companies in their barges, with streamers and firing of guns, with trumpets, shawms and regals. She shoots the Bridge at two, at the still of the ebb. She will spend two nights in the Tower, and then on Saturday proceed back to Whitehall through the city, for her coronation at Westminster on Sunday, 1 October.

Arrangements are in the hands of Arundel, as they were for Edward's coronation. Commissioners have been appointed to sort out the hereditary claims of the old aristocracy (or what remains of the old aristocracy: it was halved by the Wars of the Roses, and since has been halved again by ordinary mortality). Arundel himself, who will be High Constable for the day, claims the office of Chief Butler, Norfolk claims High Usher, Sussex Chief Shewer (who sets out the tables at the banquet, places the guests and brings in the dishes), and Oxford claims Great Chamberlain.

Less in accordance with custom are private preparations Mary has been making. She sent urgently to the Pope some while ago for some newly blessed oil: the old oil, used ever since Henry IV's coronation (150 years ago) and originally given to Thomas Becket by the Virgin Mary, might well have lost its efficacy by use at heretic Edward's coronation. In case the new oil does not come in time Renard is procuring from Flanders some blessed by the Bishop of Arras. And she does not want to be crowned in the chair used by Edward, the usual one containing the stone of Scone. The Pope is thought to be obliging with a new one but it is difficult to see how he can get it to her in time.

It is customary for the sovereign on the eve of her coronation to make Knights of the Bath. Arundel deputizes for Mary. On Saturday morning the chosen gentlemen plunge naked into a wooden bath in the chapel of the Tower, the Norman chapel on the second floor of the White Tower, and kiss Arundel's shoulder. Afterwards they serve the Queen at dinner.

Immediately after dinner the procession begins to form up. It is much the same as it was for Mary's half-brother, father and grandfather. Queen's Messengers, foreigners, trumpeters and government workers are in front. Then gentlemen and knights on horseback, in silk with showy linings, and most of the fine horses with velvet trappings to the ground. Then a medley: judges, doctors of divinity, bishops in their robes, and peers and the Council, some in gold, some in silver, with their horses covered in plates of the same metal. Then foreign ambassadors, each paired with an Englishman: the Hanse, Cleves, Venice, Poland, France, the Empire. Then two persons dressed up as dukes, symbolizing the duchies of Normandy and Gascony, ghost possessions of the Crown. Then thirteen Knights of the Bath in their robes; and Gardiner and Paulet, with the Seal and the Mace carried before them. Then the Lord Mayor, Barne, carrying the Sceptre. Then Arundel carrying the Sword, with Oxford, Lord Great Chamberlain, on his right, and Norfolk, High Marshal, on his left.

Then comes Mary, in a golden chariot open on all sides, drawn by six horses trapped in gold and with a gold canopy held over it by knights on foot. She is in mantle and skirt of cloth of gold trimmed with ermine, with a gold tinsel cloth on her head, and on the cloth a jewelled crown; but the crown is so heavy or so insecure that her hand is constantly at it. Around her chariot are four important ladies on horseback – Courtenay's mother, the Marchioness of Exeter, and the wives of Norfolk, Arundel and Paulet – and after the chariot is her horse, led by the Master of Horse, Sir Edward Hastings.

Then there is another chariot, with four horses and silver canopy. In this are Elizabeth facing forwards and, facing backwards, Anne of Cleves, still enjoying ex-queenship. They are both in cloth of silver, in the French fashion with wide sleeves and the gown open in front to show a rich skirt.

Then come thirty-four peeresses, ladies and gentlewomen, some in chariots, some on horseback, the leading group in red velvet and the rear in red satin. And still more peers and peeresses, gentlemen, ladies, maids, chamberers, in red velvet or satin or damask in accordance with rank, and at the tail the henchmen and the Guard. The whole procession flanked by Pensioners, Yeomen of the Guard and Archers.[1]

ii

The procession sets off at 3 p.m. along Tower Street, to the sounds of firing guns from the Tower, and ringing bells from churches. The cobbles have been sprinkled with gravel for the horses, and with grass and flowers.

Mary holds on to her crown. Her subjects cheer, some behind rails put up along the right-hand side of the street, some from windows hung with banners and streamers.

The procession passes Allhallows Barking, goes past Sydon Lane, rather an expensive street, and turns right up Mart Lane. A heretic area. On the left is Allhallows Stane where they were so enthusiastic in breaking images and monuments last year that expenditure on brooms rose to 12s, and as well the church-wardens had to pay for the stone and brass to be carried away. Cheers. No hostile demonstrations.

The procession turns up Fenchurch Street. Here the Genoese merchants have set up a 'pageant', a tableau on a triumphal arch. This one is especially fine and large. There are four great giants, and two men carry a throne from which a boy dressed as a girl speaks a salutation.

At the end of Fenchurch Street, where it crosses Gracechurch Street and becomes Lombard Street, there is a pageant by the Hanse from which four children standing on a mountain speak an unintelligible greeting. An acrobat flies down from the top of the mountain. A small conduit runs with wine. The Hanse want to impress.

The procession turns right, up Gracechurch Street, passing on the left another Allhallows, rebuilt on a larger scale earlier this century, like St Andrew Undershaft. The single bell in the tower is ringing like mad.

Where Gracechurch Street meets Cornhill, with Leadenhall on the right, there is another pageant by Italian merchants, this time the Florentines. Very big and very high. At the top there is an image of an angel, with a trumpet, and hidden inside is a real trumpeter. The image puts its trumpet to its mouth and blows a fanfare. Everyone is delighted. Six persons in the structure, in long coloured gowns, wish Mary good luck, and there are four statues – of Mary Tudor, Pallas Athene, Judith and Tomyris, each of whom saved her people by cutting off a head.

The procession turns left down Cornhill, where at the conduit (this one also is running wine) is the first of the pageants put up by the City. Trumpets ring out from the top, and three children, dressed as Grace, Virtue and Nature, kneel one by one as Mary passes and sing complimentary verses which are difficult to hear.

All along the great street as far as the Little Conduit in Cheap both sides are lined by the Companies in their best liveries, with hoods on shoulders, and Masters and Wardens in front in silk and with chains of gold. The rails and windows are hung with tapestries, and cloth of gold and silver, and velvets and damasks and satins.

At the pageant at the Little Conduit, where the aldermen are drawn up, one of the children gives Mary another salutation and an oration (again difficult to hear with all the shouting and clapping and bell-ringing), and the Recorder makes a speech, and Mary is given by the City a purse of 1,000 marks (£666 13s 4d). Further along, the stone Standard in the middle of the street has been newly painted, and the half-dozen City Waits play music on it. And the Cross has been burnished.

The procession turns left into Paul's precinct where at the east end, outside the schoolhouse, there is another pageant, with Thomas Heywood, playwright and humorist, sitting under a tree and delivering to Mary an oration in Latin and English, and a choir sings.

Everyone looks up at Paul's steeple. On the top there is one Peter, a Dutchman. He has set out eight streamers with the red cross and sword of the City upon them. He stands on the very ball of the weathercock, holding a streamer five yards long in his hand, and then standing on one leg he shakes the other, and then kneels down on the ball. He was supposed to light some torches but there is evidently too much wind up there.

At the west end of the precinct outside the Dean's house there is another pageant, with the choristers of Paul's holding perfumed tapers and playing on viols and singing.

Here where the route is narrow, Edward Underhill has posted himself. He has been released from Newgate very sick, and he is supported on his horse by one of his men on either side. Lean and pale as a corpse, in a long nightgown, with double kerchiefs round his head, and a great hat on top of them, he pays tribute to his Queen.

The procession goes through Ludgate which has been newly repaired and painted and hung with tapestries, and there are minstrels singing and playing, and on down Ludgate Hill. At the conduit in Fleet Street there is at last the final pageant, children on a castle singing songs of joy.

And so, with much shouting, through Temple Bar newly painted and hung with tapestries, past St Clement Danes and, on the left, the very new architecture of the Strand front of Somerset House, the Savoy, and then the stables and domestic quarters of noblemen's houses, with tenements in between; on the right, Drury Lane and Bedford House and hostelries, with, north of them, Bedford's Convent Garden. And so to Charing Cross and the enormous Mews, the royal stables.

Then left to her palace of Whitehall. And a royal thanking of the Lord Mayor for his trouble. And a lifting of that crown off her head.

She sends an urgent message to the Imperial ambassadors to find out with the greatest dispatch whether somewhere among the papers of Charles's staff in the Low Countries there might be a copy of the sentence pronounced by the Consistory in Rome in favour of her mother's marriage to Henry, and against the divorce. Parliament will be meeting in a few days; the paper would be helpful in getting it to annul the Act which pronounced the divorce, and so declare herself legitimate and Elizabeth alone a bastard.

There has been no rudery. She has been totally accepted.[2]

iii

Next morning at Old Palace Bridge, that is to say the stairs at the south end of the old palace of Westminster, there is an assortment of nobles and gentlemen representing all the estates of the Queen's realm. The royal barge arrives with Mary, having brought her the 400 yards from Whitehall Privy Stairs. The estates of her realm greet her and escort her into the Painted Chamber, which has been richly hung. She goes on to the White Hall, normally used as the Court of Requests, part of which has been reserved for her so she can dress.

In Westminster Hall the peers are already formed up in procession in crimson, scarlet and ermine. There is much red cloth on floor and walls and on the rails of Queen's Bench and Chancery, but with a strip of blue from a throne to the door out towards the cathedral through the crowds. Mary comes down the stairs from the Court of Requests and, as symbol of being chosen by the Second Estate, is led by peers to the throne.

The procession today includes the aldermen, who were not included yesterday, and excludes the foreign representatives. First, three naked swords representing Spiritual Justice, Temporal Justice and Mercy, carried by three earls in a row. Then the Garter in Mary's coat of arms, and the Lord Mayor with the Mace. Then the sheathed Sword of State carried by the flaccid Courtenay, and then, in a row, the Crown carried by Norfolk (will his legs and bladder hold out?), the Ball by Paulet, the Sceptre by Arundel.

Mary leaves her throne and takes her place behind these three, in crimson velvet, under a canopy of cloth of gold borne by the Barons of the Cinque ports. She leans her right arm on Tunstall, her left on Shrewsbury. Her very long train is held by the Duchess of Norfolk, helped by Sir John Gage. Behind her come Elizabeth and Anne of Cleves, and the peeresses, baronesses, Mary's ladies, and then the Pensioners (sans Underhill), men at arms, and the Guard, and noblemen's servants. All in the usual crimson, scarlet and ermine, and noblemen carrying their coronets, their women wearing theirs.

The First Estate enters, the Lords Spiritual: Gardiner and ten other bishops, in mitres and gold copes, accompanied by their priests and the royal choir, singing and carrying candlesticks, holy water stoup and censers. They show their acceptance of Mary by coming and censing her and sprinkling her with holy water.

A little before eleven the procession moves along the blue cloth from the Hall to the south transept of the cathedral. There are rails on both sides, and men with long-tipped staves, to keep the crowd at a distance.

Mary is led to the right into the choir, which has been strewn with rushes and is hung with red tapestry, up twenty steps to a high platform and then up a further ten steps to one still higher, on which the Coronation Chair is draped in gold damask.

Two noblemen lead her to each corner of the dais, and at each corner Gardiner addresses the assembly: 'Sirs, here present is Mary, rightful and undoubted inheritrix by the laws of God and man to the crown and royal dignity of this realm of England, France and Ireland, whereupon you shall understand that this day is appointed by all the peers of this land for the consecration, inunction, and coronation of the said most excellent Princess Mary; will you serve at this time, and give your wills and assent to the same consecration, inunction, and coronation?'

The Third Estate, the people, answers with one voice: 'Yea, yea, yea! God save Queen Mary!'

She is led back to the Coronation Chair and then immediately to another rich chair, undesecrated by Edward, and after all the offerings, prayers, prostrations, chantings, there is a sermon by George Day, new Bishop of Chichester, the floridest speaker of the age, on the single subject on which everyone in the kingdom is agreed – the obedience due to a sovereign. Then the Oath. Traditionally she should swear to maintain 'the laws of the kingdom': instead she swears to maintain 'the just and licit laws of the kingdom', begging every question and in particular avoiding any promise to continue to act as head of the Church. If the Pope replaces her as head he will want all the alienated property back again for his Church.

The contract is complete: the three Estates have accepted her; she has sworn the Oath.

The Litany. Exits and re-entrances. Changes of garb. Then the key religious moment: she is anointed by Gardiner with her special oil, and dried by him. There is play with one of the swords and with three crowns. At last Gardiner puts each of the crowns in turn on her head. The trumpets blow before each crowning, and at the end the peers put on their coronets.

Throughout the unction and the crowning she has been in a good Catholic chair. The jewels and the regalia are brought her, and she mounts to the

Coronation Chair for the homage of her subjects, first of Gardiner.

'I, Stephen Gardiner . . . shall be faithful and true, and faith and truth bear unto you, our Sovereign Lady and Queen, and to your heirs kings and queens of England, France and Ireland; and I shall, do, and truly acknowledge the service of the lands which I claim to hold of you as in the right of the Church, as God shall help me and all saints.' Then he kisses her left cheek.

Some of the lands he claims to hold of her 'as in the right of the Church' are in Pembroke's hands. Then Norfolk makes his homage, and Paulet on behalf of marquises, Arundel on behalf of earls. Meanwhile, Gardiner goes to the four corners of the dais and pronounces a general pardon for all offenders, excluding Cranmer and all others in the Tower and the Fleet, and some of those in the Marshalsea, and Richard Grafton and some others. And then Mass. Two bishops, disapproving, withdraw, John Taylor of Lincoln and John Harley of Hereford. Mary kneels with great devotion.

More conducting here and there, more re-clothing, and at last, when it is nearly four o'clock, she is led, in crimson velvet and with the crown on her head and under a canopy, back along the blue carpet to Westminster Hall. She again has Tunstall and Shrewsbury to support her. The golden sceptre is in her right hand, and in her other she is turning and turning the gold orb. The procession behind her is the same as five hours ago, but with the ambassadors added.

She is the Lord's Anointed. She will go to her room up the stairs to rest until the banquet is ready. The populace rush forward to seize their perquisite – the rails and blue carpet of the pathway.[3]

iv

The banquet is ready. She re-enters Westminster Hall, and basins of water are brought for her to wash her hands. She takes her seat at the high table under a cloth of state. Gardiner sits at her right hand, Elizabeth and Anne of Cleves at her left, rather far off.

There are four tables 9 or 10 yards long, holding thirty or so people each, down the length of the hall. The middle two tables hold nobles, judges and foreign ambassadors, the men at the table on Mary's right, their women to her left. The table along the wall on her far right holds Councillors and Barons of the Cinque Ports; the table on her far left holds the Lord Mayor and aldermen.

The tables leave plenty of room for the Earl of Derby, High Steward of England, and the Duke of Norfolk, High Marshal, to ride round the hall throughout the banquet on chargers trapped with cloth of gold.

Henry Radcliffe, Earl of Sussex, looks after the serving to Mary of her fifty-two dishes, Sir Humphrey Ratcliffe after the fifty-two for Gardiner, Sir Anthony Brown after the fifty-two for Elizabeth and Anne of Cleves. They are all offered the same choice. For the first course: boar's head, pheasant stew, red deer, cygnets, capons, pike and so on, and custard, apple fritters, and other sweets, and there is a 'subtlety' of jelly and candied sugar representing a queen in state, with the words '*Vox populi vox dei. Vivat regina* Mary'. Second course: peacocks, roe deer, larded rabbits, grilled eel, brawn, carp in sharp sauce, larded pheasant, and so on, and sweets, and a subtlety.

After the second course Sir Edward Dymoke, the Queen's Champion, rides in, in armour with heraldic surcoat and holding a mace, with a page holding his lance and another his shield, and Chester Herald in front of him. He comes to Mary's end of the hall and in a loud voice utters his challenge:

'If there be any manner of man, of what estate, degree, or condition soever he be, that will say and maintain that our sovereign lady Queen Mary the First, this day here present, is not the rightful and undoubted inheritrix to the imperial crown of this realm of England, and that of right she ought to be crowned Queen, I say he lieth like a false traitor, and that I am ready the same to maintain with him whilst I have breath in my body, either now at this time or at any other time, whenever it shall please the Queen's Highness to appoint, and thereupon the same I cast my gage.'

He casts his gauntlet on the floor. No one moves. The herald bends down and gives it back to him, and Dymoke challenges similarly in three other parts of the hall. He comes to Mary; she drinks to him, and gives him the cup. There are then proclamations of Mary's style in Latin, French and English, all in several places. And so to a rather lighter third course, selected from crane, plovers, sturgeon, quails, pheasant in his royalty, larks, cold red deer, and so on, and water is brought to Mary again to wash.

At this point there is normally a play, performed by the Gentlemen and Children of the Chapel Royal, but perhaps there is difficulty over costumes because the detailed order to Sir Thomas Cawarden was signed by Mary only yesterday; or perhaps the ceremonies have already been over long; for whatever reason there is no play.

The Lord Mayor brings Mary a gold cup, which she drinks from and then returns to him. She calls the ambassadors to her, thanks them for their congratulations, and gives them leave to retire.

Elizabeth complains to de Noailles that she is weary of the crown she has been wearing all day. Renard notes that she has warmly greeted de Noailles every time she has been near him.

By now it is candlelight, and five o'clock. Mary withdraws upstairs to

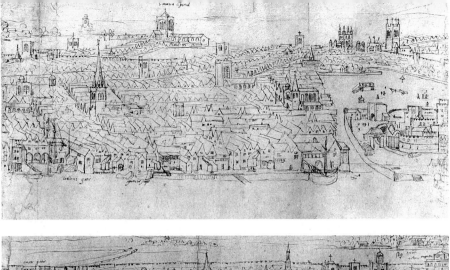

TOP Tower Wharf to Billingsgate, with
the Customs House in the centre.
Wyngaerde Panorama. (*The Sutherland
Collection, Ashmolean Museum, Oxford*)

MIDDLE London Bridge, showing the houses
and shops built on the bridge. Wyngaerde
Panorama. (*The Sutherland Collection,
Ashmolean Museum, Oxford*)

ABOVE St Paul's Cathedral from the river.
Wyngaerde Panorama. (*The Sutherland
Collection, Ashmolean Museum, Oxford*)

Mary Tudor. A painting by Hans Eworth. (*National Portrait Gallery, London*)

OPPOSITE ABOVE Holy Trinity Christchurch to Cornhill, the Stocks, Cheapside. From the Ralph Agas Map of London, produced as a woodblock between 1561 and 1570, and based on the original Copperplate Map.

OPPOSITE BELOW The north and south banks of the Thames. St Paul's Cathedral (Pole's Church) can be seen near the top. From the Ralph Agas Map of London.

The Banck

The bolle bayting

The Bearebayting

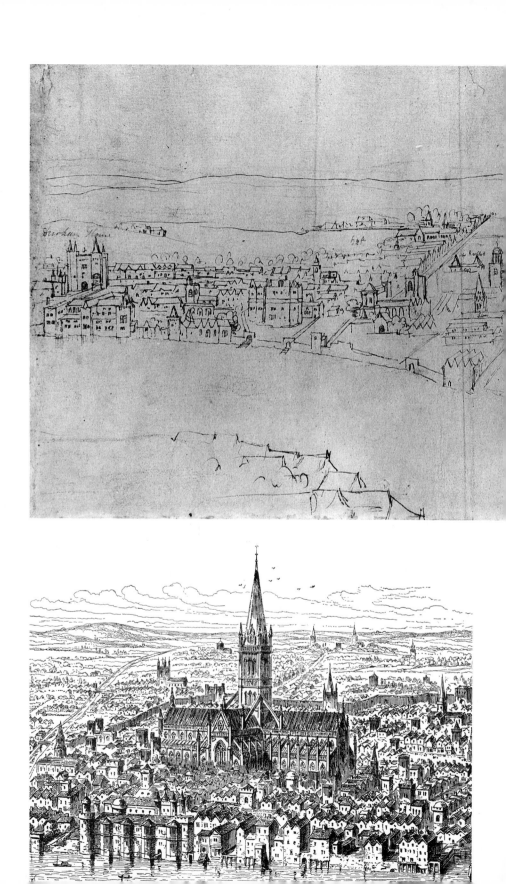

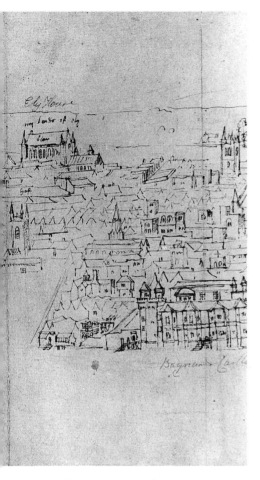

Baynard's Castle and Durham House.
Wyngaerde Panorama. (*The Sutherland
Collection, Ashmolean Museum, Oxford*)

St Paul's and the neighbourhood. An
engraving taken from Wyngaerde's
Panorama.

THE PRACTIKE WORKINGE OF
fondry conclufions Geometrical.

THE FYRST CONCLVSION.

*To make a threlike triangle or any lyne
measurable.*

AKE THE IVSTE
lēgth of the lyne with your cōpaße,
and ftay the one foot of the compas
in one of the endes of that line, tur
ning the other vp or doun at your
will drawyng the arche of a circle
against the
midle of the
line, and doo likewise with the same
cōpaße vnaltered, at the other end of
the line and wher thefe ij. croked ly-
nes doth croße, frome thence drawe a
lyne to eche end of your firſt line, and
there ſhall appeare a threlike triangle
drawen on that line.
Example.
A.B. is the firſt line, on which J wold
make the threlike triangle, therfore J
open the compaße is wyde as that line
is long, and draw two arch lines that
mete in C, then from C. J draw ij other
lines one to A, another to B, and than
J haue my purpofe.
THE. II. CONCLVSION.
*Jf you wil make a twileke or
a nouelike triangle on ani cer
taine line.*
Confider fyrſt the length that yow will haue the other fi-
des to containe, and to that fength open your compaße, and
then

The Pathway to Knowledge, 1551, by Robert
Recorde. One of the books on sale in
St Paul's churchyard.

Christ's Hospital from *The Plat of The Graye Friers*, 1617. From the archives of St Bartholomew's Hospital, London.

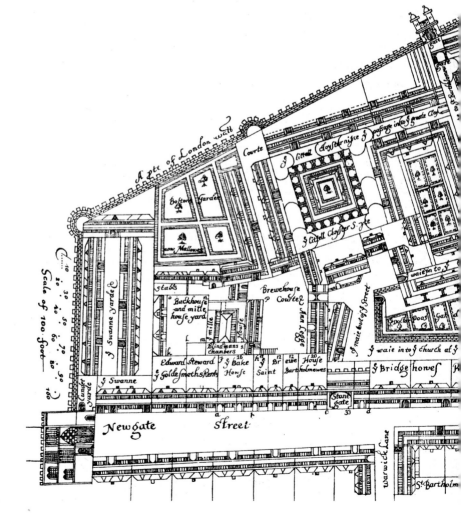

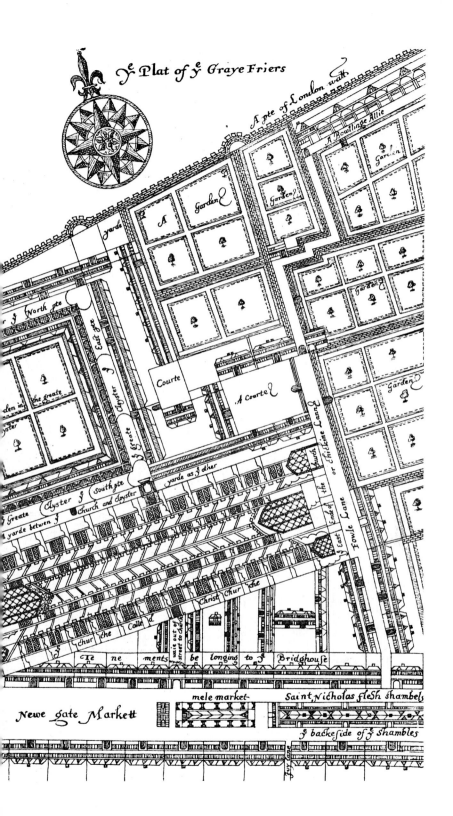

Ye Plat of ye Graye Friers

A pte of London wall

A Bowlinge Allie

Garden

Garden

Garden

Garden

yarde

Garden

the greate

Garden

ye North pte

ye East pte

Courte

A Courte

Garden

ye greate Cloyster

Church or Chickene Lane

ye South pte

yarde as ye other

Church and cloyster

Greate Cloyster ye

ye East End of the

Fowle Lane

A yarde between ye

Christ Churche

Churche Colledge

ware out of ye street to ye

Te ne ments be longing to ye Bridghouse

mele market

Saint Nicholas fleSh shambels

Newe gate Markett

ye backeside of ye Shambles

Hand and Shears to Smithfield, Bedlam,
Bishopsgate. North section of the
Copperplate Map. Only two of the fifteen
plates of the Copperplate Map still survive,
and there are no complete printed copies.
The plates probably date from 1553–9.
(*Museum of London*)

change, and then enters her barge to return to Whitehall where there is to be great feasting. Meanwhile the populace are again at their perquisites. What remains of the 156 dishes for the high table and the 1,900 for the other tables is thrown out of the temporary kitchens and scrambled for. And the kitchens themselves are then pulled to pieces and swiped.

The aristocracy will also have their perquisites, trivial expensive presents which please, and help to cement the nobility's ties to the monarch. Arundel as Chief Butler will have the Queen's best cup, and the wine remaining in the pipes and hogsheads. Norfolk will have the Queen's horse and palfrey, with the furniture on the horse, and the tablecloth used at the high table, and the cloth of estate which hung behind the Queen. Sussex will have £20, 18 yards of crimson velvet, the Queen's cloak, hat and cloak-bag, and a gelding. Oxford will have £40, 40 yards of crimson velvet, the bed Mary slept in last night with all its furniture, and her nightdress and all the room's hangings. Dymoke will have the horse he rode and its furniture, and the armour he wore, and 18 yards of crimson satin, and a full service of meat and drink of a level appropriate to a baron, to be conveyed to his lodging, and the cup from which the Queen drank to him.

A remarkable two days. The crown has been set squarely where the English believe it should be, on the loins of Henry. There has been no scrap of trouble from the heretics: in England heretics, from Cranmer to Edward Underhill and beyond, are loyal to the sovereign.

The Coronation has been a near-sacrament, to Protestants as to Catholics. For two sacramental days the English have perceived in God's new Viceroy only an inner substance which is both national and divine, and they have closed their eyes to the accidents, to this particular person's religion and marriage plans.

At this instant the English stand saved from the chaos of civil strife, united in accepting and honouring Mary Tudor.[4]

V

And Now . . .

11

Lord Treasurer, make the Crown solvent

i

And now . . . Mary must make England Catholic again. The first stages will have to be achieved by her Lord Chancellor, Stephen Gardiner, Bishop of Winchester, and then later by Cardinal Reginald Pole when he becomes her Archbishop of Canterbury. And money has to be available for the re-establishment of Church institutions: that is to say, the Crown has to be made less insolvent than it was under the former dastardly heretic government. And that must be done by her finance minister, Lord Treasurer William Paulet, Marquis of Winchester.

The Paulet who takes barge of a morning at the Three Cranes to go to the Exchequer at Westminster has his own objectives, of course, as well as the Queen's. Paulet is a self-aggrandizing survivor (he served Henry, Edward, Jane) whom Mary was very hesitant to take as her Lord Treasurer. Renard has assured her that Paulet's good sixty-eight-year-old business head can straighten out her finances, and Mary now eats out of Paulet's hand, but is Renard right?

Paulet is always working, always available. His friendly wit and sense make people believe he thinks as they do. He never does or says anything wild. A pleasant, comfortable man, the kind who gets a licence for himself and twelve friends to eat flesh in Lent and on fast days. When Queen Jane was keeping all the Council with her in the Tower, Paulet escaped to his house at Augustine Friars but was brought back. He had it in mind, men say, to decamp to Mary. It is more likely that he simply wanted to dissociate himself from a dangerous mistress, without committing himself prematurely to a new one, and that most of all he wanted to sleep in his own bed.

For his great house at the north-west corner of Broad Street he acquired and extended the priory of Augustine Friars, and managed to avoid the compulsory pulling down of the church; instead, the west end of it was granted to the Dutch to hold their Protestant services, leaving Paulet to use the choir and the lovely, slim, high, straight steeple for stowing his corn, coal, and so on. He did not at first gain the whole of the Austin friars' garden because part was got by Thomas Cromwell who had built a property south of the priory, but he gained it after Cromwell's execution.

There used to be a pathway separating Paulet's garden and Cromwell's, and it was used by the public as a short cut to Moorgate and out into Moorfields. John Stow used it as a boy. Paulet has made the gardens one, and enclosed it in a stone wall, and so destroyed the short cut. Stow is indignant: the high-handedness of great men! But Paulet has no more than a sense of property and his own rights: the gate at each end of the pathway had been closed always at night, preserving the path's private ownership.

Paulet also has, at Chelsea, the Great House, which he acquired when Sir Thomas More was attainted. And at Basing in Hampshire he has vastly, too vastly, enlarged his family seat, and has gathered into his hands all four quarters of Basingstoke town. He keeps high state, feeding poor men at his gate, and having 100 or more staff and servants in his livery of Reading tawny. He did not marry into the aristocracy but into the City, the daughter of Sir William Capell, Draper and sometime Lord Mayor.

Asked how he survives, he says: *'Ortus sum ex salice non ex quercus'* ('I'm sprung of the willow, not the oak').[1]

ii

He disembarks at Westminster public stairs, and crosses New Palace Court to Westminster Hall. The Lower Exchequer, the Exchequer of Receipt, is reached by the stairs to the first floor at the left of the entry. Its large chambers are outside the ancient structure of the Hall but adjoining it, and there are offices and storerooms beneath. Here also is the Court of the Duchy of Lancaster, which is another revenue court but not under Paulet's control. Also on this upper floor there is the Star Chamber, where he and other members of the Council sit as a court under the Lord Chancellor once or twice a week in term-time, on Fridays usually and sometimes Wednesdays, from 9 to 11 a.m.

The Exchequer of Receipt is a good place to see the English civil service of the twelfth century in operation. There are four tellers, of whom Nicholas Brigham is an example: Oxford graduate; as a hobby studies municipal law; poet, devoted to Chaucer; lives with wife Margaret and adored seven-month Rachel in a nice old house in the Abbey precinct; of utter probity, would guard with his life his iron-bound chest of the Queen's silver and gold.

Besides the four chests of the tellers there are the usual paraphernalia of an administrative office: tables, cupboards, parchment, paper, ink, seals, wax, weights, and an accounting board of green cloth.

The old routines perhaps sound over-fussy but they are not excessively so: it is their carrying out which has become tired, clogged and obstructive, making it fatiguing even to say the word 'Exchequer'. When an official from the field comes to pay in the taxes and rents he has collected (he ought to come shortly after 25 March and 29 September, but long, long delay is common), he comes to one of the tellers, who makes out a bill stating what he has paid, puts the money in his chest, and throws the bill through a hole into another office next door. The paying-in official goes next door and asks for a tally to be struck. The Clerk of the Pell enters the bill on his pell, or roll, and marks the bill *recordatur*. The Controller of the Pell checks that the entry is correct. The Auditor of Receipt enters the bill on his own pell and passes it with a tally-stick, a precisely squared stick of seasoned hazel, to one of his clerks, the *scriptor talliarum*, who writes the details of the bill on the tally. The Auditor of Receipt files the Teller's bill. The tally goes to one of the Under-Chamberlains, who cleaves it, keeping one part, the 'stock', and giving the other, the 'foil', to the other Under-Chamberlain. He then reads out the stock, and together with his fellow Under-Chamberlain and the Clerk of the Pell and the Controller of the Pell checks that the stock agrees with the foil and with the book in which the Clerk of the Pell recorded the bill, and then calls out, *'examinatur'*. The foil is thrown into the Chamberlain's chest, and the stock is given to the paying-in official as his receipt.

It is labour-intensive, but you have to pay only two fees in order to give money to the Exchequer (to the Cutter of Tallies and to the Auditor of Receipt); to get money out of the Exchequer you may have to pay more and go to a deal of trouble. As a supplier to the Crown wanting payment for goods supplied (e.g. new velvet coats supplied for the Queen's Guards, £400; spangles for 'MR' instead of 'ER', £1,000), or as a department of state wanting cash to pay wages, you may be told that no cash is available just then, so you are given a tally payable by some government department elsewhere; if they too have no cash you are passed on, perhaps to a debtor of that department. And so on.

For his annual audit, which may be delayed a year or two, an official who has collected taxes and rents comes up the other staircase, on the west side of the entry, to the Upper Exchequer, the Exchequer of Account. Here there is a large courtroom, the Exchequer Chamber, and a smaller, the Inner Court of the Exchequer. (You find this exhausting? Of course. This is the Exchequer. But persevere a while longer.) Here Paulet sits with a board consisting of the Chancellor of the Exchequer and the four Barons of the Exchequer, which deals with policy and audits accounts; and also as a court of law adjudicates disputes within its field of administration, and deals with defaulters and litigants. It is judge in its own causes, but there is appeal from its decisions to the Council.

When in due course an official comes for his audit, he has to bring with him his tallies. They will be checked with the halves in the chest, when these (for a fee) have been found. In the columns of the chequered cloth, 5 feet by 10, the amount he ought to be paying in will be represented by counters; and then below it the amounts of his tallies. Counters to the equivalent of his tallies will be successively removed from the amount at the top where, if all goes well, there will at last be nothing left: his account will be at rest, *quietus*.

Also on this side of the Hall, extending further westward, is another revenue court, the Court of Augmentations, which is not Paulet's but brings in more revenue than the Exchequer.

All the revenue courts have their own messengers, ushers, clerks, treasurers, auditors, surveyors, chancellors, and so forth, and a field staff out in the counties. Officials are allowed to appoint a deputy to do their work, and to hold several posts simultaneously.

The Exchequer is so preternaturally laborious in its practices that important and recent sources of revenue, that is to say the Courts of Augmentations, of Survey, of the Duchy of Lancaster, and of Wards have been kept out of its clutches.

Has Paulet modernized the practices of the Exchequer? No. Has he reduced the staff, over eighty altogether? No. On this October morning, is the good business head vigorously straightening out the Queen's finances? Well . . .

Watch the successful official and learn.[2]

iii

He has his eyes on uniting to the Exchequer some of the other revenue courts, as recommended by Northumberland's commission and authorized by Edward's Parliament last March. Well, not quite as recommended by the commission. The commission recommended that all the revenue courts, not some, should be united. Paulet thinks the Duchy of Lancaster might be left undisturbed: its affairs are efficiently organized, and the holders of Duchy lands would think they were going to be made subject to knight service (on which a word in a moment). And the Court of Wards should be left out: it is a special case.

Since there is a new sovereign, the uniting of the courts will have to be re-authorized, by the Parliament which is about to sit. Then the Court of Exchequer will once again be the most important financial organ of the Crown. It will include the Court of Augmentations and Surveys (which administers lands come to the Crown through the dissolution of monasteries, and so on, and through attainders) and the Court of First Fruits and Tenths (which collects from the Church those annual and other payments which used to go to the Pope).

The revenues of the courts are roughly like this:

Exchequer	£39,000	Duchy of Lancaster	£18,000
Augmentations and surveys	159,000	Wards	14,000
First fruits	24,000		
Proposed enlarged Exchequer	£222,000	Not in proposed enlarged Exchequer	£32,000

Will this be a great reform? It will get rid of a little overlapping. Will it save staff? Yes, most of the head office work of the absorbed courts can be carried by existing Exchequer staff.

And that will save money? No. For several years it may cost more. The redundant staff will need pensions, which will be about the same as their salaries. Some may be a little less because rises given by Northumberland (cost of living increases) can be ignored; others may be more because loss of fees from clients has to be compensated for. Pensions are supposed to continue only until the Crown offers alternative employment, but have a way of not stopping. So reduction of staff will probably save money only when death at last abolishes the pensions.

Will the reorganization introduce into the Exchequer the more efficient practices of the Augmentations? Not really. Exchequer business will be carried on in the old way, Augmentations business in the Augmentations way (more or less, by Exchequer staff). Paulet changes nothing unless he has to.

Then will the change benefit the Queen's Treasury? Not in the short run. But it will establish a single control over most of the Crown's revenue and expenditure. And it will bring under control Augmentations which, since Cromwell's hand was removed, has swelled in expenditure and corruption.

Will it benefit Paulet? Oh, yes. The enlarged control will be in his hands. And control of Augmentations should be worth, to him personally, several thousands of pounds a year.

So, no noses are put out of joint. Augmentations staff do no work but continue to receive much the same as before. Exchequer officials have additional opportunities for fees and sweeteners. And the Queen will not notice that her income does not increase because there is no accounting which shows that kind of thing.[3]

iv

Can the Queen's income be increased some other way? From Crown lands? The rents paid by tenants have risen in the last decades less than have the prices they receive for their crops. Rents must be put up? Certainly. But most leases are very long: there can be no sudden great increase, only a gradual one. And future leases must be for shorter periods, and as far as possible no more Crown lands must be given away to deserving courtiers or sold to meet emergencies.

Can more be raised by taxation? What about restoring 'fifteenths and tenths' to their original nature and force? Henry VII and Edmund Dudley did not do it, nor did Henry VIII and Cromwell. It is not for Mary and Paulet to dare think of it.

What about subsidies, the tax of 2s in the £ on income from land, payable over two years, 2s 4d in the £ on personal property? Assessments are falsified of course: William Cecil, for example, declares his property at 200 marks p.a. Edmund Dudley used to make people take an oath to the value of their property, but an oath is a serious matter so this was unfair and had to be dropped. And half the greatest landowners, the peers, delay paying from year to year until with luck they are released from the debt.

If Paulet tried to interfere with the low taxation of nobility and gentry he would find his head on London Bridge. What about the Wards, the second of Paulet's kingdoms? The Court of Wards is down the stairs and through the Hall to the southern end, and then up the few stone steps.

In feudal times a tenant holding lands from the Crown paid for them by serving as a knight so many days a year. If he died while his heir was still a child, his heir could not give knight service and therefore could not for the time inherit. Until the heir was of age he became a ward of the Crown: he was brought up at Court and received a courtly education, and this was paid for by his lands being temporarily at the Crown's disposal. In due course the king gave up acting himself as guardian of such a ward and appointed a nobleman or gentleman to act in his place, giving him as recompense temporary possession of the ward's lands, the right to marry the ward to whomever he pleased, and the right to sell the wardship. This recompense was valuable.

Henry VII used Edmund Dudley and Richard Empson and a newly set up Office of Wards to extract income from the sale of wardships, and Henry VIII went further. When he sold any Church property he made the purchaser hold it by knight service. Consequently many more heirs became wards available for sale and he set up the Court of Wards in 1540 in place of the smaller Office of Wards.

The Court of Wards brings the Crown at present about £14,000 a year. But it brings three or four times as much to the main beneficiaries: the successful bidders for wards, and those whose favour the bidders must seek, such as Paulet, Master of Wards, and his officials.

Surely, then, more income could be got for the Crown from the Court of Wards? Yes, by putting up the prices of wardships, and reducing the private profits; or by offering the nobility and gentry to abolish the institution in exchange for an increase in direct taxation; both methods would cause trouble. No.

The Court of Wards has several rooms besides this great chamber, the outer court. Paulet or a deputy presides over judicial business here every Monday, Tuesday, Thursday and Saturday in term-time. The officers of the court sit round a rectangular table, with Paulet or a deputy at the head under a canopy, and Thomas Anton, the clerk, at the foot. Behind the surrounding barriers wait the counsel, witnesses and so on. Anton has been with the court since it was established in 1540, and so has the messenger, Stephen Claybrooke. Claybrooke may or may not be a qualified lawyer but he is of that calibre and class, and his 4d a day, plus 26s 8d a year for cloth for his livery, is a fraction of his receipts.

Society's attitude to the Court of Wards is ambivalent. The well-to-do dread what may happen to the children when the head of the family dies. The mother has no prior claim to be guardian of her children; under Paulet about one widow in five obtains wardship of her children. Everyone hates the institution; everyone pulls every string, offers every inducement to the officials, in order to get a profitable wardship. Sir Nicholas Bacon, Cecil's brother-in-law, is a fair example: he bought ecclesiastical lands, so if his heir were young he would be subject to the Court of Wards; Bacon wants to avoid that at any cost and is going to try to get a grant from Mary that his children will be wards of his own brothers. Nevertheless Nicholas Bacon has bought wards for himself, and is one of Paulet's most senior officers in the Court, the Attorney.

The institution is not wholly evil. Many people die young, so there is much re-marriage, and a child may do better with a guardian who intends to marry him to his daughter than with his mother's second or third husband. And the Court is, theoretically, paternalistic: a socially inappropriate marriage or a too-violent cutting down of a ward's trees will stir it to action – or rather, will be acted against if some interested party pays someone to see that it is.

Has Paulet done anything to improve the institution or its practices? No. On the other hand, he has held the mastership for twenty-seven years, under four sovereigns, so nobility and gentry must feel he is about as good a master as the Court will get. But he may soon lose his profitable post. It would be a handsome reward for Mary to give one of her long-faithful Household officers. Paulet will lose it with good grace. By then re-organization of the revenue courts will have given him the Augmentations.

What about the Customs? They bring in only £26,000 a year, and have actually declined in the last decade in spite of increase of trade and rise of prices. They would bring in five times as much if the rates were brought up to date. But they cannot be raised now, not before the Queen has been longer established. And not before the City can be bargained and nudged into acquiescence.[4]

V

If the income cannot be increased, can it at least be unreduced by corruption and embezzlement? There are difficulties. Much revenue, in the Augmentations, for example, comes through officials out in the counties, far from the head office eye and close to local pressures and temptations. And in the London Customs could there really be closer supervision of 'customers', who assess cargoes, and of 'watchers', who watch for smuggling? Free Englishmen are not happy about being supervised: it interferes with men's right to earn a dishonest living.

Another difficulty is the backwardness of English arithmetic and accounting. Eyes do not run as sharply as they might over a page of figures. Arabic numerals are often used for totals, but roman almost always for the figures which have to be added. Addition, using counters or fingers, is slow, unconfident, usually unchecked, often wrong.

And accounts are simple records of transactions, and never give a whole picture. Double entry has been used by Italian firms in London for a century or more, but has hardly entered English practice. Payments of arrears are easily concealed, either accidentally or on purpose, because they are all lumped together, totals of new arrears-payments are added to the totals of old, and individual payments can be forgotten. It was by omitting to enter payments for arrears that a recent Receiver-General in Paulet's own Court of Wards, John Beaumont, embezzled £11,823.

Incidentally, Beaumont also held on to £10,000 received on behalf of the Court instead of paying it in: he did not embezzle it, just held on to it. It is the custom for treasurers of revenue departments to hold on to some of their receipts for a few years instead of paying them in every half-year, so they always have a few thousands of capital for their own investments. Paulet has not put an end to this custom: if he did, the Receiver-General's income would be less than the messenger's.

Taking it all in all, Paulet must judge the prospects of the Queen having more revenue in the next few years to be poor. So he must persuade her to keep expenses down, not to give back to the Pope his First Fruits and Tenths, nor to monastic orders their lands, nor to reward faithful followers with lands belonging to the Crown, and above all not to get involved in war.

And borrowing will have to continue on a considerable scale. The new regime is suspicious of Sir Thomas Gresham, so a new agent in Antwerp has been appointed, Christopher Dauntsey, Mercer and Merchant Adventurer. Dauntsey is a goodish business man but is borrowing at more than 14 per cent, according to Gresham. Self-publicizing account-cooking Gresham will have to be re-appointed.

Is Paulet depressed? Why should he be? He will flourish – wise, witty, of exceptional reliability; not officiously reformative, not unacceptably stick-in-the-mud; seeker of long-term advantage to Crown and self, without short term disturbance; like willow flexible, like bay evergreen. Will he make the Crown solvent? He will press it in the general direction of solvency cautiously, gradually, profitably.[5]

12

Lord Chancellor, make England Catholic

On 5 October, the Thursday morning after the Coronation, the whole Court forms up in procession at Whitehall Palace for the opening of Parliament. After an hour or two the Lord Chancellor takes his place. In this Parliament he has to lay the legal basis for Mary's counter-revolution.

Stephen Gardiner is not the man he was before his five years in the Tower, but prison did not crack him. At seventy he still has a quick head, quick tongue, quick temper. Vigour and assertiveness are still in his eyes, and humour and good opinion of himself in his mouth. It is over twenty years since, under Henry, he first signed himself 'Ste. Winton', Stephen Bishop of Winchester, princely prelate with £4,000 p.a. He accepted the substitution of king for pope since he was the King's loyal and ambitious servant, and a patriot. He accepted the dissolution of the monasteries since the law of the realm required it, and the monks were, he said later, just 'belly-gods'. But under Somerset he would not accept changes in the Mass, and he opposed the destruction of images, 'the books of the illiterate': the Protestant revolution would destroy religion and the order of the state. It is for him now, late in life but under a Catholic queen, to reverse it.

He has the ability. He is the most formidable civil and canon lawyer in the country, and the most formidable orthodox theologian and controversialist. And he has the experience. He was Wolsey's right-hand man, Henry's Secretary, Henry's chief negotiator with the Pope, the Empire and France, and one of Henry's most capable administrators and heresy-hunters. But he is not an easy member of a team, nor an easy leader. An unmarried peremptory lawyer, lacking warmth. And the Queen does not care for him.

Mary takes her place, on a mule and in her Parliament robes. Trumpets blow and the procession moves off down King Street: all the other bishops besides Gardiner; Paulet and the Council, and the peers; heralds, and

Hastings, Master of Horse, leading a horse; and the Pensioners, noble ladies, the Guard. Into the old Abbey church for a sung Mass. After Mass into Westminster Palace.

Mary goes to her privy chamber, the Lords to the Painted Chamber, the Parliament House, where the ecclesiastics sit along the wall to the throne's right, the temporal peers to its left and also across the hall facing the throne and some way in front of it. Immediately in front of the throne is the Chancellor's woolsack, but Gardiner does not sit on it today: he stands at the right of the throne. On the three woolsacks making up a rectangle with the Chancellor's are the judges.

Mary enters. The Commons are summoned from St Stephen's chapel, and as many of them as can squeeze in enter the chamber. Gardiner declares on behalf of the Queen the general objectives of the session: the resumption of the union of religion, and the repeal of the iniquitous religious laws of recent years. He knows how to be indefinite. He may mean a return to the Catholicism of Henry's last years, or he may mean a return to the Papacy. He neither implies that the peers and burgesses are to lose their Church property, nor that they are to keep it. And he makes no mention of marriage for the Queen.[1]

ii

Next day, Friday, Gardiner takes his barge again from Winchester House to Westminster to commence his second task, to purge the civil courts of heretics. In the Hall, in his Court of Chancery at the far end on the left, he is to administer the oath of office to the judges before the Michaelmas term opens on Monday. Will he purge the bench this morning? No, it would leave too many vacancies. Will he do nothing then? It is not like Gardiner to do nothing. Watch.

The oaths are taken, pleasantly and with good will. Until the turn of Sir James Hales, Judge of the Common Pleas, who was odd man out last June when he refused to sign Edward's devise as contrary to law. Gardiner will have a good word for him?

Gardiner: Master Hales, ye shall understand that like as the Queen's Highness hath heretofore conceived good opinion of you, especially for that ye stood both faithfully and lawfully in her cause of just succession . . . so now, through your own late deserts against her Highness's doings, ye stand not well in her Grace's favour; and therefore, before ye take any oath, it shall be necessary for you to make your purgation.

133

Hales: I pray you, my Lord, what is the cause?

Gardiner: Information is given that ye have indicted certain priests in Kent for saying Mass.

Hales: My Lord, it is not so, I indicted none; but indeed certain indictments of like matter were brought before me at the last assizes there holden, and I gave order therein as the law requireth. For I have professed the law, against which in cases of justice I will never, God willing, proceed nor in any wise dissemble, but with the same show forth my conscience.

Gardiner: Yes, Master Hales, your conscience is known well enough. I know you lack no conscience.

Hales: My lord, you may do well to search your own conscience, for mine is better known to myself than to you. And to be plain, I did as well use justice in your said Mass case by my conscience as by the law, wherein I am fully bent to stand trial to the uttermost that can be objected.

Gardiner: Why, master Hales, although you had the rigour of the law on your side, yet ye might have had regard to the Queen's Highness's present doings in that case. As it should seem, that which ye did was more of a will favouring the opinion of your religion against the service now used, than for any occasion of zeal of justice. I will presently make an end of you. The Queen's Highness shall be informed of your opinion and declaration, and as her Grace shall thereupon determine ye shall have knowledge. Until such time ye may depart as ye came, without your oath, for as it appeareth ye are scarcely worthy the place appointed.

Now, that is odd. Gardiner has never forgotten or dissented from a decision of judges in Henry's time that, although the King might wish for a certain course of action, Parliament must authorize it first. How can he now withhold the oath from a judge who refuses to jump the law? Because he holds to the Mass, law or no law. And because he enjoys the petty bullying and the overriding of law and regulation made possible to him by power. And because he is irritated by the self-righteousness of destroyers of the Mass, reformers whose day is over. And because, by a single demonstration, he will probably frighten the whole pack of judges out of using the law to delay return to Catholicism.[2]

iii

Heretic preachers are a greater problem than heretic judges. When one especially catches his eye, as does, inevitably, Thomas Mountayne, the Dick-

Whittington-digging-up incumbent of St Michael in the Tower Royal, he summons him to Winchester House.

On Wednesday, 11 October Mountayne is brought to the great chamber. Gardiner is standing at a bay window, with a crowd of followers and suitors around him.

Gardiner: Thou heretic! how durst thou be so bold to use that schismatic service still, of late set forth? seeing that God hath sent us now a Catholic queen, whose laws thou hast broken, as the rest of thy fellows hath done, and you shall know the price as I do live. There is much abominable company of you, as is able to poison a whole realm with your heresies.

Mountayne: My lord, I am no heretic, for that way that you count heresy so worship we the living God . . .

Gardiner (to Sir Anthony St Leger, Lord Deputy of Ireland, who is standing by): God's passion! did I not tell you, my Lord Deputy, how you should know a heretic? He is up with 'the living God' as though there were a dead God. They have nothing in their mouths, these heretics, but 'the Lord liveth . . . the living God ruleth . . . the Lord . . . the Lord . . .,' and nothing but 'the Lord!'

Gardiner takes off his cap, and rubs his forehead up and down where a lock of hair insists on standing up. He always does this when he fumes.

St Leger encourages Mountayne to submit himself and win favour, but Mountayne bites his head off.

Someone else tells Gardiner to waste no more time on Mountayne: 'He is not only a heretic but also a traitor to the Queen's Majesty, for he was one of them that went forth with the Duke of Northumberland and was in the open field against her Grace; and therefore as a traitor he is one of them that is exempt out of the general pardon, and hath lost the benefit of the same.'

Gardiner calls for a text of the general pardon, and asks Mountayne his name.

'Thomas Mountayne!'

'Thou hast wrong.'

'Why so, my lord?'

'That thou hast not mounted to Tyburn or to such like place.'

'I beseech your lordship be so good lord unto me as to let me know mine accusers . . . . As for the laws of the realm I trust I have not offended or broken any of them.'

'No? I will make thee to sing a new song ere thou and I have done, for these two be always linked together, treason and heresy, and thou hast, like a shameless man, offended in both.' And to one of his gentlemen Gardiner says in a loud voice, 'I pray you, master Hungerford, take this traitor heretic, and have him to the Marshalsea.'

Gardiner has found that a simple summons to Winchester House has frightened into flight several of the foreign Protestant preachers he has particularly wanted to see the back of. Many hard-line English Protestants have fled too to Germany or Switzerland, and he wishes they would all go.

He detests the Reformers for what he considers their licentious doctrine of justification by faith alone, irrespective of good works, for their constant presumption of superior scholarship in God's utterances and intentions, and for their hatred-filled invective: 'Your learning cannot be good that preach so like the devil.'

Their religion as a whole is anathema to him because in Europe he sees Lutheranism as having led to anarchy. And, unpeaceful man that he is, he has an obsession with orderly peace, and has indeed made, he thinks, a nutshell of peace at Winchester House. There are no quarrels among his servants: 'for in them I punish that fact without examination of the cause.'[3]

iv

London is so crowded – with Parliament, and the law term, and Convocation (through which Gardiner has to lead or drive the Church back to orthodoxy) – that for the next Sunday's Paul's Cross sermon bars are put up at the gates of the Churchyard to keep down the numbers and keep out horses. There is excitement in some of the churches: a priest is almost killed for blackguarding the Reformed Religion, another for preaching the True Presence.

On Monday, 16 October Convocation is opened in St Paul's. It will sit each Monday, Wednesday and Friday for several weeks. The Upper House, consisting of Gardiner and the score of other bishops, sits in the partitioned-off second bay on the north side of the nave, while the rest of the nave continues with its usual trafficking. There is apt to be more action in the Lower House, in the Lady Chapel. Something over 100 persons attend officially: the dean and provost of each cathedral, two archdeacons from each diocese, and so on.

Gardiner has always been in two minds about Convocation. In Henry's time he defended its right to decide religious affairs almost without regard to the King, and he has always believed (at any rate since he became a bishop himself) that Church leaders should be rich and powerful enough to have some independence. On the other hand he wrote for Henry *de vera obedientia*, a strong defence of the King's divine right to the total obedience of his subjects, in religious matters as well as lay. The inconsistency is massive, but Gardiner finds it not unportable. Convocation need not now conflict at all with its sovereign: it obediently but unenthusiastically turned the Catholic Church Protestant, and it will now, he hopes, turn it back again with joy.

On Monday the session is opened by Nicholas Harpsfield, returned refugee, civil and canon lawyer, first Regius Professor of Greek at Oxford. He lauds Mary, lauds Gardiner and other bishops, and castigates Protestant preachers, of whom there are six present. One of them is John Philpot who, when a boy at Winchester with Harpsfield, bet him he would write 200 Latin verses in a night, with not more than three mistakes, and won the bet. Hugh Weston, Dean of Westminster, is chosen as Prolocutor, to chair the Lower House and act as link between Lower and Upper. That is all for the day. The real business will start on Monday, 23 October.

On the Monday there is a great crowd, including peers and MPs because Parliament has been prorogued for the day so that they can attend. Parliament, incidentally, has not yet done anything dynamic in relation to religion, although Mary would have liked it to sweep away instantly all laws since 1529 with any reference to religion. This would have done away with the Act of Supremacy, the annulment of Henry's marriage to Catherine, Cranmer's Prayer Book, and the dissolution of the monasteries and chantries; the Papacy would be back, the Mass restored, Mary legitimate. But Convocation has to utter first, and the Lords are reluctant: they want the changes to be made bit by bit. And no interference with property.

Weston told Convocation last week that it was the Queen's pleasure that they debate matters of religion and propose laws accordingly, which she and Parliament would then ratify. Conclusions could be arrived at quite smoothly by majority vote. Very reasonable and normal.

He went on to say that it would be lawful for everyone to speak his mind, so that all doubts on the True Presence of Christ in the sacrament of the altar could be removed, and everyone fully satisfied. Very proper. But the Protestants' doubts can never be removed, and if Weston is not careful they will talk Convocation's hind leg off.

And, before this grand audience, that is what happens. Religious mysteries are wrangled over and chop-logicked, with quotations from Scripture and the Fathers hurtling from one side of the Lady Chapel to the other. Disputation is an unilluminating spectator sport. The opposing views on, for example, transubstantiation have been more clearly summed up in considered writings by Gardiner and Cranmer.

Cranmer: 'As Christ is a spiritual meat, so is he spiritually eaten and digested with the spiritual part of us, and giveth us spiritual and eternal life, and is not eaten, swallowed, and digested with our teeth, tongues, throats and bellies.'

Gardiner: 'I know by faith Christ is present, but the particularity how he is present, more than I am assured he is truly present, and therefore in substance present, I cannot tell. The ways and means whereof no man can tell, but humble spirits, as they be taught, must constantly believe it.'

This of Gardiner's is endearing. The lawyer-bishop, so forceful in argument, confesses in the end that he has no argument, that he is a child with a loved toy, a miracle, which he wants everyone to enjoy and love. And he will burn anyone who does not, as soon as Convocation and Parliament allow. He means this but in this passage does not say it, and it is not endearing.

Philpot and the other Protestants argue and argue, but Convocation votes overwhelmingly to restore the old religion. Gardiner should be happy. But he is not. He can handle Parliament, the courts, and Convocation, but not the happy and obstinate Queen.

Mary has removed from Richmond to Hampton Court, and as a result Gardiner and the Council spend much time barging up there. As does Renard. Past Chelsea, Fulham, Chiswick. Autumn colours. Past empty Syon and its park, and Richmond park and the empty palace. Past Teddington, the limit of tidal water. Then the first bridge above London Bridge, at Kingston. Then immediately, on the right, Hampton Court park, and across it the towers and pinnacles of the palace, not stone like Richmond, but red brick. It is a palace which impresses visitors.

But not by its architecture. The south front, which is seen first, is to continental eyes confused and crude, and the north-west front where one enters is to English eyes dull, except for its phantasmagorical chimney stacks. Its distinction is its furnishings. Wolsey procured for it hundreds of hangings from the Low Countries, of silk and gold, sometimes with pearls and stones; they cover the walls of every chamber and gallery in the five large courts and five small. And he loved carpets: he once got Venice to present him with sixty from the Levant. And there are wonderful beds, chairs, chests, linen and, of course, plate.

Besides the great churchman's wealth, one is surrounded at Hampton by Henry's arbitrariness. His purloining of the palace from Wolsey was immediately celebrated by having Tudor roses and portcullises embossed on all the walls, so heavily and in such numbers they are like spots before the eyes, and his successive marriages by successive embossings of ladies' initials and emblems.

Mary is happy on Sunday, 29 October because, not only has Convocation voted itself Catholic, but the House of Commons has during the week passed all three readings of a Bill to make lawful the marriage between Henry and Catherine of Aragon 'notwithstanding any sentences or Acts of Parliament to the contrary'. Mary is no longer a bastard. Elizabeth still is.

Mary is obstinate. A few days ago, accompanied by Rochester, Walgrave, Englefield and Southwell – Gardiner's chief but low-powered allies – her Lord Chancellor came to her and told her the country would not accept a foreigner as her husband. Parliament, Gardiner told her, was virtually unanimous. She said that Courtenay was not to her taste.

She is not confiding in Gardiner at all. She confides instead in Renard, who in return slanders Gardiner as being hopelessly unsuccessful with the Council, and timid and suspicious as if prison had affected his mind.

As odd as the Queen's attitude towards her chief minister is her attitude towards state secrets. She delights to give Renard, for onward transmission to Charles V, all the secret dispatches she receives from Wotton, the English ambassador in France. Patriot Gardiner would be shaken if he knew.

He would be even more shaken if he knew what his sovereign is doing on the evening of Sunday, 29 October. In an oratory in her privy apartments, in the presence of Renard, she is kneeling before the sacrament and swearing that she will marry Philip, and nothing, nothing, nothing will stop her.[4]

13

City: *Domine dirige nos*

i

While monarch and central government have been absorbed in their important activities, as if everyone's spiritual and material well-being depended on them, the City of London has grumbled and prospered. There have been one or two bankruptcies; there was even, last year and the year before, a recession after exceptional boom. But now business booms again. *Domine dirige nos*. It is as if *dominus* translated into 'sound finance', and the City guided by its Lord were more sure-footed than the men of state.

The City has not had to destroy minutes; it has not had to destroy personnel; it has not had undignified public disputations. When a new Lord Mayor was due to be elected, on 29 September, it simply elected a Catholic: Thomas White, sixty-one, the very prosperous, respected and pious Merchant Taylor who years ago went to Newgate rather than serve as alderman.

Monday, 30 October is the day of his swearing-in and his banquet. At eight in the morning the aldermen and sheriffs come to his house in Tithe Lane, close to St Michael Cornhill, in scarlet gowns furred, and with their cloaks. With his Company leading the way in their liveries, he is brought across the Stocks Market, along Poultry, and to Guildhall. There, waiting, is the outgoing Lord Mayor, Sir George Barne.

Meanwhile, a mighty procession of liverymen of all the Companies other than the Merchant Taylors has formed up at Grocers' Hall in order of the Companies' precedence. This procession links up with the Lord Mayor's and – with the Merchant Taylors at the head – rides White down to the Three Cranes. At about nine the citizens take their barges. The Lord Mayor's barge comes first, then the Merchant Taylors', then the sixty or so other Companies in order of precedence: Mercers, Grocers, Drapers, Fishmongers, Goldsmiths, Skinners . . . The Companies do not own their barges, they rent them. The Companies are all in their different liveries. The barges are all decorated.

Small guns bang off both from shore and from barges. Musicians in the barges (members of the Guild of Musicians) vigorously drum and fife.

And so, on the chilly water, past Bridewell and the Savoy, and the gardens of the Temple and of the noblemen's houses, past Whitehall, to Westminster.

Normally the Merchant Taylors and the Skinners lash their barges together as they approach Westminster, and drink to 'The Merchant Taylors and Skinners, Skinners and Merchant Taylors: root and branch, may they flourish for ever!' This custom was started seventy years ago to put an end to their feud over precedence. Today the Merchant Taylors are half a dozen barges ahead of the Skinners, indisputably having precedence. There is another custom, that the Stationers' barge rows across to Lambeth Palace and is regaled by the Archbishop: wine and cakes for the livery, beer and bread-and-cheese for the watermen. But Archbishop Cranmer is in the Tower.

At Westminster Bridge the Companies put on their cloaks (for dignity, not warmth), enter Westminster Hall and go right round it making courtesy (the courts are in session). And so up the stairs to the Upper Exchequer where, in relative quiet, the Lord Chancellor waits. On behalf of the Queen, Gardiner approves the election of Thomas White and administers the oath. From this moment the status of White when he is outside the city is next below the Councillors; within the city he has precedence over every subject of the sovereign, including her own family. Then down the stairs to the Common Pleas and the Queen's Bench. They take off their cloaks and go around the kings' tombs in the Abbey church, and then to barge again, and the Three Cranes.

The procession re-forms in Paul's churchyard, and at about noon sets off for Guildhall. In front are two tall men carrying streamers of the Merchant Taylors' arms, then a drum and a flute, and then the way-clearers – two great wild men, in green leaves and with big beards and long hair, with long staves headed with spurting squibs. Then sixteen trumpeters; then eighty poor men (sixty are a more usual number), all in blue gowns and caps and hose, each carrying a javelin and a shield bearing the Merchant Taylors' arms. Then a devil; then all the 'bachelors', selected yeomen, in livery and scarlet hoods. Then a pageant of John the Baptist, patron saint of the Merchant Taylors, 'gorgeously and with goodly speeches'. Then all the Queen's trumpeters, in scarlet caps with banners. Then the livery men of all the Companies, then the City Waits playing hautboys (oboes), and so on, then the Lord Mayor's officers, and Thomas White himself, attended by the Swordbearer and the Common Crier, and then the aldermen and sheriffs. And so to Guildhall.

Between 300 and 400 from the procession go to the banquet in the Great hall of Guildhall: the wardens of all the Companies and a varying number of liverymen – a dozen from the Drapers, four from the Bakers. There are some guests – Councillors and important officers of the Crown, foreign merchants, foreign ambassadors.[1]

ii

The master and wardens and some liverymen of the Merchant Taylors have seen to the arrangements in the hall and supervise the feast, and a dozen or so of the bachelors help with the service.

Barne, the retiring Lord Mayor, sits with the chief guests at the high table on the hustings, the dais, at the east end of the hall and 'keeps the feast'. White, when he comes in, greets Barne and the guests at the high table, and those at the Lady Mayoress's table and the gentlewomen's table, and the judges, but then goes out into the Chamberlain's court and dines *à six* with a couple of the senior aldermen, the Recorder and the sheriffs. The sheriffs in succession to Garrard and Maynard are Thomas Offley, an unusually short man, and William Hewitt, the Clothworker of London Bridge. The Recorder is always one of the MPs for London, and Robert Brooke has been Recorder and MP for eight years. By the time those in the hall are almost through their second course White and his company have finished their dinner and returned into the hall. White greets Barne all over again, and everyone else in the hall, amid general acclamation.

Why do the major elected officials undertake their civic work, which is after all very heavy? The Queen's Councillors and the senior Crown officers can hope for gifts, bribes, the profits from embezzlement, grants of land, grants of offices, grants of wards, the benefits of patronage. The Lord Mayor, sheriffs and aldermen get little, little that is material. White will be given £40 towards his year's expenses, but the year will cost him a great deal more than that. What they all receive is prestige, and the advantages and pleasures of exercising power among their fellows – administering the law, collecting taxes, selecting for military service, and regulating all manner of activities. There are business benefits in close association with key people and potential customers. And it would be unlike public life in 1553 if they got no irregular income: the Chamberlain, the City's treasurer, like the treasurers of the Queen's revenue courts, has the temporary use for his own purposes of any funds he has in hand, and everyone with power receives gifts. But of squeeze and embezzlement there seems truly to be little.

Are these men here then a superior type of human being? Improbable – they fiercely keep down wages and prices in their own interests, exploit and defend their monopolies, and keep the yeomanry of their Companies in their traditional subservience.

It is the City organism which constrains and encourages them to responsible behaviour in civic matters. They can only conduct business by being a member of a Company and a citizen, involving a commitment, strictly enforced, to accept office in the Company or City if elected. Their feeling for their Company and City is constantly nourished by their fellows and by the continual committees and consultations, banquets and processions and church services; and by the tight little rules and practices which are imposed with a firmness which is clean, not vengeful, never shirked.

The City is structured for the production of capable, loyal and contented governors. And under its governors it usually finds for itself paths of secure and profitable rectitude. When White takes his seat as Lord Mayor in Guildhall, his first words will always be *Domine dirige nos*, and these will be his words whether God is legislated into being Catholic or Protestant.[2]

iii

What is talk about at dinner? It has been a good wheat harvest, for the second year. The price of wool is down, right down, two-thirds of last year, a half of 1550 and 1551. They have been loading cloth for the November fair at Barrow (which is English for Bergen-op-Zoom). Cloth exports have risen sharply after the two-year slump. Merchant Adventurers complain that the Queen, like Edward before her, will take most of the foreign exchange they earn and pay them in sterling. She needs it, for servicing her debts, and the Adventurers do not, because their imports are modest. But they complain: they might want to increase their imports.

There is bound to be talk about the Hanse, who will soon be back in the market in a big way. Meetings between the Hanse delegation and the Queen's commissioners, headed by Gardiner, ended last Tuesday: the Queen is restoring their privileges to the level before Northumberland reduced them last year. Again they are to pay 1s duty on each broadcloth exported, as against an Englishman's 1s 2d and any other alien's 1s 9d, and pay nothing on general commodities against an Englishman's 1s in the £ and other aliens' 2s in the £. But they can export unfinished white cloths only by licence, like everyone else, instead of quite freely. In general they will be competing here for cloth much as of yore, so prices will go up: good for Clothworkers, bad for Merchant Taylors and Merchant Adventurers.

London will half forgive the Hanse their preferential terms if only they stick to the treaty: if the Hanse truly export only to their own towns and not to Antwerp and elsewhere, and if they truly open their own towns to English traders, and cease to block English trade in the Baltic. But all this has been promised in previous treaties and not carried out. Can the Queen persuade her cousin Charles to make them stick to the treaty? He probably would not and could not.

If the Queen were to marry Philip, would control of the Hanse be any easier? Would there be any trade advantage? For example, would England be allowed into Spain's trade with her colonies? England's interests would always come second to those of Spain and the Empire.

The single advantage to the men in this hall would be the certainty of peace with the Netherlands. But this would be balanced by the quasi-certainty of war with France, with inevitable taxation and interference with trade.

And outside business no one is in favour of the marriage. Too many have seen the Inquisition in the Netherlands, Spain, Portugal. It is one thing to burn Anabaptists – everyone does that – and it is one thing to burn in a moderate English way an occasional hyper-active Lutheran or Zwinglian or Calvinist, but it is another to destroy, in the wholesale Spanish way, Protestants of much the same faith as most of the men and women in the hall.

Although MPs (the City's four MPs are here) are supposed not to speak of parliamentary affairs outside the House, it is certainly known by everyone here that Parliament is against a marriage to Philip but that, marriage or no marriage, Catholicism and the Papacy are, step by step, to be wholly restored. Which means that, sooner or later, heresy laws will return, and that the heretics in this hall are likely to be much disturbed in possession of life and property.

The banquet has brought together, at the high table, Renard and de Noailles. Renard, after his closeting with Mary at Hampton Court yesterday evening, probably looks like a cat which has eaten a fish. De Noailles finds that Renard talks, quite interminably, of the desirability of peace between Charles and Henri.

In due course the banquet ends and the procession lines up again to go to Paul's for Mass, and afterwards it goes, with trumpets and hautboys blowing, round the choir and the body of the cathedral, and then, still blowing and blowing, and with the eighty old men in blue now and carrying torches, home to White's house. What hours are spent in these City ceremonies!

14

Parliament: *La Reyne le veult*

i

Next morning, Tuesday, 31 October, 8 a.m. In St Stephen's Chapel Sir John Pollard is in the Speaker's chair. There are first readings of several Bills: about the practice of archery; the giving of lands to grammar schools; some legal practices out of term. A fourth is in the interest of manufacturers and merchants of London and other towns, a requirement that all artificers in certain crafts should dwell in a town and therefore be under closer control.

A fifth is to restore Catholic doctrines and practices but not the monasteries or Papal supremacy. The paper text is read to the House by Seymour, the Clerk. Any member who wants to study the text for himself must look at it in Seymour's office, or pay for Seymour's assistants in the Lobby to make him a copy. At a first reading there is normally no discussion, but there may be queries or comments or, now and again, postponement or outright rejection.

Does it pass its first reading? No problem. The second and third may be different.

Has Mary, unlike Northumberland, been able to pack the House? No, but loyalty to a newly anointed sovereign has made the country delight to return members of her entourage and followers of her religion. On the other hand the group of Councillors and Crown servants sitting on Pollard's right are only a moderately persuasive and forceful team. A pity Gardiner has to be in the Lords.

On Friday the Bill has its second reading. There is discussion, much standing up bareheaded to indicate a desire to speak (members at other times wear their hats in the House). On Saturday there is further discussion. It is rare for discussion to overflow to a second day. On Sunday morning Feckenham, chaplain to Bonner, Bishop of London, preaches at St Mary Overy, and tries to persuade any MPs in the congregation to ease the Bill's passage. There are disturbances. And in the afternoon he preaches similarly at St Stephen Walbrook, with similar disturbances. How could it be otherwise? It is remarkable there are no serious riots.

Who are these MPs on whom so much depends? About a quarter of the House, ninety members, are 'knights of the shire', each county in England being represented by two, elected by those who hold land to the value of 40s a year. They are not necessarily 'knights' but they are certainly gentlemen, socially dominant in their counties, or nominated by the socially dominant. Usually county elections are not contested, because persons of social eminence do not like to risk public defeat. The two or three leading families settle the matter between them. To be even the junior county member holds more prestige than being member for a borough. Councillors Englefield, Rochester, Hastings and Sir Richard Southwell are senior members for, respectively, Berkshire, Essex, Middlesex and Norfolk.

The borough seats are ostensibly for burgesses, who are not gentlemen, but boroughs happily elect gentlemen from other areas instead. To maintain an MP a borough has to pay a burgess 2s for every day, including his travelling time, but a gentleman, recommended to a borough by some important person and therefore not a nobody, is expected to cost the borough nothing. Some boroughs choose a burgess for one seat and accept a free-gift gentleman for the other. London accepts no free gifts as its four members: Sir Rowland Hill and Recorder Brooke are regarded as 'knights of the shire' and are paid 4s a day each and are allowed two attendants each; John March and John Blundell 2s a day and one attendant; all four have a livery allowance and the cost of boat hire.

Legal men also fill a fair number of borough seats. Parliament displays their talents, brings them (fare paid) to Westminster, and does not interfere too greatly with attendance in court in Westminster Hall, although the hours of the Commons and the courts are the same, 8 to 11 a.m., Monday to Saturday.

The House has been slower than the City to develop a strong corporate sense: its members come from the four corners of the kingdom, and at the end of a session scatter again. Nevertheless, wherever they sit (in general they sit where they like) they find relatives and friends: their marriage links and business links criss-cross over half England. And in the last twenty years the House has got to know itself better through some very long sessions, and through the same members being returned repeatedly.

These gentlemen, burgesses and lawyers, already conscious of their local or professional importance, have these last decades been pressing their importance as members of the House. They have now extended their privilege of freedom from arrest to include their servants, and once a week on average the Serjeant-at-Arms is sent to have a member's servant released.

But they are aware that they are of a lower order of nature than the noblemen in the Upper House, and they have no touch of divinity as has the Sovereign. And their corporate sense has a wedge driven in it by the group of Councillors and Crown servants whose service is to the Crown rather than the electorate or the House.

ii

On Monday the House decides that the Bill dealing with religion shall be engrossed on parchment in the expectation of an undiscussed third reading. The third reading is on Tuesday, and there is discussion after all. There is further discussion on Wednesday, 8 November before master Speaker says: 'As many as will have this Bill pass, in manner and form as ye have heard, say 'Yea'.

The greater part of the House say 'Yea'.

'As many as will not have this Bill pass, let them say 'No'.

About eighty say 'No'.

A handsome majority. But nearly a quarter of the House are determined enough to let themselves be marked as heretic.

So, by the Bill, after 20 December there will be no more of the Reformed Religion, no more English services. The Mass and images and vestments and candle-carrying processions will be back universally. And no married priests are to minister or sing Mass, so the 4,000 wives of priests must become secret mistresses, or be wholly put away, or see their husbands deprived of their livings.

Gardiner should be pleased: the doctrinal changes have been agreed before the Queen's marriage plans have disastrously troubled the waters.

For the best part of a week the House has wanted to present a petition that the Queen shall marry within the kingdom, but she has declared herself too sick to receive them. The sickness may have been nervous and diplomatic but she may also have been genuinely upset by the cold weather. Surely she will receive them now, or next week?

So far John Seymour has not entered in the House journal any mention of the Queen's marriage or of a possible petition, but the anxiety is considerable. It is one thing to accept reversion to the country's old religion, with all its implications, but quite another to accept a foreign King, a Spaniard, with Spaniards being presented to every lucrative office, the country's trade being made subject to Spanish interests, and Englishmen being sent abroad to fight in Spain's wars while Spaniards are brought to occupy England and tell any Englishmen who remain what to do and what not to do.

On Monday, 13 November Cranmer and Jane, with Guildford and the other Dudley boys, are taken from the Tower to Guildhall for trial. They are on foot, with the Axe before them, Jane in black and attended by two of her women. The new Lord Mayor presides. They are all found guilty of treason and are condemned. No awkward demonstrations.

iii

On Thursday, 16 November the Commons presents to the Queen by the mouth of the Speaker its deferred and passionately felt petition. Sir John Pollard is accompanied by the Duke of Norfolk, the Earls of Arundel, Shrewsbury, Derby, and Pembroke, the Bishops of Durham, Winchester and Norwich, the Lords Privy Seal and Paget, and several other noblemen. This is more than the Commons; this is Parliament.

He dwells on the present state of the succession, the strife that would arise if she were to die without issue, the opening that would be afforded to the Scots, and the desirability of leaving an heir of her own. He sets forth all the disadvantages, dangers and difficulties of her choosing a foreign husband.

It is a lengthy piece, and the Queen sits down. She becomes so offended that she answers the speech herself instead of having her Lord Chancellor answer it, and answers it at length, concluding that if she marries against her will she will not live three months, and will have no children. All her affairs, she declares, have been conducted by divine disposition, so she will pray God to counsel and inspire her in her choice of a husband, beneficial to the kingdom and agreeable to herself. According to God's inspiration she will choose, for she always thinks of the welfare of her kingdom, as a good princess and mistress should.

iv

Mary's intention to marry Philip is believed – by wider and wider circles, and soon by everyone – to be fixed. Renard fears, de Noailles hopes, that these violent changeable people will make trouble. But the days go by. There is no confrontation between Parliament and Crown. The strength of the country's feeling has usefully been made known to the Queen and the Council, and through Renard to the Emperor and Philip. The Queen must now have her way; but the marriage treaty must be so tight that the country cannot be over-run by Spaniards or dragged into the Emperor's wars.

There is furious talk. Numbers of people who welcomed Mary say they would rather die than let the Spaniards in. But whatever may be said in taverns and Paul's Walk, and although some people make oblique inquiries of de Noailles about financial and armed help from the French, it is not easy actually to do anything. To do something is treason.

Work goes on. Parliament has meetings even in the afternoons in an effort to finish the session in November. On the afternoon of Monday, 27 November Paulet's Bill for reorganization of the revenue courts has its first reading, and by the following Monday has passed through all its stages. There is a Bill to confirm the bishopric of Durham to Tunstall, but reserving Durham House for Elizabeth's use. There is a Bill confirming the attainders of Northumberland and his sons, and of Jane, Cranmer, Northampton and others. Norfolk tries to get back some of the lands lost by his own attainder under Henry VIII, but their new owners object and the matter goes to arbitration. There is a Bill to deal with people who disturb church services or do not come to church.

There is anxiety, rumour. In the country two priests are killed; another is fired at in a village church while celebrating Mass. The ambassadors – Imperial, French, Venetian – prestigious, jumpy expatriates, are not a tranquillizing influence on any minds they reach.

On 1 December Renard receives from Charles a draft set of marriage articles based on a set he himself worked out with Paget; on 2 December, Saturday, Mary has a copy sent to the Council. It is intended that some of the peers shall be told of it before they disperse with the dissolution of Parliament.

The last readings of Bills in the Commons are finished by Tuesday, 5 December. On Wednesday afternoon Mary in her Parliament robes enters the Parliament Chamber where the peers are already assembled. The Commons are admitted. Pollard makes obeisances and an oration. Mary tells Gardiner to reply on her behalf.

He says Her Majesty is displeased. In the morning a dog was found in her Presence Chamber, with its head shaven like a priest's and a rope round its neck, and a note attached saying priests and bishops should be hanged. Gardiner tells Parliament that such acts may move the Queen to a kind of justice further removed from clemency than she would have wished.

At his little table between the woolsacks the Clerk of the Crown reads the titles of the Bills passed during the session by both Houses. As each is mentioned the Clerk of the Parliaments (an official who also acts as Clerk of the Lords) consults a paper signed by Mary and gives her decision. She consents to thirty-one Bills. With a private Bill he says *'Soit fait comme il est desiré'*; with a public, *'La Reyne le veult'*.

In due course Gardiner says: 'It is Her Majesty's pleasure that this Parliament shall be dissolved; and she giveth licence to all knights, citizens and burgesses to depart at their pleasure. And so, God save the Queen!'

The Commons say a loud Amen.

On religion the country, as represented by Parliament, has decided of its own free will to be Catholic again.

On marriage the Queen, against representations by Parliament, has decided – with divine guidance – to marry the handsome young Spanish prince.

Bishopsgate Street, Three Needle Street,
Walbrook, the Crane in Vintry. Detail of
south section of Copperplate Map. (*Museum of
London*)

ABOVE Westminster Abbey, with the
King's Palace to the left. *Aide memoire*
drawing by Wyngaerde. Panorama from the
Sutherland Collection, Ashmolean Museum,
Oxford.

Jane the Quene

The signature of Lady Jane Grey, as Queen.

OPPOSITE ABOVE The palace at Richmond,
from Richmond Green.

RIGHT The Tower of London from the
Ralph Agas Map of London *c.* 1560.
(*Guildhall Library, London*)

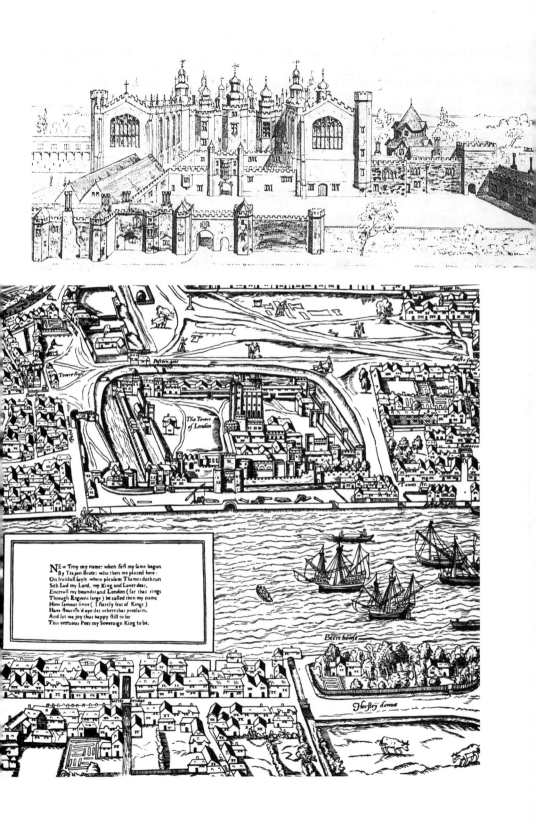

NEw Troy my name: when first my fame begun
By Trojan Brute: who then me placed here:
On fruitfull foyle where pleasant Thames doth run
Sith Lud my Lord, my King and Lover dear,
Encreaft my bounds and London (far that rings
Through Regions large) he called then my name
How famous since (I stately feat of Kings)
Have flourifh'd aye: let others that proclaim.
And let me joy thus happy ftill to see
This vertuous Peer my Soveraign King to be.

The coronation procession passed from
Cheapside around the south of St Paul's and
down Ludgate Hill towards Fleet Street.

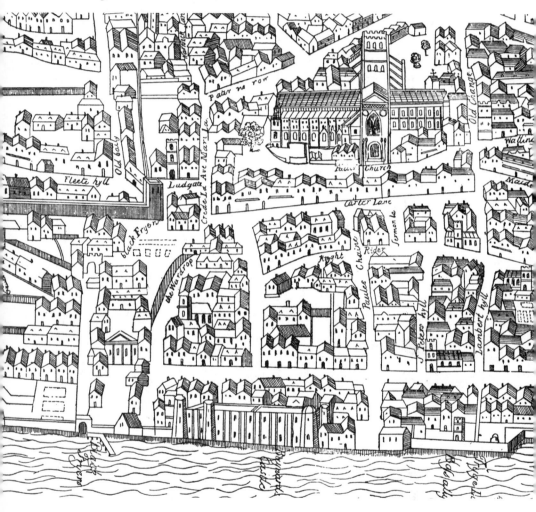

The signature of Mary Tudor, as Queen.

Archbishop Cranmer, painted by Flicke in
1546. (*National Portrait Gallery, London*)

Bishop Gardiner's doodle (*Public Record Office*)

OPPOSITE Wyatt's route: St George's church – number 56 on map – around the east past part of Southwark to the Bridge. Detail from plan in the Duchy of Lancaster Records, *c.* 1542.

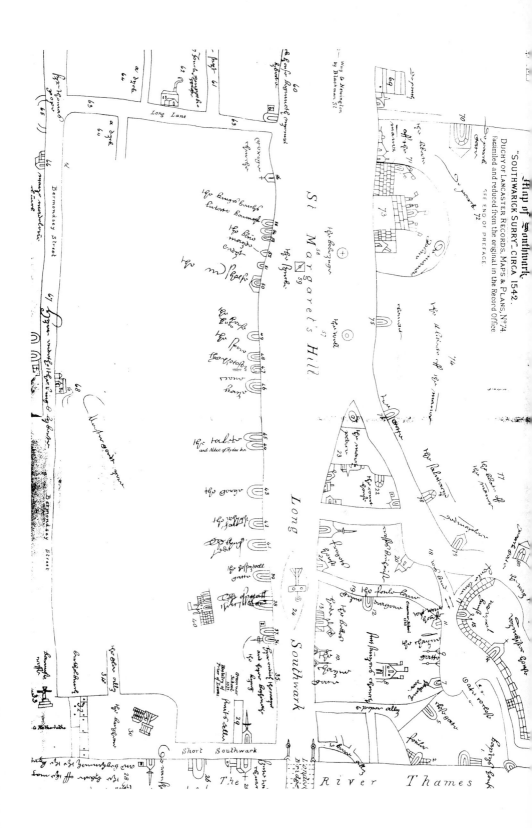

Map of Southwark.

"SOUTHWARK SURRY", CIRCA 1542.

DUCHY OF LANCASTER RECORDS, MAPS & PLANS, No 74

Facsimiled and reduced from the original in the Record Office

SEE END OF PREFACE

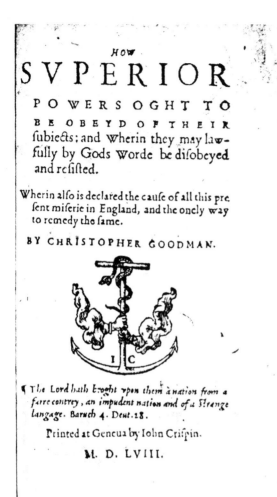

HOW

SVPERIOR

POWERS OGHT TO
BE OBEYD OF THEIR
fubiects; and wherin they may lawfully by Gods worde be difobeyed
and refifted.

Wherin alfo is declared the caufe of all this pre
fent miferie in England, and the onely way
to remedy the fame.

BY CHRISTOPHER GOODMAN.

¶ The Lord hath broght vpon them a nation from a
farre contrey, an impudent nation and of a ftrange
langage. Baruch 4. Deut.28.

Printed at Geneua by Iohn Crifpin.

M. D. LVIII.

ABOVE Christopher Goodman's *How Superior Powers Ought To Be Obeyed*, published in 1558.

BELOW The Strand front of Somerset House, after the drawing by John Thorpe. (*Sir John Soane Museum*)

VI

Crisis Again

15

Approach to crisis – again

i

The following day, Thursday, 7 December, the treaty is considered by the Council, Gardiner in the chair. Charles has realized the treaty must give the English everything they could possibly want if it is to be accepted. Philip is to assist Mary in the task of government, subject always to England's laws, privileges and customs. He relinquishes all claim to dispose of offices and benefices, which are to be bestowed on natives. All business is to be conducted in the languages which have been used of old in the kingdom, and by natives. Mary is to be admitted to share in Philip's realms and dominions; and for as long as the marriage endures, and until her death if she survives Philip, she is to receive annually £60,000 Flemish. The children born of the marriage are to succeed to Mary's rights to England and to Philip's rights to the Netherlands and Burgundy. Philip's rights to Spain and its American empire, the two Sicilies, Milan and other Italian territories are to go to his son, Don Carlos, and his heirs; but if that line becomes extinct they come to the descendants of the marriage. There is to be wholehearted fraternity, union and confederation between the Emperor, his heirs and dominions, and Mary and her dominions; and they are to assist one another in accordance with the treaty of 1542 and the declaration of 1546.

Gardiner has withdrawn his opposition, and the Council agrees the terms subject to insignificant amendments. Special envoys are expected from Charles at the New Year; they will agree the final text, and then the excellent terms will be published.

Two days later Gardiner is rowed up-river past Westminster. He is going to Syon, which has been Crown property since last Wednesday when Mary assented to the Bill for Northumberland's attainder. In August commissioners (Sir Thomas Pope, Sir Robert Southwell and others) inventoried the goods and paid off the servants. What is Gardiner doing with the commissioners at

Syon today? Perhaps looking it over with an eye to its being returned to the Bridgettines.

During their talk Gardiner doodles. He experiments with his signature, 'Ste Winton'. Writes the year when the Bridgettines were founded, '1345'. And *'Edwardus'*. And 'July 1553' when Northumberland was *'Stultus'*, a fool. And look, the Lord Chancellor kicks himself for a *stultus*: *'Ego sum'*, I am. *'Ego'*. By opposing the marriage for so long he has perhaps wholly lost the little confidence the Queen had in him. And there could be good for both himself and the country in having the disciplined and immensely powerful Philip as the King. Instead of 'Ste Winton' Gardiner should be 'Stulton'.

In the following days he works loyally to forward the marriage. He tells a gathering of peers the terms. Lord Windsor, not usually given to assertive good sense, comments: 'You tell us many fine words on the part of the Queen and many large promises on the part of the Emperor and his son, but if it happens that they choose not to carry out what they promise, what pledges and assurances will you have of them to compel them to hold by their agreements?'

It is a pity the terms cannot yet be officially published. There is too much rumour. In London there are leaflets and violent talk. A man is put in the pillory in Cheap for seditious words against the Queen and the Council. Renard keeps thrusting at Paget information about conspiratorial meetings, day and night, between heretics and Frenchmen. He thinks, and so does Mary, that the kingdom is full of rebelliousness and French intrigue, with Princess Elizabeth up to her neck in it. Renard would like Elizabeth in the Tower, Mary would like her explicitly excluded from the succession. There are rumours of French ships gathering in Normandy to intercept Philip on his way from Spain, and of Plymouth and Exeter declaring they will not let the Spaniards land.[1]

ii

The situation holds irreconcilable contraries. People do not want the marriage, but that is now tantamount to not wanting the Queen. They do not want to betray the Queen, but the marriage would betray England.

Most of the English, busy trying to make a living, or a bit more than a living, find that irreconcilable contraries can be lived with for a long time, but there are educated men who, if under-employed, convince themselves they cannot live with them, and they prick around for relief in talk or action. Some of those pricking around in this cold winter are: Sir Peter Carew, ex-Sheriff of Devon, given to loud gestures and bad timing; Sir Nicholas

Arnold, ex-Sheriff of Gloucestershire; Sir Edward Warner MP, who was in charge of the Tower under Jane, and his stepson Sir Thomas Wyatt, ex-Sheriff of Kent; Sir James Crofts, ex-Lord Deputy of Ireland; Sir Nicholas Throgmorton, who was in favour with Edward; William Winter, Surveyor of the Navy; Sir George Harper, Sir Edward Rogers; William Thomas, ex-Clerk of the Council, Italophile, who knows what Machiavelli would say – 'Kill the Queen' – and he knows a man with an assassin's face, John Fitzwilliams. All these gentlemen declare the safety of England is at stake.

Elizabeth, especially if married to Courtenay, would be such a convenient alternative to Mary that Mary and Renard inevitably fear both of them. Which terrifies Courtenay, and he thinks of fleeing to the Continent. Elizabeth, at her house at Ashridge Park, near St Albans, keeps very low, watches her tongue and pen, and asks Mary to send her copes and chasubles and chalices and crosses for her chapel.

With a certain stiff aristocratic excitement, de Noailles listens to the scraps of information which come to the French mission. Some come, unsolicited, from well-born Englishmen. Some from professional spies and double-spies for a fee. Some from the well-informed Venetian Ambassador: Soranzo is against the marriage because Venice wants neither the Empire nor France to gain advantage. Some from an interpreter employed by Renard; from an equerry of Courtenay's; from a French artist in Mary's household who has access also to Paulet's; from a French bookseller who has contacts with Renard's household; from a Flemish servant of Paget's; from contacts of de Noailles's Scots groom and of the English wife of one of his cooks. He puts two and one together to make five and, through the English-speaking Secretary of his mission, sympathizes with the disgruntled, impatient, unrealistic, potential rebels and their intermediaries, and implies that French help would be available to them, hoping that Mary and her Council will hear enough to make them think Henri will fight to prevent a marriage.

There is fuss. Many words. Much unease. Mary tells the whole Court she trusts them to do their duty, and her women are in a flurry.[2]

iii

Meanwhile, Paul's has its candles and processions again, and the sacrament is hung over the high altar under a canopy of gold. Every church is required to restore Mass, rebuild its altar, and get its cross before St Thomas's Day, in time for Christmas.

In the Tower, Jane is allowed to walk in the Queen's Garden and on the hill, and Robert and Guildford Dudley to walk on the leads of the Bell Tower: great relief for all of them.

Underhill, who still feels himself very sick, is able to walk about the streets again, his pale lean face wrapped up. He is sure people are thinking he is up to no good and are saying, 'Daren't he show his face?'

It is very cold. Wood and coal are dear: faggots are 5s or 6s a hundred; coal sells from the cart at 10s a sack, from the horse at 14d or 15d a bushel. The Lord Mayor arranges for lighters of coal to be brought to Billingsgate and Queenhithe and sold at 4d a bushel.

The Court is merry at Christmas, with George Ferrers Lord of Misrule as for Edward's last two Christmases. But Gardiner suffers an irritation. The heretics bring out over the Christmas season a translation of his *De vera obedientia*, which he wrote for Henry against Papal supremacy.

On 1 January the entourage and servants of the Emperor's envoys arrive. Almost 400 of them. With baggage. As they ride through London they are snowballed by ribald children. The following day the Prince of Gavre and the other envoys, recovered from a very sick crossing, arrive at Tower Wharf, and are greeted by a great peal of guns and by Lord William Howard, who is now Lord Admiral instead of Clinton, and by Sir Anthony Browne, both gorgeously dressed. On Tower Hill, Courtenay and other lords greet them and conduct them through Cheapside to their quarters at Durham House. To an English eye the crowd seem to take no pleasure in their arrival, but the envoys write off to Charles that there was a great gathering of people 'who seemed to us to rejoice at our coming'.

Sir Thomas White (he was knighted three or four weeks ago) sends them gifts on behalf of the City, and there are daily festivities. They watch bearbaiting. They dance. They dine at Gardiner's with all the Council. They hunt at Hampton Court, killing all manner of animals with hounds and swords.

A gentleman is put in prison for saying the match will not have the desired result. One or two notices are stuck up saying that Philip is already betrothed to the Infanta of Portugal. Renard advises Mary to deal exemplary justice because the heretics are poisoning the people against the nobility and foreigners. He writes to Philip suggesting he should send Mary a present, and he should come before Lent because Mary refuses to marry in Lent itself and the English give trouble after Lent, in the summer.

On 12 January the treaty is signed.

iv

A week ago, in Spain, there was a small ceremony.

Juan Vasquez de Molina:
In the noble town of Valladolid, on the 4th of January 1554, in the presence of me, Juan Vasquez de Molina, Secretary, member of his Majesty's Council and notary public in all his realms and dominions, and of the witnesses mentioned below:

The very high and mighty Prince Philip, first-born and heir to the realms and dominions of the Crown of Spain, stated that his Majesty the Emperor and King, his father, had on account of his marriage with the very high and mighty Lady Mary, Queen of England, granted certain articles, the tenor of which is here declared, and he (Prince Philip) was about to grant a power in due form to the Prince of Gavre, Count de Lalaing, MM de Courrières, Prince Nigri and Simon Renard to enable all and each one of them to ratify and swear to observe the said articles in his name. He would thus be obliged to ratify and swear to them in the manner contained in the power and in the writing of confirmation, in the terms here set forth.

Until the articles had been drawn up and granted by his Majesty (Prince Philip continued), he had not known of them, and he intended to grant the said power and swear to observe the said articles in order that his marriage with the Queen of England might take place, but by no means in order to bind himself or his heirs to observe the articles, especially any that might burden his conscience.

And because by his own free will he had never agreed and never would agree to the articles, he protested, before me, the Secretary, and the other witnesses mentioned below, against the articles and everything contained therein. And, wishing to make valid this protest and revocation, he protested once, twice and thrice, or as many times as it was necessary to make the act legal, and to ensure that the power and confirmation that he was about to grant should be invalid and without force to bind him, as things done against his will and only in order to attain the aforesaid object.

This he swore by Our Lord, by Saint Mary and by the Sign of the Cross, as it stands here †, on which he bodily laid his right hand, and by the words of the Holy Gospel where they are set out at length: that he would not be bound by the said ratification to be made in his name, nor by his own promise to observe or keep anything contained in the said articles, especially if it went against his conscience to do so.

This he swore to in good and true form before me, the Secretary, and before the witnesses named below, and protested that he would demand of the Holy Father to be freed from his oath as often as it might be necessary to do so.

Witnesses who were present: the Duke of Alva, of his Majesty's Council and his Master of the Household; Ruy Gomez de Silva, his Highness's Chamberlain; and Licentiate Minjaca, of his Majesty's Council.

I, the said Juan Vasquez de Molina, was present together with the witnesses, and at his Highness's bidding I here declare that the act took place as here described, wherefore I set my mark in witness of the truth. Juan Vasquez.

One need not feel concern about the English Queen being deceived. She has already dispatched a message to Philip through Charles that he is not to worry about the terms of the treaty – everything, in secret, shall be done according to his wishes.[3]

V

Two days after the signing of the treaty, on Sunday, 14 January, Gardiner eloquently expounds and praises the treaty to an assembly of Councillors, nobility and gentlemen in the Presence Chamber at Whitehall. The following day he makes a similar speech to the Lord Mayor, sheriffs, aldermen and forty London commoners, who have been summoned before the Council. He desires them to behave themselves like subjects with all humbleness and rejoicing.

And, while they are there, he chides and threatens them because religion is very slackly set forth in London. He has already, ten days ago, had to summon to him the churchwardens and principal citizens of thirty parishes to inquire why they have not Mass and service in Latin in their churches. To the impatient Gardiner progress does not seem fast. Moreover, now that the marriage is a certainty, the threat of trouble seems more serious and more immediate.

Those 400 Spaniards are still here. Why so many? 'The Spaniards will flood the country,' is being said more and more. Should not some true Englishman seize the Tower before the Spaniards do? Should not everyone arm to defend their properties and families and rights? And to change the Queen's advisers?

Sir Peter Carew went off to Devon some while ago, talking of arming against the Spaniards and holding Exeter. Machiavellian William Thomas has gone in the same direction. Sir Nicholas Throgmorton has said firmly and audibly in London that it is a damnable marriage.

Renard tells Mary on Thursday, 18 January all he knows, or thinks he knows, of evil plotting by the French, evil plotting by the heretics. The following day Sir Thomas Wyatt, ex-Sheriff of Kent, goes down to his Allington Castle to talk with his neighbours about saving the country and seizing the Tower. Sir Peter Carew, whom the Council has summoned back from Devon, has not obeyed, suspecting they suspect him. He says he has no horses and cannot come. The Council issues a warrant for his arrest.

Six months ago Londoners declared for Mary against Jane, prompted by dislike of Northumberland and obsessed with the single issue of legitimate succession, ignoring the religious consequences. If there comes another moment of truth, will Londoners declare for Elizabeth, prompted by dislike of the Spaniards and obsessed with the single issue of patriotism and well content with Elizabeth's religion?

Will the Council change sides if the country moves under their feet towards Elizabeth? None of them is wedded to the marriage. Is Paget? He is an opportunist. Is Arundel? He is a stubborn patriot, and he has that ambiguous man Crofts staying at Arundel House. Pembroke? He has no convictions, and too much wealth to risk loyalty to anyone. Gardiner? The last of all the Council to acquiesce. The peerage are not for the marriage, nor the gentry, nor the townsmen.

Is Mary, for her heart's desire – her middle-aged maidenly lust – giving away her miracle?

Elizabeth is very near, just 30 miles away at Ashridge.

England faces civil war again. How will God's people deal with it this time?[4]

16

O Lord, save thy people – again

i

On Saturday, 20 January news, or rumour, reaches London that in Devon Sir Peter Carew and the Sheriff of Devon, Sir Thomas Dennis, are 'up', and they have taken Exeter and its castle. Rebellion has reared its head at last. How widespread? Where does everyone stand?

On Sunday Gardiner sends for Courtenay. This frightens some. Courtenay will give names of everyone he can remember who has talked with him about religion or marriage. With the West up, any old unbuttoned remarks will be taken as evidence of plotting. Courtenay tells Gardiner he does not intend to marry Elizabeth; he would rather go back to the Tower.

Monday. The Council sends Sir John St Leger to Devon to take charge and report. On Tuesday the guard on the gates of the city is strengthened, and the streets are patrolled. On Wednesday Renard tells Gardiner, who probably knows at least as much as he does, that there is a plot to seize the Tower. Warner, ex-Lieutenant of the Tower, is involved, and a dozen other heretics. Elizabeth, he says (as if Gardiner would not agree), should be put in the Tower as quickly as possible. Not the right place if there is danger of it being seized. On Thursday morning, the twenty-fifth, news comes that in Maidstone Sir Thomas Wyatt has called to arms against the Queen's marriage, and similar proclamations have been made elsewhere in Kent. The Lord Chamberlain, Sir John Gage, informs the Lord Mayor, and White calls the Court of Aldermen for the afternoon. The Council has the Tower re-victualled and its artillery overhauled. So, a rising in the south-east to add to the rising in the south-west.

The Council sends down to Sheen for the Duke of Suffolk: perhaps to send him down to Kent to deal with the Wyatt trouble, perhaps because they suspect he may be involved. Suffolk fears the worst: he rides away to his own country, the Midlands, trying on the way to raise a little money and a man or two. So, are the Midlands going to rise too?

The Council decides to put the Marquis of Northampton under lock and key since he is a heretic and lodges with the suspect Warner. In the evening Northampton is taken by White and sheriffs Offley and Hewitt to White's house in Tithe Lane, and Warner is taken to Hewitt's; in the morning they will go to the Tower. White rides about the city to check the Watch.

Friday, 26 January. Suffolk is proclaimed a traitor, and Huntingdon is sent after him.

Saturday the twenty-seventh. Paulet goes to Guildhall and asks officially for 500 well-harnessed men. A Common Council is summoned for the afternoon, and assents: the men are to be ready by 6 p.m. The Companies summon their quotas – for example, Merchant Taylors thirty, Bakers eight. Most of the equipment comes from store but the Merchant Taylors have to spend nearly £15 to make up the full number of German rivets (a rivet is a body armour of which the front and back plates are held together by straps, so it does not have to be made to measure), salads (headpieces fastened under the chin by a strap), bows, bowstrings, arrows, bracers (to guard the left arm against the bowstring), shooting gloves, swords, daggers, bills; and to give the men 2s each enlistment money, and some welcoming beer.

Bonner moves John Rogers, heretic and therefore suspect, from his house next door the Bishop's Palace and into Newgate. Rogers in any case no longer has a right to the house since he has been deprived of his prebend.

During the night two aldermen ride about to check the Watch. There is to be a similar check as long as the emergency lasts.

Next day, Sunday, the 500 Whitecoats assemble at Leadenhall under five captains, and proceed by barge to Gravesend. One of de Noailles's agents, a Scotsman named Broughton, has been in touch with these captains, but it is doubtful whether so untrusted a foreigner as a Scot can have affected their loyalty. Some of the Guard also go down to Kent. The old Duke of Norfolk is in command. Too old for the task? But he is loyal.

It is cold damp weather for a river trip; cold damp weather for a rebellion. The rebels rifle Sir Henry Sidney's armoury at Penshurst, and gather strength; against them the Sheriff of Kent, Sir Robert Southwell (brother of Sir Richard), with Lord Abergavenny (of a great Kentish family), has been able to raise only 600 men.

In London it is being said that the West has been pacified, but 200 French ships are about to bring troops to help Wyatt. Guns are put at every gate of the city. Gardiner writes gleefully to Petre that he has taken in suspicious circumstances Sir John Harington, one of Elizabeth's household, and is clapping him in the Tower.

The pacification of the West has proceeded apace for a good reason. There has been no rebellion. Carew and Dennis were not 'up'. For a month there had been talk in Devon of the threatened coming of the Spaniards, who would undoubtedly rob one of lands and chattels, and rape one's wife and daughters; and the talk had been attributed by the authorities, that is to say by the Sheriff, Dennis, to agitators: naturally, heretic agitators: naturally, Carew and his friends. Carew had been talking widely as always, and had not damped down local excitement as a responsible gentleman does. When there is prospect of invasion or civil disorder everyone sees to his arms, but Carew had been noisy and seen to his arms ostentatiously. Dennis in his anxiety harassed the Carews, and garrisoned Exeter since it is always more heretic than the countryside. And Carew fled: he would be in trouble with the Sheriff if he stayed, and he may have known that the Council had issued a warrant for his arrest. No swords have clashed, no shots have been fired. There has only been precautionary action by Dennis, noise and precipitate flight by Carew, and misreporting in London.

Sunday, 28 January. The Council sends out a letter to the counties about Suffolk's treason, saying he wants to make Jane queen again. Neither he nor anyone else wants any such thing. There has been no rising in the Midlands, which are not in the least stirred to revolt by the flight into their midst of the Duke.

In Kent Sir Robert Southwell, the Sheriff, has defeated a small rebel force, and Wyatt is promptly deserted by Sir George Harper and one or two other associates. Less happily for the Queen, Sir Thomas Cheyne, Lord Warden of the Cinque Ports, says he doubts if his own people will follow him against the rebels, and Lord Abergavenny is having difficulty getting food for his men.

Monday, 29 January. Paget assures Renard that Carew has been caught, the affair in Kent will be over in two days, and Suffolk and his two brothers are the only remaining anxiety.

In Kent the Duke of Norfolk and his men face Wyatt near Rochester. The London Whitecoats under their senior officer, Alexander Brett, shout 'A Wyatt! A Wyatt!' and 'We are all Englishmen, we are all Englishmen.' Wyatt and his horse ride into Norfolk's ranks calling to the Londoners and the rest to come and join them. And all the Whitecoats, some of the Guard, and most of the others, do so. Including Sir George Harper, who changes sides again.

Norfolk and his residue return to London, including those of the Guard who have not joined Wyatt – Londoners are delighted to see they are in wretched condition and without arrows or bowstrings.

Half a dozen or so heretic prisoners are moved from the Tower into the Marshalsea in Southwark, to make room for new traitors and suspects.

Next day, Tuesday, 30 January, the Duke of Norfolk retires to Norfolk, and Pembroke is appointed Lieutenant-General of the Queen's forces. He promises, God willing, never to look the Queen in the face before he brings up the rebels dead or captive. Sir Nicholas Throgmorton says Pembroke will neither oppose the rebels nor join them.

In Kent, Lord Abergavenny's forces leave him on hearing about the Whitecoats; he still has not heard from Cheyne, the Lord Warden, who seems to be doing nothing. There is no longer armed opposition to the rebels.

Wyatt sets out for London. He now has some of the Queen's ordnance, and assurance from the Whitecoats that London will open its gates to him. He takes Lord Cobham's castle at Cowling. George Brooke, Lord Cobham, is Wyatt's brother-in-law and has so far been energetically inactive on both sides of the conflict. He knows for a fact, he says, that the Gentlemen Pensioners and the Guard and the Londoners will all join Wyatt.

Mary is worried by the Council's seeming inactivity. She has been trying in vain to get them to provide troops to defend her, additional to the normal peacetime Guard (most of whom went into Kent) and the Pensioners.

A mailbag of de Noailles's is seized and contains a copy of a letter Elizabeth wrote to Mary three days ago. This is conclusive proof, says Renard, that Elizabeth is communicating with the French: she must be arrested at once. She is not arrested.

On Wednesday, 31 January Wyatt is at Deptford, 3 miles from London Bridge. Mary, to temporize, sends Sir Edward Hastings to him. At the west end of Deptford, Wyatt has his ordnance. When Hastings dismounts, Wyatt steps in front of his men with a partisan in his hand, and prevents his men from hearing what Hastings has to say. Sensibly.

Hastings says that the Queen will appoint a commission to discuss the marriage grievance, and will offer pardon to all who go home within twenty-four hours. He asks what security Wyatt wants for the performance of these offers. Wyatt asks for possession of the Tower and the person of the Queen.

Wyatt is in his early thirties, a family man, married since he was sixteen; ten years ago he inherited Allington Castle and considerable property and debts from his father Sir Thomas Wyatt, courtier, ambassador, friend of Anne Boleyn, poet. Just before he inherited he was put in the Tower for a memorable window-smashing escapade in London with the Earl of Surrey, but he is not wild: he is eminently respectable, and did bravely and soundly in the French wars. At the time of the 1549 rebellions he was shocked by the lack of reliable English troops at the disposal of the Council, and he put up to Somerset a sensible militia scheme. It is difficult to know how far he is Protestant like his father, perhaps not at all. He certainly was one of the first in Kent to declare for Mary. There are elements of a slightly elevated purity in him, and of over-confidence in his own military science and capacity for leadership, but he is a responsible young man.

Hastings returns to the Court. A rising is expected hourly in London. Mary is advised to withdraw to the Tower, or to Windsor.

It looks like the end for Mary, seven months after the beginning.[1]

ii

Next morning, 1 February, proclamation is made in Cheapside, at Leadenhall and at St Magnus corner, where Thames Street meets Bridge Street, with a herald, a trumpeter and the Common Crier, together with Lord William Howard and Lord Mayor White, and Sheriffs Offley and Hewett, that Suffolk and his two brothers have had to disguise themselves as serving men and will soon be caught; that Sir Peter Carew has escaped to France; and that anyone who brings in Wyatt dead or alive shall have lands worth £100 a year for himself and his heirs for ever.

The Emperor's three marriage-envoys this same morning set out at last for home, with all haste and a last-minute request from the Council for a loan of £50,000. They take their boats at the Queen's Stairs, pick up their baggage at Durham House, and embark at St Katharine's, below the Tower.

As soon as they are out of the way, Mary rides with her lords and ladies, knights and gentlemen, heralds and constantly blowing trumpeters, along the Strand, through Ludgate and to Guildhall. At about 3 p.m. White and the aldermen welcome her; she goes up to tidy herself in the Council Chamber where the aldermen usually meet, and then comes down into the Great Hall. On the hustings, standing under a cloth of state, she addresses the Common Council, the commons of the city, assembled in their liveries. She says her piece, very manly and with good spirit, and with so loud a voice that everyone in the hall hears her.

Queen Mary:
I am come unto you in mine own person, to tell you that which already you do see and know, that is, how traitorously and seditiously a number of Kentish rebels have assembled themselves together against both us and you.

Their pretence (as they said at first) was only to resist a marriage determined between us and the Prince of Spain . . .

The marriage is found to be the least of their quarrel. For they now swerving from their former articles, have betrayed the inward treason of their hearts, as most arrogantly demanding the possession of our person, the keeping of our Tower, and not only the placing and displacing of our Councillors but also to use them and us at their pleasures.

Now, loving subjects, what I am you right well do know. I am your Queen, to whom at my coronation, when I was wedded to the realm, and to the laws of the realm (the spousal ring whereof I have on my finger, which never hitherto was, nor hereafter shall be, left off), ye promised your allegiance and obedience unto me.

And that I am the right and true inheritor of the crown of this realm of England, I not only take all Christendom to witness, but also your Acts of Parliament confirming the same. My father (as ye all know) possessed the regal estate by right of inheritance, which now by the same right descended unto me.

And to him always ye showed yourselves most faithful and loving subjects, and him obeyed and served as your liege lord and king: and therefore I doubt not but you will show yourselves likewise to me his daughter. Which if you do, then may you not suffer any rebel to usurp the governance of our person, or to occupy our estate, especially being so presumptuous a traitor as this Wyatt hath showed himself to be. Who most certainly, as he hath abused my ignorant subjects to be adherents to his traitorous quarrel, so doth he intend by colour of the same to subdue the laws to his will, and to give scope to all rascal and forlorn persons to make general havoc and spoil of your goods.

And this further I say unto you in the word of a prince. I cannot tell how naturally a mother loveth her children, for I was never mother of any; but certainly a prince and governor may as naturally and as earnestly love subjects as the mother doth her child. Then assure yourselves that I, being your sovereign lady and Queen, do as earnestly and as tenderly love and favour you. And I thus loving you cannot but think that ye as heartily and faithfully love me again. And so, loving together in this knot of love and concord, I doubt not but we together shall be able to give these rebels a short and speedy overthrow.

And as concerning the case of my intended marriage, against which they pretend their quarrel, ye shall understand that I entered not into the treaty thereof without advice of all our Privy Council; yes, and by assent of those to whom the King my father committed his trust, who so considered and weighed the great commodities that might ensue thereof, that they not only thought it honourable, but expedient, both for the wealth of our realm and also of our loving subjects.

And as touching myself (I assure you) I am not so desirous of wedding, neither so precise or wedded to my will, that either for my own pleasure I will choose where I lust, or else so amorous as need I must have one. For God I thank him (to whom be the praise thereof) I have hitherto lived a virgin, and doubt nothing but with God's grace shall as well be able so to live still.

But if, as my progenitors have done before, it might please God that I might leave some fruit of my body behind me to be your governor, I trust you would not only rejoice thereat, but also I know it would be to your great comfort.

And certainly if I either did know or think that this marriage should either turn to the danger or loss of any of you my loving subjects, or to the detriment or impairing of any part or parcel of the royal state of this realm of England, I would never consent thereunto, neither would I ever marry while I lived. And in the word of a Queen I promise and assure you that, if it shall not probably appear before the nobility and commons of the high court of Parliament, that this marriage shall be for the singular benefit and commodity of all the whole realm, then I will abstain, not only from this marriage, but also from any other whereof peril may ensue to this most noble realm.

Wherefore now as good and faithful subjects pluck up your hearts, and like true men stand fast with your lawful prince against these rebels, both our enemies and yours, and fear them not: for I assure you that I fear them nothing at all.

And I will leave with you my Lord Howard, and my Lord Treasurer, to be your assistants, with my Lord Mayor, for the defence and safeguard of this city from spoil and sackage, which is the only scope of this rebellious company.

She comes down from the dais, goes up to the Council Chamber, drinks, and prepares for the return journey. Quite a number have wept.

Remarkable woman. Not the most truthful, but the most bravely persuasive speech the century has so far seen.[2]

iii

White, Paulet and Lord William Howard get to work. All the Companies are to provide additional contingents, twice as big as before, a thousand householders in all. And there are to be none but householders guarding the Bridge and the gates – no unreliable substitutes. Every householder in the city must get himself his white coat (1½ yards at 8d a yard) with the cross of red kersey before and behind. It costs the Companies a good deal more than the previous call-up, the Merchant Taylors four times as much because this time none of the rivets (12s each) can come from store. The Companies' contingents meet at their halls by candlelight to be equipped and have a drink.

The following day, Friday, 2 February, Candlemas Day, the justices at Westminster are in harness, and the lawyers plead in harness. In London most of the householders are in harness, and White's officers serve him at dinner in harness. Usually on the afternoon of Candlemas Day the City attends at Paul's, but instead every alderman musters his ward.

Councillors raise greater numbers of equipped men than does the City. Arundel provides sixty horsemen and 800 foot. Even Petre provides 142 of his tenants and servants in red coats, and spends about £100 in arming them; in addition two cartloads of equipment for them are brought from the Tower to his house in Aldersgate Street.

Saturday, 3 February. By drum Pembroke's men, principally the forces provided by noblemen, are commanded to be at St James's Park before noon, and the City men, under Howard and White, are to be in Finsbury Field. Citizens are commanded to be in harness, shut their shops and shutters, and stand at their doors. There is a great clearing away of goods on street stalls, a great running here and there for harness and weapons; men look stunned, women weep, children run home, doors are slammed. Much tumult, much terror. There is about 'to be a sacking of the city – the fire, sword and rape which invariably accompany an invading army. The gate at the southern end of the Bridge is shut. The drawbridge over the seventh arch is cut down and towed away to Paul's Wharf. All boats have been taken to the north side of the river and commanded to stay there, on pain of death.

It must be getting on for four when there are shots from the Tower cannon. From the White Tower Wyatt's force of a couple of thousand men has been spotted approaching Southwark along the Kent road. There are half a dozen shots, that is all. Some overshoot, some fall short; all miss.

Wyatt sets up one of his precious cannon by St George's Church, from whence London Bridge is half a mile north. Some of his men go down past the Tabard and the White Hart to London Bridge.

Does anyone resist them? No. No fighting. All friends together.

Meanwhile Wyatt himself with the remainder of his force makes a tour of the east part of Southwark. He marches back east from St George's Church along Long Lane, towards the very large mansion of Sir Thomas Pope, which used to be Bermondsey Abbey. He turns left along Bermondsey Street northward, past St Mary Magdalen and another fine house or two, until he reaches Bermondsey Cross where the street joins an east-west road, Short Southwark. He turns west along Short Southwark, passes the inn and tenements at Battle Bridge (where the abbots of Battle had their London house), goes across an open space with a pillory and cross in the middle, and past on the right the Bridge House, of which the other face is upon the river. Then past the fine old stone house of Sir Anthony St Leger (still another abbot's London house – of St Augustine's, Canterbury), and St Olave's Church close to the Bridge foot.

Why this curious tour? To check on the presence of government troops and the attitude of the people. There are a few of Howard's men but they are not hostile. There has been no resistance, only welcome.

At the entrance to the Bridge he lays two pieces of ordnance and digs a great trench between himself and the Bridge; he puts another cannon on his left flank at Gardiner's Winchester Place, and another on his right to command Bermondsey Street.

The half-dozen shots fired from Sir John Brydges's cannon at the Tower have been the only signs of opposition to Wyatt's men. The armed men join them, the inhabitants entertain them.

Wyatt drums a proclamation that no soldier is to take anything without paying for it: he has come simply to oppose the coming of the Spanish prince. Nevertheless, some of his men, led by an unknown gentleman, begin to ransack Gardiner's house, looting food and drink, wrenching open locks, and tearing to pieces the books in his library: they become almost up to their knees in leaves. Wyatt stops the destruction and puts into the looters fear of God and of being hanged on the Bishop's wharf.

He sends one of his chaplains to the Marshalsea to ask if Dr Sandys, Mountayne and other religious and political prisoners want to be released. They thank him, but they are there for their consciences and will await lawful discharge. He does not offer to release the common prisoners, who are mostly pirates and London watermen and other marine offenders.

But are the Londoners going to open to him? The southern gate of the Bridge remains shut, there are three pieces of ordnance standing at the city side of the drawbridge gap, and there seem to be some hundreds of citizens guarding the Bridge, with Lord William Howard making sure they do.

In the evening there is suddenly the noise of two shots. Are the Kentish men going to assault? False alarm.

What is happening in the city and at Court? Is the Queen properly guarded? Are the Pensioners defaulting?[3]

iv

Pensioner Underhill's post was filled by someone else last October but he is still receiving his pay (the Lieutenant of the Pensioners favours the Gospel). Does such a one default or does he go on duty?

Edward Underhill's story:
When Wyatt was come to Southwark, the Pensioners were commanded to watch in armour that night at the Court, which I hearing of thought it best in like sort to be there, lest by my absence I might have some quarrel picked unto me, or at least be stricken out of the book for receiving any more wages.

After supper I put on my armour as the rest did, for we were appointed to watch all the night.

So being all armed, we came up into the Chamber of Presence with our poleaxes in our hands, wherewith the ladies were very fearful; some lamenting, crying and wringing their hands, said:

'Alas, there is some great mischief toward; we shall all be destroyed this night! What a night is this, to see the Queen's chamber full of armed men; the like was never seen nor heard of.'

Then master Norris, who was a Gentleman Usher of the Outer Chamber in King Henry the Eighth's time, and all King Edward's time, always a rank Papist, and therefore was now Chief Usher of Queen Mary's Privy Chamber, he was appointed to call the watch, and see if any were lacking; unto whom Moore, the clerk of our check, delivered the book of our names, which he perused before he would call them at the cupboard, and when he came to my name.

'What,' said he, 'what doth he here?'

'Sir,' said the clerk, 'he is here ready to serve as the rest be.'

'Nay, by God's body!' said he, 'that heretic shall not be called to watch here; give me a pen.'

So he struck out my name of the book.

The clerk of the check sought me out, and said unto me, 'Master Underhill, you need not to watch, you may depart to your lodging.'

So departed I into the Hall where our men were appointed to watch. I took my men with me, and a link, and went my ways.

When I came to the court gate, there I met with master Clement Throgmorton and George Ferrers, tending their links to go to London . . .

As we went, for that they were both my friends, and Protestants, I told them of my good hap and manner of discharge of the watch at the Court.

When we came to Ludgate it was past eleven o'clock, the gate was fast locked, and a great watch within the gate of Londoners, but none without, whereof Henry Peckham [*son of Sir Edmund Peckham*] had the charge under his father, who belike was gone to his father or to look at the waterside [*i.e. to piss*].

Master Throgmorton knocked hard, and called to them saying, 'Here are three or four gentlemen come from the Court that must come in, and therefore open the gate.'

'Who!' quoth one. 'What?' quoth another, and much laughing they made.

'Can ye tell what you do, sirs?' said master Throgmorton, declaring his name and that he had been with the Queen to show her Grace of the taking of the Duke of Suffolk, 'and my lodging is within, as I am sure some of you do know.'

'And,' said Ferrers, 'I am Ferrers, that was Lord of Misrule with King Edward, and am sent from the Council unto my Lord William who hath charge of the Bridge, as you know, upon weighty affairs, and therefore let us, or else ye be not the Queen's friends.'

Still there was much laughing amongst them.

Then said two or three of them, 'We have not the keys, we are not trusted with them; the keys be carried away for this night.'

'What shall I do?' said master Throgmorton, 'I am weary and faint, and I now wax cold . . . I shall perish this night.'

'Well,' said I, 'let us go to Newgate, 'I think I shall get in there.'

'Tush,' said he, 'it is but vain, we shall be answered there as we are here.'

'Well,' said I, 'an the worst fall I can lodge ye in Newgate, you know the acquaintance I have there, and the keeper's door is without the gate.'

'That were a bad shift,' said he, 'I should almost as lief die in the streets; yet I will rather than wander again to the Court.'

'Well,' said I, 'let us go and prove. I believe the keeper will help us in at the gate, or else let us in through the wards, for he hath a door on the inside also; if all this fail I have a friend at the gate, Newman the ironmonger, in whose house I have been lodged, where I dare warrant you we shall have lodging, or at the last house-room and fire.'

'Marry, this is well said,' sayeth Ferrers.

So to Newgate we went, where was a great watch without the gate, which my friend Newman had the charge of, for that he was the constable. They marvelled to see three torches coming at that time of night.

When we came to them, 'Master Underhill,' said Newman, 'what news that you walk so late?'

'None but good,' said I, 'we come from the Court, and would have gone in at Ludgate and cannot be let in, wherefore I pray you if you cannot help us in here, let us have lodging with you.'

'Marry, that ye shall,' said he, 'or go in at the gate, whether ye will.'

'Godamercy, gentle friend,' said master Throgmorton, 'I pray you let us go in if it may be.'

He called to the constable within the gate, who opened the gate forthwith.[4]

v

On Sunday morning a great cannon is shot off at the Tower. Excitement and much fear among the populace of Southwark. False alarm again: only the usual discharge at the changing of the watch.

In the evening two men are seen rowing away from Gardiner's wharf. Half a dozen of Wyatt's arquebusiers shout to them to come back. The boat rows on, the arquebusiers shoot, one of the men is killed. The other rows the boat with difficulty through the Bridge and to Tower Wharf. Immediately the Tower ordnance is trained on Southwark, but nothing more happens.

London does not open to Wyatt; neither does anyone fight Wyatt; neither does Wyatt make any move.

Monday morning: again nothing happens. The guns are seen to be still trained on Southwark, but they do not fire. Southwark people make a clamour to Wyatt: their lives and property are in danger. He says, 'God forbid that ye, or the least child here, should be hurt or killed in my behalf.'

The number of his men does not seem to have increased. If anything, the reverse. He tells his men he will not pay them again until he does it in Cheap.

There is a rumour that Sir Robert Southwell, Lord Abergavenny and at last Lord Cheyne are at Blackheath with 3,000 men.

In the evening Wyatt has a wall broken down in a house adjoining the southern gatehouse of the Bridge, so that he can get on the leads and then down into the porter's lodge. It is about 11 p.m. and the porter is asleep, his wife and some others are sitting round a fire. Wyatt with a few men goes through the lodge as far as the drawbridge gap. Without being seen, he watches on the further side Howard, White, Sir Andrew Judd and others, and listens to them discussing the defence of the Bridge, and notes the three cannon eight or nine paces beyond. He comments, 'This place is too hot for us.'

Before six next morning, Shrove Tuesday, he takes his force out of

Southwark. 2,000, or rather fewer, march along the low-lying muddy February road to the south-west. Slow going. After 6 miles they cross the Wandle at the village of Wandsworth (notable in more normal times for its salmon). Up and over Putney Heath. Then Wimbledon Common on the left, Richmond deer park to the right. And down into Kingston and glad of it. It is four in the afternoon. Ten hours for 12 miles.

The bridge is quite undefended. It is a narrow wooden causeway, railed in on either side, and resting on rows of piles. About 30 feet of the causeway has been taken away, but the piles are still there. Wyatt bargains with two watermen to swim over and bring a barge to him. It is already dark. He has the causeway rebuilt, with planks, ladders, beams, tied together with rope. It takes time, but the time is useful for getting food in Kingston, and resting up.

By about 10 p.m. the bridge is fit to bear his ordnance and transport as well as his men. By eleven they are all on their way back to London. Never at any time have they been opposed.

North and then east. In 3 miles they are at Twickenham and crossing the Crane. They are making better time than yesterday. In another 3 miles they have passed Syon House somewhere in the darkness on the right, and crossed the river Brent at Brentford. Through the narrow High Street, without time really for the Three Pipers or the Red Lion. A mile and a half and they are at Gunnersbury Manor.

A wheel of one of the gun-carriages breaks. Should he hurry on or wait for the repair? A single cannon might make all the difference later on. And they could all do with a rest.

By the time they are at Turnham Green there are signs of dawn. At 6 or 7 a.m. they are entering West Town, one of the four manors of Kensington (over to the left is another, Notting Bourne, which is Paulet's; to the right another, Earl's Court; ahead the other, Abbot's Kensington, once belonging to the abbots of Abingdon).

Past Kensington Church all the land on the left of the road is Hyde Park, which Henry took over for his hunting, and paled. The land on the right is Neat Park, stretching down to Tothill Fields and the Thames, which Henry took for hunting from the Abbey of Westminster.

Between eight and nine there is a halt at a bridge, Knight's Bridge, which crosses the Westbourne.[5] Chester Herald approaches. He has been sent by Pembroke to say that, if Wyatt submits to save bloodshed, Pembroke will be a mean to the Queen for his pardon. Wyatt does not submit.

Things are very quiet. There has been no firing of cannon or of small arms.

vi

Meanwhile what has been happening in Court and City?

Yesterday afternoon, in London, a trumpeter went around warning that the Queen's forces were to be in St James's field at six this morning. In the night someone brought news to the Court of Wyatt's sudden approach: he had mended the bridge at Kingston and moved on much more rapidly than expected. Mary and the Court are said to have been 'wonderfully affrighted'. The Council met at the Queen's bedside. She accepted their advice to go to the Tower for safety, and then changed her mind. She said she had confidence in Pembroke and Clinton (who seven months ago were very much Northumberland's men), and would stay and see the uttermost. Drums were sent out at 4 a.m. to assemble her forces.

It was thought that Wyatt would come from Brentford to Kensington, and on to Hyde Park Corner. From there, either he would continue along the main road up the slope, passing the windmill, towards St Giles and Holborn, and so to Newgate or the northern gates; or else he would take the causeway which leads direct to Charing Cross, and from there go on to Ludgate or turn south to Whitehall Palace.

White and Howard have assembled the Londoners to defend London, all the gates from Ludgate round to Bishopsgate. Pembroke has assembled the horsemen and foot-soldiers of noblemen and Councillors and the Queen's ordnance in the fields west of St James's Palace to defend the Court. His ordnance is at the middle and highest point of the causeway which runs east from Hyde Park Corner, directly facing Wyatt's likely advance. His main body of foot, with arquebuses and pikes, bows and bills, is on the causeway and just south of it, behind the ordnance, and he has more foot further south-west. He also has two bands of horse under Clinton: the heavier in a field north-west of the most south-westerly foot, and the light horse north-west of the heavy, in the lane going up the east side of Hyde Park. He himself is with his main body of horse and the Queen's standard on the slight hill between the causeway and the main road from Hyde Park Corner to St Giles. These seem to be the dispositions he intends, but his troops are not fully in their positions at the time he sends Chester Herald to Wyatt.

In Whitehall Palace Mary goes to Mass, which is sung by Weston with harness under his vestments.

Some short time after ten, Pembroke's forces are all ready.

Wyatt has moved a little nearer Hyde Park Corner, to the lazar house of the Holy Trinity, and has planted his ordnance on slightly higher ground to his north-east. As they come there has been some scrimging from a detachment of Pembroke's arquebusiers and pikemen, but there has been no serious attack. It is about eleven.

Pause. For ale? For dinner?

A little before two there is a move. Wyatt sets off with the bulk of his force, all foot, along the causeway. At the sound of a trumpet, Clinton's horse attack from both sides. They press between the leading part of Wyatt's force and the less disciplined and worse-armed crowd of Kentish men behind, of whom some are killed, a few score wounded, and the rest driven away westward.

Wyatt turns right, off the causeway, on foot and with four or five of his leading ensigns (an ensign is 100 men), and marches across the gateway of St James's Palace towards Charing Cross; at the same time a couple of ensigns under William Knevett, with Thomas Brooke (Lord Cobham's younger son) and William Vaughan, turn south through the back yards of St James's and down across the park to Tothill, and so east to Westminster and then up King Street to the Court, the gates of which are open.

Meanwhile, the ordnance on both sides has been shooting freely. There have not been many casualties, but there have certainly been three: a single ball hit the heads of three of Wyatt's men as they were going along the wall of St James's, and then went through the wall.

Pembroke's men watch Wyatt's as they march along to Charing Cross. Pembroke has some ado to make his men stand where they are, let alone fight. He entreats them bareheaded. At any distance from him they express their attitude by saying Wyatt intends no hurt except to the foreign enemy. Pembroke does not bother about Knevett's troop making for the Court, or does not know about them, or knows but can do nothing.

At Charing Cross Wyatt's 400 or 500 men are encouraged by a sermon from the vicar of Kingston-on-Thames, and then push past 100 or 200 Court servants and others under the Lord Chamberlain, Sir John Gage, who scrimge at them and then hurry down towards the Court.

Wyatt pursues his way unopposed along the Strand to Temple Bar, and along Fleet Street to Ludgate. In Fleet Street they meet 300 men of Paulet's coming in the opposite direction; Paulet's men are on the opposite side of the street and take no notice of them. Householders in harness stand at their doors on both sides of the street, and watch. Whatever may have been said earlier by Chester Herald, Wyatt's men call out as they go along Fleet Street: 'The Queen has pardoned us!', 'A Wyatt! A Wyatt!'. 'God save Queen Mary! The Queen has given us pardon!'

Henry Peckham's guard, who the other night kept Ludgate closed against Underhill, now have Ludgate wide open. However, a Merchant Taylor named John Harris recognizes Wyatt's banners, and the gates are closed just in time. Wyatt knocks, calling to come in. Lord William Howard from the other side says: 'Avaunt, traitor! Thou shalt not come in here.' Wyatt sits down, on a bench outside the inn on the north side of the gate, the Belle Sauvage.

Meanwhile, there has been excitement at Whitehall. When Sir John Gage and his minions reached the palace, the gates were open, and from the opposite direction arrived Knevett's rebels. The Queen was in the gallery which is on the right as one enters the gates. The Guard, or some of it, were in the Great Court. Everyone thought from the rush of Gage's men that Pembroke had joined Wyatt and there were shouts of 'Treason! Treason!', and shrieking, and running, and shutting of doors, and general noise.

Edward Underhill, unable to keep away, was with the other Pensioners, in armour, in the Hall which had been appointed their base.

Edward Underhill:
Then came Knevett and Thomas Cobham [*Thomas Brooke*] with a company of the rebels with them, through the gatehouse from Westminster [*he means the Holbein Gate, spanning King Street*], wherewith Sir John Gage and three of the judges, that were meanly armed in old brigandines [*quilted leather jackets covered with iron plates*], were so frighted that they fled in at the gates in such haste that old Gage fell down in the dirt and was foul arrayed: and so shut the gates. Whereat the rebels shot many arrows.

By means of the great hurly-burly in shutting of the gates, the Guard that were in the court made as great haste in at the Hall door, and would have come into the Hall amongst us, which we would not suffer. Then they went thronging towards the watergate, the kitchens and those ways.

Master Gage came in amongst us all dirt, and so frighted that he could not speak to us; and then came the three judges, so frighted that we could not keep them out except we should beat them down.

With that we issued out of the Hall into the court to see what the matter was; where there were none left but the porters; and the gates being fast shut, as we went towards the gate, meaning to go forth, Sir Richard Southwell came forth of the backyards into the court.

'Sir,' said we, 'command the gates to be opened that we may go to the Queen's enemies, we will else break them open; it is too much shame that the gates should thus be shut for a few rebels; the Queen shall see us fell down her enemies this day before her face.'

'Masters,' said he, and put his morion off his head, 'I shall desire you all as you be gentlemen, to stay yourselves here that I may go up to the Queen to know her pleasure, an you shall have the gates opened; and, as I am a gentleman, I will make speed.'

Upon this we stayed, and he made speedy return, and brought us word the Queen was content we should have the gates opened.

'But her request is', said he, 'that you will not go forth of her sight, for her only trust is in you for the defence of her person this day.'

So the gate was opened, and we marched before the gallery window, where she spoke unto us, requiring us, as we were gentlemen in whom she only trusted, that we would not go from that place.[6]

vii

By the time the Pensioners begin to parade up and down outside the Palace, Knevett's troop, having shot arrows into the windows and courtyard of the palace without hurting anyone, have gone up the street to Charing Cross. There they fight with a force of as many as 1,000, sent by Pembroke 'to rescue the Court'. There ensues some of the chief fighting of the day, hampered by the difficulty both sides had in identifying their opponents, by no means everyone having any regular distinguishing mark. However, all Wyatt's men have mud on them, so Pembroke's shout: 'Down with the daggle-tails!' A dozen or score of the rebels are killed, and the remainder flee north-east towards St Giles or south-east to the river.

By this time Wyatt has given up hope that London will open to him. He says, 'I have kept touch!' gets up from outside the Belle Sauvage, and turns back along Fleet Street. He and his men are not stopped until, at Temple Bar, they meet some of Pembroke's men, including horse, come on from fighting at Charing Cross. There is some scrimging, but Wyatt's dwindled force are outnumbered (and tired) and stand 'as men amazed' in the gate of Temple Bar.

For some time both sides make as if to fight, but do not. Clarencieux Herald harangues Wyatt and tells him to save bloodshed by surrendering. Wyatt surrenders to the herald, as to the Queen. It is no more than an hour and a half since he made his move from Hyde Park Corner. He gets up behind one Sir Maurice Berkeley who happens to be riding towards London, and is ridden to the Court.

In another hour he is on his way to the Tower by water. By about five Wyatt, William Knevett, Thomas Brooke and Alexander Brett are all at the Tower. Muddy rebels are being taken in streets and houses. They will be stored in the prisons and, when those are full, in churches. Probably not more than forty or fifty people have been killed in the field.

Mary's host march through London in goodly array. At no time has sectarianism been appealed to. At no time has Wyatt implicated Elizabeth.

Once more an English miracle, this time an almost bloodless non-revolution. It can be said that, apart from the staunchness of Mary and something of the young hero in Wyatt, there has been only a confusion of incompetence and pusillanimity, shaky loyalty, and plain inactivity. If the protagonists had been more efficient, bellicose, stiff-necked, energetic, they would have caused much bloodshed and destruction, and in the end uttered probably no clear message. As it is, out of contention the English have achieved, with minimal loss and disruption – consensus.

Put together, the actions and inactions of rebels and Queen's forces have made some national statements:

(a)   Our rightful queen is Queen Mary, and we do not propose to replace her, even by Princess Elizabeth;

(b)   We do not want the Spanish marriage, but we want civil strife even less;

(c)   The marriage goes ahead – *La Reyne le veult.*

viii

Across the Channel they may be right: England's brains are perhaps too foggy to analyse and intellectually resolve a crisis. It is England's belly which, with help from Northumberland, Mary and Wyatt, has dealt with it twice in half a year.

They have been saved twice from self-destruction but not from anything else? True. They know their priorities. Other salvations can be thought about later.

Since the Spanish marriage will go ahead, the English will need – when they can get around to it – salvation from Spaniards. A third salvation will have to be from piffling military feebleness. A fourth from the insolvency of the Crown. A fifth from the narrowness of the nation's commerce. A sixth from its poverty of culture. A seventh salvation – most needed of all, Edward would have said – must be from Papistry.

The amusing and Protestant Catherine Bertie, Dowager Duchess of Suffolk, now a refugee on the Continent, likes to say: 'God is a remarkable man'. If the English are his Chosen People, will not that remarkable man see that before many years have passed they will gain not just one salvation, but all seven? Or at least take significant steps towards them?

Of course. But how many years must pass? Thirty? Forty? No, no. Less.

A prophecy. The six further salvations will be achieved, or significantly begun, within the lifetime of Mary Tudor. Papistical and unpatriotic as she has appeared, she has a courageous core, and other characteristics besides, weaknesses as well as strengths, which like Northumberland's may combine to serve the nation.

Such a prophecy cannot be fulfilled in a short life. Long live Queen Mary!

VII

Yea!

17

Salvations

Move forward to Christmas 1558. Queen Mary died a month and a half ago. Consider how she and the English fared in her reign of five years and a few months. A very short reign.

She had much good fortune. She acceded against all the odds. She restored her kingdom to her own religion. She married a man she adored, and had him with her for the whole of their first married year, and then last year for another three months – many women have their husbands for not so long, or too long. She had no children, but continued always to have hopes of them.

Apart from the small Wyatt rebellion, which was useful as a purgative, she had no serious plots or revolts, only trifles. Nor was she invaded by foreign armies (no more than border raids), unlike most rulers. By great good luck the French captured Calais (attacking unsportingly over the Christmas holidays), so that a place which had become a strategic, commercial and financial liability was got rid of without serious casualties or expense. The only possible cause for regret was that Mary had not sold it to the French as Northumberland's Council sold Boulogne.

She was not a great popular figure like her father, but she was not unpopular except with her religious enemies. She was respected as a devout woman, charitable and often thoughtfully kind – helping a child to an apprenticeship, getting a collier paid expeditiously for his cart which had been pressed by a royal purveyor, and so on. In larger matters she was clement by international standards: when Wyatt collapsed she killed no more than 300 or so rebels. The war against France at Philip's behest was unpopular at first, but when the nation was jolted by losing Calais and by Mary Queen of Scots marrying the Dauphin, it realized afresh the whoreson nature of the French. And anyhow there were soon peace negotiations. Mary's only serious offences were the Spanish marriage itself, and a recent succession of wet summers.

Have the English been as fortunate as their Queen? There were six salvations they still needed.[1]

ii

Salvation Two, from Spaniards.

Four years ago London streets were awash with Spaniards. What happened to them? Poor fellows! Their property began to disappear as soon as it was landed at Southampton. Then children began to ask why they had brought so much baggage for such a short stay. They loved the castles and country houses, the woods, streams, delicious meadows, but found the people even more barbarous than they had anticipated. They were charged twenty times the proper price for everything they bought, everything. They were studiously ill-served wherever they ate or drank. They had stones thrown at them. They were so attacked, robbed, stripped, they feared to go out after dark. The friars ceased to go out at all. Philip had told them to forget Spain, but in spite of the English countryside they thought lovingly of the thin stubble fields of Toledo. Philip had said they should live like Englishmen, but they found Englishmen beer-drinking boors. Philip's graciousness, lack of pomp and stream of presents soothed a little the sullenness and suspicion of English courtiers, who continued, however, their habit of being accompanied everywhere by a page carrying their shield, and followed by armed servants, so that they could deliberately, contemptuously, clash with Spaniards.

And English women! Outside in the streets and in the country there were lovely women, but in the Court none. Court ladies wore layers and layers of thick material, vilely cut; their dancing was strutting and trotting; and when they walked they showed their black-stockinged legs up to the knees.

Mary was a saint. But for child-bearing she was old, unhealthy, and not of fertile stock. What would be the good of the whole affair if she did not have a child?

Philip acted always with consideration towards Mary herself, and to the English as a whole: for example, since troops and expatriate wives are major causes of offence to natives, he allowed none to be landed. Nevertheless, with the Imperial responsibilities which descended on him from his father, he must have wearied sometimes of the English. They kept him sternly to the terms of the marriage treaty, so the already infinitely indebted Imperial crown had to carry his double staff, English and Spanish (the English bedchamber gentlemen did not share with him a common language and soon ceased to turn up, but they still had to be paid), the expenses – all the expenses – of himself and his courtiers, and the pensions and gold chains necessary to confirm the loyalty of the English Councillors.

In recompense, the military help he got in his war with France was delayed, first until he had paid for the English light ordnance, then until he had supplied seventy horses to draw it, then until he had given 210 carts. The English finally came up to fight, not in his great victory outside St Quentin, but afterwards, in time to loot the town. Then they had completed their statutory three months service and had to be paid off. There was similar masterly foot-dragging over his coronation: the English called him King, sent him notes of Council discussions, let him sign with Queen Mary appropriate documents, and made an ink stamp with both names, but never got around to crowning him.

He may have wondered even about his half-English wife: her failure to have him crowned, and niggling incidents. At the wedding feast he ate off silver plate, Mary off gold. After his state entry into London, when he and Mary reached Whitehall Palace and they parted in the Presence Chamber, each to the correct Privy Lodging, who went to the King's Side? Mary. To the Queen's? Philip. A Tudor queen is a queen is a king.

Bishop Gardiner, before he died in 1555, became a devotee of Philip, and secretly advised him on how to hold England permanently for the Habsburgs. However, every Spaniard who could has fled the abominable English, and with Mary dead there has been no place for Philip himself, because Elizabeth will have none of him. A pity in some ways: the Spaniards have much to teach the English.

A salvation nevertheless. Salvation Two.[2]

iii

Salvation Three, from the military wretchedness which appalled Philip, with a militia governed by the thirteenth-century Statute of Winchester, drafted before the introduction of firearms. This last January there was a new Act, prompted by the humiliation of Calais, the rude comments of Spaniards, and probably pressure from Philip personally. Note that the new Act was introduced not under the great Henry, but under his poor, weak, unmilitary daughter. It recognizes the arquebus (not the caliver, which is expensive), and its concomitant the pike. Admittedly the man with only £5-£10 a year in land still has to provide himself with the old long bow, but if he has £10 p.a. he must provide a less efficient but more fashionable arquebus. The man with £1,000 p.a. must provide – along with horses, halberds, thirty long bows, and so on – twenty arquebuses. This will not bring the English militia into 1558 but it should bring it into the sixteenth century, just, if it is carried out.

And it is being carried out. In May, Paulet was appointed Lieutenant of all troops raised south of the Trent. This did not mean that the comfort-loving septuagenarian was girding himself to lead troops in battle: he is an administrator. Within a month Philip was being asked to license export from the Netherlands of 8,000 corslets, 8,000 arquebuses and 8,000 pikes.

Another recent Act lays down fines for pressing unfit men simply so that they will bribe themselves out, fines for drawing pay for troops who have been discharged or are dead, fines for supplying sub-standard rations. An Act is not action, of course, but it indicates that there is the thought in several Parliamentary minds that action might one day be a good thing. Action will surely come – a century hence, two centuries . . .

Paulet has also been administering the navy since January of last year. He has put its finances in order. And its technical management is now under an exceptional group of officials, headed by Clinton. Clinton, like Paulet, identified with Northumberland's Protestant government, had earlier been replaced as Lord Admiral by cheerful, bawdy, Catholic Lord William Howard; now he is back in his old job and doing everything well (except providing navigational aids in the Thames). Until the end of 1555 there had been a five-year stop on naval renovation and construction owing to shortage of money. Then, under Philip's prompting, repairs were put in hand and two new ships built, the 500-ton *Philip and Mary* and the 600-ton *Mary Rose*. Another 500-ton ship, the *Lion*, was built last year, an 800-ton ship has been started, and rebuilding of the 300-ton *Jennet* has begun.

This petticoat government has taken real steps to head the navy back to excellence and to improve England's slight military power. Salvation Three is not fully achieved by any means but significant steps have been taken.

How has the money been found? Salvation Four was needed, from an insolvent Crown.[3]

iv

Under Edward, Crown income was less than expenditure, in peacetime, by £60,000 p.a. Mary did not debase the currency, nor did she part with more than a minimum of Crown lands. How could she, and Paulet, bring the books into balance in a mere five years?

The cost of the Household was above the cost of Edward's in her first year, with the Coronation, and in her second, with Philip's coming and the wedding, but finally it has been reduced to £36,000 against £52,000 in

Edward's last year. However she spent more on Wardrobe than he, £6,200 against £5,400. On balance, a saving of say £15,000, reducing the deficit from £60,000 to £45,000.

Peacetime garrisons were reduced even further than under Northumberland, and Ireland cost only £18,000 instead of £43,000 in the last year of Edward. A saving of more than £25,000, reducing the deficit of £20,000.

She restored to the Pope his first fruits, and to the Church in England the clergy's tenths, making a loss to the Crown of say £25,000. But Crown pensions, not now including monastic pensions, fell from £20,000 to £5,000. On balance she was £10,000 worse off, making the deficit £30,000.

Paulet has revised the administration of the Augmentations Office of the Exchequer, and raised some rents, increasing revenue from £27,000 to £48,000, with an extra £1,000 from the Duchy of Lancaster. The deficit becomes £8,000.

Customs were bringing in something under £30,000 p.a. At last, in May this year, a new book of rates was issued. It was tactically a suitable time, and the City complained not more loudly than could be borne. In a full year, if there is no reduction of trade or increase of smuggling due to the higher rates, there should be an additional £25,000 of revenue. Call it only £18,000. The deficit under Edward of £60,000 has become a surplus of £10,000.

The figures are of course shaky, and they ignore interest payments, but in peacetime, as long as a sovereign continues Mary's thrifty habits, the Crown is solvent. Note the place of Mary's qualities in this. Although unfledged and bigoted, she saw Paulet's virtues and trusted him, and on the whole did what he advised. Salvation Four.

What next? A narrow-based commerce.[4]

V

In five years one cannot expect a great broadening of commerce. Philip might have allowed the English into the Americas – he might have, but he did not. There might have been a significant development in English manufactures – woollen cloth is still overwhelmingly the most important manufactured export – but there has not. Nevertheless, there are signs of salvation.

That expedition under Sir Hugh Willoughby which left the Thames in 1553 to find a north-eastern passage to the Far East did not get to Cathay but it reached Muscovy, where there are now three bases for the sale of English woollen cloth, and the purchase of wax, tallow, whale-oil, ropes and cables. The trade, by the standards of the Italians and the Hanse, is small beer, but it is organized in a new way which may be useful at other times in other places: the Muscovy Company is a joint-stock company which has a continuing existence, not being dispersed at the end of a single voyage, and determined to keep interlopers of any nation out of its monopoly.

Cathay has not been forgotten. An expedition led by Anthony Jenkinson has now left Moscow and gone right down the Volga to the Caspian; away east at Bokhara he is hoping to find caravans from and to Cathay.

Ships have continued to go to the Guinea Coast of Africa for gold and peppers, and made good profits, although losing many lives until they respected the seasons. These voyages are quite different from those to Muscovy: they are *ad hoc* speculations, and the English are interlopers in a Portuguese monopoly. The Portuguese asked Philip, who became their king a few years ago, to order the English to keep away. Which he did. But the English did not: neither the Council nor Queen Mary (she was alone on her double throne at the time) wanted to cramp English enterprise in the name of Iberian interests. Indeed, some of Mary's own ships went to Guinea. Queenship has made Mary more English.

These extensions of trade depend on marine capability. There is now among the English greater skill in navigation; longer voyages are making for greater ships, and greater ships for longer voyages. London merchants nowadays spread their risks by taking shares in a number of ships instead of being sole or part owner of one or two. And marine insurance, rather late, is developing in London.

But what boot the Muscovy and Guinea trades if much of the more valuable Antwerp trade is still in the hands of aliens? It is no longer. The Italians and the Hanse are allowed still, if they are graciously permitted licences, to send English kerseys to their home markets via Antwerp, but they are not allowed to sell them in Antwerp. The City at last has effective monopoly of selling English cloth in Antwerp. And, wonder of wonders, English merchants are taking more interest in imports. Imports of silk, for example, have been tumbling out of Italian hands into English. This is not a sensational broadening of commerce, but there is greater confidence and power, and that invention of the joint stock company. We are talking of only five years. Not salvation, but some steps towards salvation.

Next, cultural poverty. How could anything have happened in five years?[5]

vi

A country's literature is taken as indicative of its culture as a whole, and English literature is painfully poor, the English language itself being too crude for the elegance and sensitivity of civilized thought.

Some would say there is good writing in the English translation of the Bible and in Thomas Cranmer's prayers, but they are *hors concours* as being heretical (or alternatively as having received special assistance). The best of their other prose – More's, Ascham's – is self-conscious and stiff. Their drama – Udall's, Heywood's – is wretched in the extreme. In poetry there has been no one of real stature since Geoffrey Chaucer, who lived in the century before last and can scarcely be understood or even pronounced.

However, in June last year, 1557, a Fleet Street printer, Tottel, brought out *Songs and Sonnets by the Earl of Surrey, and others*. This was the Earl of Surrey with whom Wyatt once went on a window-smashing spree. Only two of his poems had been published before; here are forty.

Take this sonnet. It is a translation from Petrarch, so the thought is not Surrey's, but the English words carry it with almost the ease of Italian or French. And notice Surrey's rhyme scheme, confidently different from Petrarch's *abba abba cde cde*, and sounding very right in English.

Henry Howard, Earl of Surrey:

Alas, so all things now do hold their peace,
Heaven and earth disturbed in nothing:
The beasts; the air; the birds their songs do cease;
The night's chair the stars about do bring.
Calm is the sea, the waves work less and less:
So am not I, whom love alas doth wring,
Bringing before my face the great increase
Of my desires, whereat I weep and sing
In joy and woe, as in a doubtful ease.
For my sweet thoughts sometime do pleasure bring,
But by and by the cause of my disease
Gives me a pang, that inwardly doth sting,
When that I think what grief it is again
To live and lack the thing should rid my pain.

No, it is not perfect. But the words put themselves in a line without kicking one another, and there is poise, and variety of rhythm. Tottel has also just published a translation by Surrey of two books of the *Aeneid* – in unrhymed iambic pentameters, another novelty in English which comes off.

In the earlier book there are some eighty poems by Sir Thomas Wyatt, the father of the rebel Wyatt. His name is not with Surrey's on the title page because it was the same as his son's. His songs are even cleaner and lighter than Surrey's. Give a man a lute and he will sing them.

Sir Thomas Wyatt:

Disdain me not without desert,
Nor leave me not so suddenly,
Since well ye wot that in my heart
I mean ye not but honestly.

Refuse me not without cause why,
Nor think me not to be unjust,
Since that by lot of fantasy
This careful knot needs knit I must.

Mistrust me not, though some there be
That fain would spot my steadfastness.
Believe them not, since that ye see
The proof is not as they express.

Forsake me not till I deserve,
Nor hate me not till I offend.
Destroy me not till that I swerve,
But since ye know what I intend,

Disdain me not that am your own,
Refuse me not that am so true,
Mistrust me not till all be known,
Forsake me not now for no new.

One must not exaggerate. Wyatt and Surrey were not Petrarch and Dante, nor do two poets make a *Pléiade.* But they showed there is nothing in the language to stop the English from being poets, and civilized persons. Culture in prospect – Salvation Six.

But what of the last, salvation from Papistry?[6]

vii

In November 1553 the House of Commons voted by a large majority that Protestant rites must be replaced by Catholic, and priests must get rid of their wives. A year later it voted, with a single dissentient, that the kingdom should be reunited with Rome. Reginald Pole, the Papal Legate, absolved England for its previous disobedience. Without a division the Commons voted to reintroduce the burning of heretics. For some years Mass has been sung in the churches, and some monasteries have been re-established. For two years Westminster has been again a Benedictine abbey, with thirty or forty monks, and there are Franciscans again at Greenwich, Dominicans at St Bartholomew's, Carthusians at Sheen, and Bridgettines at Syon. One has to look hard to find the Protestants. Is this at last a salvation quite unwon?

No. Those re-founded monasteries contain only 100 religious in all: there has been no rush of applications from the 1,500 ex-religious in the country, or from the young. Those Westminster monks process with their abbot Feckenham in dignified manner, but their processions smell to London only of superstitious and clerical pomp. And Westminster sanctuary, for which Feckenham has fought hard and successfully, and which once had value, reminds now only of the clerical power the English want never to return.

The renewal of Catholicism has been in the hands of Cardinal Pole, who besides being Papal Legate has been Mary's Archbishop of Canterbury, greatly loved and trusted by her — gaunt, gentle, a lover of books and principles. But not a toucher of common hearts, no administrator, of little vitality even when young, and by the time he came to Lambeth Palace, careworn. He died the same day as Mary. Time has been short for the production of a vigorous priesthood: fine plans have been put on paper but not realized. There might have been more to show if there had been even a little of a new Catholic spirit blowing in England. There has been none, neither in the people (there are fewer going to Mass than a year ago) nor even in Mary or Pole, whose gestures have not been trumpets and whose actions have been sincere but not always sensible.

Mary used symbolically to wash the feet of twelve poor every Maundy Thursday, and did it with such devotion that her ladies wept. But the significant action for the poor in the 1550s is in the City's welfare schemes, and in those she took no interest. She re-founded the Savoy, and her ladies provided bedding and linen, and Feckenham provided plate and a chalice. Bless their instincts. And damn their brains: they have left the Savoy grossly under-endowed, and organized just as it used to be, convenient for easy milking by neglectful on-the-make master and chaplains.

Pole was a holy man. Nevertheless, he indecently had himself consecrated Archbishop of Canterbury the very day after the see was made vacant by Cranmer being burned. His commissioners had the corpse of Martin Bucer, a moderate man and Regius Professor of Divinity at Oxford, dug up, condemned when it did not apostasize, and burned. Not only indecent but silly. The corpse of Peter Martyr's wife was dug up and thrown out on a dungheap. If Pole did not initiate these actions, he condoned them. They would have smirched him less if they had been outshone by many public actions of some nobility. He did none.

Was Mary more successful negatively, in suppressing Protestantism? Yes, most people have conformed to Catholic rites, as they used to before 1547. No, suppression was unsuccessful, not only because the Protestants were English and stubborn, but because the Catholics were more English and decent than Roman (or Spanish) and ruthless.

Take last year, 1557. The Government made what purported to be a special drive to round up heretics, and a commission was authorized to search premises as it wished and force witnesses to give sworn evidence. The object was not to burn, of course, but to punish and convert, but if the drive had been wholehearted there would inevitably have been an increase in the number of seized heretics who refused to be saved from the stake. But the number of heretics burned remained, in 1557 as in 1556 and 1555, about eighty in the country as a whole.

Are eighty many? Yes, it is more Protestant martyrs in a single year than all the Protestant and Catholic martyrs in the whole thirty-eight-year reign of Henry VIII. No, it is not many. It compares with four times that number executed each year for theft, which is presumably a less serious crime. It compares with a yearly average of 1,500 heretics whom Charles V manages to burn or otherwise do away with in the Netherlands.

Too few heretics were taken, and the stage-managing of the burnings took no account of the God-filled courage of the actors or the mood of the people. The first to be burned was John Rogers. The crowd was sensation-seeking, yes, but grieving too – he was a good and loved man. And, of all things, the crowd was rejoicing – rejoicing because Rogers, it felt, was proving its faith as well as his own.

The French ambassador was right: it was as if the little man was being led to his wedding. He was chained by the waist to the stake, which was a little above the bundles of wood so that he would burn properly. The flames were put to the reeds. In due course, the wood caught. In due course, the fire took hold of his legs and shoulders. It is uncertain whether any friend had hung a bag of gunpowder round his neck to quicken the end, but it is likely. When a pigeon or two flew out from St Bartholomew's (perhaps because of a bang of gunpowder) the faithful rejoiced that the Holy Spirit had descended in its usual likeness. As the limbs were consumed they grew lighter and rose in the fire's heat or, as the faithful said, Rogers washed his hands in the flames as if the fire was cold water, and then lifted them to heaven. Afterwards there was a rush for souvenir bones.

If Rogers had been burned by the Inquisition in Spain, he would have first been held so tightly in prison that no writings would have escaped from him (from English religious prisoners writings have issued in a continuous stream

– English Catholics are so God-inspired lax they do not annihilate dissidence). When at last he was brought out and shown to the public he would have been a cloaked and hooded figure, painted with devils and flames, in a very large and disciplined *auto-da-fé* calculated to strengthen the orthodox and discourage everyone else. And when he was burned, it would have been in a business-like operation away from the *auto-da-fé*, with a gag in his mouth and no attendant sympathetic crowd.

But from England reports of heretics' arrests, examinations, imprisonments and martyrdoms have been finding their way across the Channel to John Foxe in Basle, who is even now feeding to a printer a book of martyrs likely to be a second Bible to English Protestants.

English Protestants could not possibly have had a better Catholic queen.[7]

viii

A year ago, before it seemed likely that Mary would shortly die, Papistry was already weaker than it should have been, and Protestantism stronger, but with time Catholicism might have won through. To secure a Catholic succession Philip and Mary made new attempts to beget an heir but had no success. In any case Mary might have died in childbirth and the child in infancy. Something more had to be done. If it was not, Elizabeth would succeed and there would be 1553 again, but in reverse.

So did they have Parliament approve the only strong Catholic candidate, Mary Queen of Scots? No. Because a Scot married to the Dauphin of France would be even less welcome than Elizabeth the Protestant. Patriotism took precedence over Papistry. Or did they have Elizabeth killed, as a necessary preliminary to adopting a weak Catholic candidate? No. Mary had had five years to kill her and had not done so. What happened, then? As in 1553, the nation mulled things over somewhere out of sight, in its belly. Then suddenly, as with the proclamation of Mary, all became clear. Notice how impeccably everyone acted as part of the organism.

On Saturday, 6 November, when the doctors admitted the Queen was going to die, the Councillors came to her and asked her to declare Elizabeth her successor in accordance with Act of Parliament. They came to her not a moment too soon, when she would have refused to nominate Elizabeth, and not a moment too late, when she could not have nominated anyone. She agreed. Elizabeth had become her father's daughter, and family took precedence over Papistry. A Tudor queen is a Tudor is a Tudor.

Next day, the Sunday, the Comptroller Sir Robert Rochester and the Master of the Rolls Sir William Cordell went to Elizabeth at Hatfield and said the Queen was willing that, if she died, Elizabeth should succeed, but requested of her two things: that she would maintain the old religion as the Queen had restored it and that she would pay the Queen's debts.

Mary made no conditions; she simply requested.

Elizabeth said yes, she would do those things. No humming or hawing: the straight lie. Immediately it was permissible to pay court to Elizabeth. Cecil, the all-competent, came out of the wings. Ten days later, having given ample time for dispositions to be made, Mary died, between five and six in the morning, adoring the Mass.

Later in the morning the Lords summoned the Commons. The Lord Chancellor Nicholas Heath, Archbishop of York, told them that God had taken the Queen to his mercy and had furnished them with another Sovereign Lady, his Lady Elizabeth's Grace. He willed the knights and burgesses to resort to the Palace, where the Lords would come and cause her Grace to be proclaimed Queen of England.

There was nothing special in that? There was. Heath knew, and the peers and bishops and knights and burgesses knew, that if Elizabeth was Protestant, as they believed, then Heath and the bishops would find themselves in prison again as they were under Edward, and all would have to toe a new religious line; and there was again a queen, and the Lord knew whom she would marry. Again, no humming or hawing: a clean statement.

With heralds, trumpeters, clerks, lords, knights, and Norfolk, Paulet, Shrewsbury, Bedford, the Lord Mayor and the aldermen, Elizabeth was proclaimed at the Cross in Cheap. In the afternoon, bells; in the evening, bonfires, and tables in the streets.

The imperious lusty young woman rode towards her city from Hatfield, attended by 1,000 or more nobles and gentlemen. They included, for work, the professional administrators – Cecil, Paulet, Nicholas Bacon – for play, her Master of Horse, Northumberland's boy, Robert Dudley.

She went for a few days to the Charterhouse, then to the Sovereign's Lodgings at the Tower, a few days later to Whitehall. Was there as much enthusiasm as there had been for Mary? St Michael Cornhill paid its ringers twice as much, and afterwards had to mend the clapper of the great bell.

Salvation from Papistry? Yes, inch by inch. The first sermon at Paul's Cross was Protestant. This Christmas Day the Queen told the bishop who was to officiate at Mass in her chapel that he was not to elevate the Host.

Seven salvations.[8]

18

Super-salvations

There are two more salvations, super-salvations, which England needs, as do those countries across the Channel.

The first is from absolute monarchy. With every change of monarch, the people have to change their religion, as if they were beefeaters changing their spangles. English Protestants have not believed that arms should be taken up against a monarch, even if he or she is anti-Christ: one should obey, or else disobey and die. Or one can flee, but one does not rebel.

On this subject some of those Protestants whom Gardiner was so pleased to see become refugees in Europe, have been goaded – by lack of money, cramped living, isolation, idleness, inability to see any end to their exile – to change their mind. They have now decided that a sovereign is not a sovereign: he must be subject to the laws and to the axe or rope like everyone else. The godly are justified in rebelling against a monarch who is idolatrous. Not all the refugees have decided this but the hardcore have, the 'Puritans'. Besides, it is not an unattractive idea to do away with the sovereign's practical divinity (as distinct from symbolic divinity). It is no longer needed: it has been useful as an instrument for taming the nobility and the Church, but that was done by Henry VII and Henry VIII, and now the headpiece of government could be Parliament.

Super-salvation One is not yet born in England in 1558, but it has been conceived. Gestation may require a century or so, and a succession of unacceptable monarchs, but it will come.

Super-salvation Two, from monopolistic religion, has also been conceived. It would not do if England were saved from the fire of Papistry only to fall into the pot of Protestantism. There are walls of intolerance round the empires of the two religions, but there are interlopers making holes in the walls.

In Paul's Churchyard William Turner's *Avium praecipuarum* is on sale, a book on birds. Also his *A New Herball*. Innocuous? No, more dangerous than his heretical *A Preservative, or Triacle, Agaynst the Poyson of Pelagius*. Interlopers. The meticulous study of plants and creatures, and their precise description, are not a better celebration of God and his creation than the rituals, myths, literature and art of the Catholics and Protestants, but are in an alternative and attractive interloping mode. And they strengthen sense of material fact, to which the laws and lore of religious empires are vulnerable.

Look too at Robert Recorde's *The Castle of Knowledge*, and consider the comet and eclipse of 1556. The great Protestant ex-bishop John Ponet declared that these celestial happenings signified the great wrath and indignation of God at the wrong-doings of Catholics. In the presence of such knowledge and skill as Recorde's, ecclesiastics must be more careful how they identify and interpret God's messages.

Mathematical thinking is often regarded (especially by mathematicians) as the thinking of God. Mathematics does not contradict the dogmatic religions, but it is another manner of approach to the divine which is not under their imperial control.

Still another is architecture, considered by many (especially architects) as the greatest of the arts. Not the old architecture of pointed arches but the new architecture according to Alberti and the rediscovered texts of Vitruvius, which is based on mathematical principles of proportion, and operates in the imagination – for example, the Strand front of Somerset House, and in due course, it is said, a great house at Longleat in Wiltshire. The new architecture relates, without ecclesiastical assistance, to cosmic harmonies.

Similarly music. In Rome at the present time the music of Pierluigi Palestrina does its duty in carrying Catholic dogma, but it also carries a wholly musical non-ecclesiastical message of balance, proportion, calm. Music of the spheres. In England the Chapel Royal has no Palestrina, but it has Thomas Tallis and John Shepherd, and there are promising youngsters like John Byrd's fifteen-year-old William.

A monopolistic state religion has now to operate in competition with these secular interlopers, at a time when (in England) its civil powers and perquisites have already been halved, or quartered. It is in competition too with smaller religions and near-religions, from the Anabaptist to the Hermeticist, which sometimes speak with tolerance, gentleness, generosity. It is too early to say that the laughable intolerances of the monopoly religions are about to be blown away by gales of English laughter – the horrors have been inhibiting laughter somewhat – but there are seeds for those gales in the jokes of such as Catherine Bertie, who pulled the leg of (safely incarcerated just then in the Tower) Stephen Gardiner at least once, and often pulled that of her (safely enskied) God, 'a remarkable man'.

Seven salvations, two super-salvations. Happy, happy England!

Is not God a remarkable man? Are not the English – the uncivilized, stubborn, confused, exasperating, brains-in-the-belly English – his Chosen People?

Indubitably.

Notes

The following sources have been used so much that they are mentioned in these Notes only when there is verbatim quotation from them: Stow's *Survey of London*; *Calendars of State Papers*: Domestic, Spanish, Venetian; *Acts of the Privy Council*; de Noailles's *Ambassades*; Nichols's *Chronicle of Lady Jane*; Machyn; *Greyfriars Chronicles*; Wriothesley; Grafton; Holinshed; Foxe; *Dictionary of National Biography*. Cuts in verbatim quotations are not always indicated by dots. Numbers (i), (ii), etc. in the notes refer to the Bibliography.

Introduction
1 Harrison; Perlin; Robertson-Scott. Cardano so describes London speech. The blood-red hail is mentioned by Froude quoting Baoardo, *History of the revolution in England on the death of Edward VI* (Venice, 1558), but it is not mentioned in Grafton, Greyfriars, Holinshed, Machyn, Nichols (ii), Stow (i) or Wriothesley. The phenomenon, caused by sand blown from the Sahara, recurs every now and again, e.g. on 1 July 1969.

1 Gravesend to Greenwich Palace and Billingsgate
1 Addison; Bellow; Cruden; Harbison (i); Harris, G. G.; Perlin; Philp.
2 Cardano; Dunlop; Edward VI; Kirby; Strype (ii); Survey (ii).
3 Barclay; Bindoff (iii); Dunlop; Harbison (i); Read.
4 Barclay; Bayley; Challis; Davey (ii); Dunlop; Gould; Kirby; Ramsey (iii); Willan (i). Ponet gives Gardiner's nostrils as 'like a horse'.
5 Beer; Hoak; Hurstfield (i); Pollard; Sturge.
6 Broodbank; Gras; Ramsay (i), (ii), (iii); Ramsey (ii); Stern.
7 Besant; Chandler; Hearsey.
8 Davis. Suburbs add a further 90,000 or so to the population. High tide at London Bridge was at 9.23 a.m. (Dr John Vassie, Institute of Cosmographic Science).

2 Billingsgate to the Three Cranes and Whitehall Palace
1 Broodbank; City (i) Rep 13 (1); Thrupp.
2 Bennett, Eric; Pearce, Arthur; Ramsey (ii); Stern.
3 Perlin; Simon.
4 Cook; Muller; Philp; *Survey* (iv).
5 Bennett, H. S. (i); Chambers; Cowie; O'Donoghue (ii); Prest. Description of Mary largely from Soranzo, *State Papers* (ii).
6 Bates; Needham & Webster; Nichols, J. G. (ii); Somerville; *Survey* (iii).
7 Beer; Davey: Stone, quoting Rosso.
8 Challis; Dunlop; Gould; Knoop & Jones; Outhwaite (ii). For fares: Parliament (ii), 6 Henry VIII 7.

3 Aldgate to Cheapside and Guildhall
1 Atkinson; Dickens (i), (ii), (iii).
2 Mullins; O'Donoghue (ii); Perlin.
3 Bowden; Burgon; Herbert; Jarvis; Mullins; Overall; Rogers (iii).
4 Dobb; Herbert; Perks: Ramsay (iii); Rogers (i), (ii).
5 Beaven; City (i) Rep 13 (1); Jones; Masters, B. R.; Unwin (i), (ii).
6 Hobhouse.
7 Fisher; Ramsay (i), (ii); Willan (i), (ii); Williamson (i).

4 The Saracen's Head to St Paul's, Christ's Hospital and Newgate
1 Bennett, H. S. (i), (ii); Cook; Maclure.
2 Cook; Mullins.
3 Bennett, H. S. (i); Howes; Kingdon; Pearce, Arthur; Pearce, E.H.
4 Dobb.

5 The Hand and Shears to Smithfield, the windmills, Bedlam and Bishopsgate
1 Beck; Hall, M. B.; Moore; Vicary.
2 Beer; Holmes (i); Masters, Anthony; O'Donoghue (i); Oman; Walker, G. G.

6 The Crane in Vintry to Westminster and Syon
1 Bell; Brayley and Britten; Neale; Saunders.
2 Alsop; Beer; Fanshawe; Outhwaite (i); Richardson; Roseveare; Saunders.
3 Ridley (i); Stanley; Thornley; Westlake.
4 Aungier; Batho; Read; Stone, quoting Rosso; *Survey* (i). Syon pensions are in Augmentations, Court of.

7 'O Lord God, save thy chosen people of England!'

1 Holinshed.

8 In time of miraculous revolution

1 Beer; Davey; Stone, quoting Rosso; Tytler.
2 The Tower journal is in Nichols, J. G. (iv).
3 Kitto; Nichols, J. G. (ii); Overall; Tittler (iii).
4 City (i) Rep 13 (1); Fuller (ii); Nichols, J. G. (ii); Pearce, E. H.; Read.
   Jane's letter to Mary is in Stone, translating from the Italian of Rosso. The
   original text seems to be missing. The letter to Gilbert Potter is in
   Nichols, J. G. (ii).
5 Underhill.
6 Underhill.
7 Mozley; Read; Ridley (i). The elegy on Edward is in *Harleian Miscellany*.

9 Truth on Tower Hill, truth on Paul's door

1 de Guaras.
2 Graziani; Nichols, J. G. (ii).
3 de Guaras; Perlin.
4 Chancellor.
5 Cave-Browne; Ridley (i). Cranmer's statement is in Foxe.

10 'Yea, yea, yea!'

1 de Guaras; *Rutland papers*.
2 de Guaras; Nichols, John; Underhill.
3 de Guaras; Planché.
4 de Guaras; Planché; *Rutland papers*.

11 Lord Treasurer, make the Crown solvent

1 'Ortus sum . . .' is from Naunton.
2 Alsop; Elton (ii); Fanshawe; Outhwaite (i); Richardson; Roseveare;
   Saunders; Stopes (ii).
3 Alsop; Dietz (i); Richardson.
4 Bell; Dietz (i); Hurstfield (ii); Miller.
5 Hall; Hurstfield (i); Ramsey (i).

12 Lord Chancellor, make England Catholic

1 Muller.
2 The Hales interview is in Foxe.
3 Mountayne.
4 Dixon; Foxe; Law; Muller; Parliament (i).

13 City: *Domine dirige nos*
1 Nichols, J. G. (i), (iii); Sayle (i), (ii); Unwin (i).
2 Beaven; Nichols, J. G. (iii); Ramsay (i), (iii); Ramsey (ii); Unwin (i); Williamson (i).

14 Parliament: *La Reyne le veult*
Main sources: Neale (i), (ii), (iii); Parliament (i), (ii), (iv). The Lords Journals for this session are missing.

15 Approach to crisis – again
1 The terms are in *State Papers* (iii) vol XII. Gardiner's doodle is in Augmentations (i).
2 Harbison (ii); Loades (i).
3 *State Papers* (iii) vol XII.
4 Loades (i).

16 O Lord, save thy people – again
Proctor's pro-government account and Nichols, J. G. (iv) are main sources, and Loades (i) is useful. The events of Ash Wednesday, and their timings and locations, are not at all clear. There are no minutes of the Court of Aldermen for the days of the rebellion.
1 Clode; Cruden; Harbison (ii); Hist.Mss Comm. (i); Kennedy.
2 Kennedy. Mary's speech is in Wriothesley.
3 Rendle.
4 Underhill.
5 Knight's Bridge was close to the present Albert Gate.
6 Underhill.

17 Salvations
1 Clifford; Prescott.
2 Ferrers; Hume.
3 Boynton; Glasgow.
4 Dietz (i); Willan (iv).
5 Hakluyt; Ramsey (i), (ii), (iii); Rich; Scott; Willan (iii); Williamson (i).
6 Tottel.
7 Chester; Foxe; Haile; Holinshed; Huggarde; Hughes (i); Knowles; Mozley; Pogson; Schenk; Somerville; Thornley.
8 Nichols, John; Overall; Parliament (i); *State Papers* (iv).

18 Super-salvations
Donaldson; French; Garrett; Goodman; Hall, M. B.; Jordan; Ponet; Raven; Recorde.

Bibliography

Addison, W. W., *Thames Estuary*, London, 1954.

Alsop, J. D., 'The theory and practice of Tudor taxation', *Eng. hist. rev.*, XCIX, 1982.

Arber, Edward, *An English garner*, vol iv, Birmingham, 1882.

Atkinson, A. G. B., *St Botolph Aldgate*, London, 1898.

Augmentations, Court of, Public Record Office MSS (i) E 101 631 44; (ii) E 315 261.

Aungier, G. J., *History and antiquities of Syon monastery*, Nichols, Westminster, 1840.

Aydelotte, Frank, *Elizabethan rogues and vagabonds*, Oxford, 1913.

Barclay, John, 'Icon animorum', *Trans. Greenwich & Lewisham Antiq. Soc.*, vol iv, pt 1, 1936.

Bates, L. M., *Somerset House*, London, 1967.

Batho, G. R., 'Syon House', *History today*, vol vii, 1957.

Bayley, John, *The history and antiquities of the Tower of London*, 2 vols, London, 1821.

Beaven, A. B., *The Aldermen of the City of London*, London, 1908.

Beck, R. T., *The cutting edge: early history of the Surgeons of London*, London, 1974.

Beer, B. L., *Northumberland: the political career of John Dudley, Earl of Warwick and Duke of Northumberland*, Kent State Univ. Press, USA, 1973.

Bell, H. C., *An introduction to the history and records of the Court of Wards and Liveries*, Cambridge, 1953.

Belloc, Hilaire, *The river of London*, London, 1912.

Bennett, Eric, *The worshipful company of the Carmen of London*, London, 1961.

Bennett, H. S., (i) *English books and readers 1475–1557*, Cambridge, 1952; (ii) 'Notes on English book-prices 1480–1560', *The Library*, 5th ser vol v, Dec 1950.

Besant, G. B., *London Bridge*, London, 1927.

Bindoff, S. T., (i) *Kett's rebellion*, Hist. Ass. pamphlet, 1947; (ii) *Tudor England*, London, 1950; (iii) 'A kingdom at stake 1553', *History today*, vol iii, 1953.

Bowden, P. J., *The wool trade in Tudor and Stuart England*, London, 1962.

Boynton, Lindsay, *The Elizabethan militia 1558–1638*, London, 1967.

Brayley, E. W. & Britton, John, *The history of the ancient palace and late houses of Parliament at Westminster*, London, 1836.

Brinkelow, Henry, *Complaynt of Roderyck Mors*, ed J. M. Cowper, Early Eng. Text Soc., extra ser xxii, 1874.

Broodbank, J. G., *History of the port of London*, vol ii, London, 1921.

Burgon, J. W., *The life and times of Sir Thomas Gresham*, 2 vols, London, 1839.

Burn, J. S., *The history of the French, Walloon, Dutch and other foreign Protestant refugees settled in England from the reign of Henry VIII to the revocation of the Edict of Nantes*, London, 1846.

Burnet, Gilbert, *The history of the Reformation of the Church of England*, ed N. Pocock, Oxford, 1865.

Cardano, Girolamo, 'Dialogue with death', *Strange island*, by F. M. Wilson, London, 1955.

Cave-Browne, J., *Lambeth Palace, and its associations*, 2nd ed, Edinburgh, 1883.

Challis, C. E., 'The circulating medium and the movement of prices in mid-Tudor England', *The price revolution in 16th century England*, ed P. H. Ramsey, London, 1971.

Chambers, E. K., *Notes on the history of the Revels Office under the Tudors*, London, 1906.

Chandler, M. I., 'London Bridge before the Great Fire', *Guildhall Miscellany*, 1, Jan 1952.

Chester, J. L., *John Rogers*, London, 1861.

City of London, (i) Repertories of Court of Aldermen, City Records Office MSS; (ii) Journals of Common Council, ibid; *The Corporation of London*, London, 1950.

Clifford, Henry, *Life of Jane Dormer*, ed J. Stevenson, London, 1887.

Clode, C. M., *The early history of the guild of Merchant Taylors*, 2 vols, London, 1888.

Cobb, H. S., 'Books of rates and the London Customs 1507–1558', *Guildhall Miscellany*, 4, 1971.

Cook, G. H., *Old St Paul's Cathedral*, London, 1955.

Cowie, L. W., 'Blackfriars in London', *History today*, vol xxiv, Dec 1974.

Cranmer, Thomas, *Writings and disputations of Cranmer relative to the sacrament of the Lord's Supper*, ed J. E. Cox, Parker Soc, 1844.

Creighton, Charles, *A history of epidemics in Britain from A.D. 664 to the extinction of the plague*, 2 vols, Cambridge, 1891.

Crewdson, H. A. F., *The worshipful company of Musicians*, London, 1950.

Cruden, R. P., *The history of the town of Gravesend and the port of London*, London, 1843.

Cunningham, Peter, *A handbook for London*, 2 vols, London, 1849.

Cunningham, W., *Alien immigrants to England*, London, 1897.

Davey, R., (i) *The nine days' queen*, London, 1909; (ii) *The Tower of London*, London, 1910.

Davis, E. J., 'The transformation of London', *Tudor studies presented to A. F. Pollard*, London, 1924.

Dickens, A. G., (i) 'The Reformation in England', *The Reformation crisis*, ed. Joel Hurstfield, London 1965; (ii) *Reformation and society in 16th century Europe*, London, 1966.

Dictionary of National Biography, ed. Leslie Stephen & Sidney Lee, London, 1885–1903.

Dietz, F. C., (i) *English government finance 1485–1558*, Univ. of Illinois, 1920; (ii) *English public finance 1558–1642*, New York, 1932.

Dixon, R. W., *History of the Church of England*, vol iv, London, 1891.

Dobb, Clifford, 'London's prisons', *Shakespeare in his Age*, ed. Allardyce Nicoll, Shakespeare survey 17, Cambridge, 1964.

Donaldson, Peter, 'Bishop Gardiner, Machiavellian', *Hist. jl.* XXIII, 1980.

Dudley, Edmund, *The tree of commonwealth*, ed. D. M. Brodie, Cambridge, 1948.

Dunlop, Ian, *Palaces and progresses of Elizabeth I*, London, 1962.

Edward VI, *Literary remains*, ed. J. G. Nichols, Roxburghe Club, 1857.

Ellis, H. ed. *Original letters illustrative of English history*, London, 1824–1846.

Elton, G. R., (i) *The Tudor revolution in government*, Cambridge, 1953; (ii) *England under the Tudors*, London, 1955.

Emmison, F. G., *Tudor Secretary – Sir William Petre at Court and at home*, London, 1961.

Evans, A. H., *Turner on birds*, Cambridge, 1903.

Fanshawe, Thomas (att.), *The practice of the Exchequer Court*, London, 1658.

Ferrers, George, 'The winning of Calais by the French, January 1558', *An English garner*, vol iv, ed. Edward Arber, Birmingham, 1882.

Fisher, F. J., 'Commercial trends and policy in 16th century England', *Econ. hist. rev.*, vol x, 1939–40.

Fox, John, *Acts and monuments of the English martyrs*, ed. S. R. Cattley & George Townsend, London 1847–41.

French P. J., *John Dee: the world of an Elizabethan magus*, London, 1972.

Froude, J. A., *History of England from the fall of Wolsey to the death of Elizabeth*, vol vi, London, 1860.

Fuller, Thomas, (i) *The history of the worthies of England*, ed. J. G. Nichols, London, 1811; (ii) *Church history of Britain from the birth of Jesus Christ until the year 1648*, ed. J. S. Brewer, Oxford, 1845.

Glasgow, Tom, Jr. 'Maturing of naval administration 1556–1564', *The Mariner's Mirror*, vol lvi, 1970.

Gardiner, Stephen, *Letters of Stephen Gardiner*, ed. J. A. Muller, London, 1933.

Garrett, H. E., *The Marian Exiles*, Cambridge, 1938.

Goodman, Christopher, *How superior powers ought to be obeyed*, repro. from 1558 ed. Facsimile Text Soc, Columbia, 1931.

Gould, J. D., *The great debasement: currency and the economy in mid-Tudor England*, Oxford, 1970.

Grafton, Richard, *Chronicle*, ed. H. Ellis, London, 1809.

Gras, N. S. B., *The early English customs system*, Cambridge, Mass., 1918.

Graziani, A. M., *La vie du Cardinal J. F. Commendon*, trans. M. Flechier, Paris, 1694.

Grey (Dudley), Lady Jane, *Literary remains of Lady Jane Grey*, ed. N. H. Nicholas, London, 1825.

Greyfriars chronicle of London, ed. J. G. Nichols, Camden Soc. liii, 1852.

Griffet, Henri, *Nouveaux éclaircissements sur l'histoire de Marie reine d'Angleterre*, Amsterdam, 1766.

de Guaras, Antonio, *The accession of Queen Mary*, trans. Richard Garnett, London, 1892.

Hakluyt, Richard, *The principal navigations, voyages, traffiques, and discoveries of the English nation*, vol ii Muscovy, etc., vol vi Guinea, etc., Glasgow, 1903, 1904.

Haile, Martin, *Life of Reginald Pole*, London, 1910.

Hall, A. R., 'Military technology', *A history of technology*, ed. Charles Singer, E. J. Holmyard, A. R. Hall, T. I. Williams, Oxford, 1957.

Hall, M. B. (formerly Marie Boas), *The scientific renaissance 1450–1630*, London, 1962.

Harbison, E. H., (i) *Rival ambassadors at the court of Queen Mary*, Princeton, 1940; (ii) 'French intrigue at the court of Queen Mary', *Amer. hist. rev*, vol xlv, April, 1940.

Harleian miscellany, ed. W. Oldys, vol x, London, 1813.

Harman, T., *A caveat or warening for common curseters vulgarely called vagabonds*, ed. John Awdeley, E.E.T.S. extra ser ix, 1869.

Harris, A., *The oeconomy of the Fleet*, ed. August Jessop, Camden Soc., new ser xxv, 1879.

Harris, G. G., *The Trinity House of Deptford 1514–1660*, London, 1969.

Harrison, William, *Description of England*, ed. F. J. Furnivall, New
Shakespeare Soc., 1871.

Hay, Denys, 'P. Vincentius, the *Narratio historica*', *Eng. hist. rev.* lxiii, 1948.

Hearsey, J. E. N., *Bridge, church, and palace in old London*, London, 1961.

Herbert, William, *The history of the twelve great livery companies of London*,
London, 1837.

Hexter, J. H., *Reappraisals in history*, London, 1961.

Historical Manuscripts Commission, (i) vol 45 Letters from London during
Wyatt's rebellion; (ii) vol 70 Report on MSS of Magdalene College,
Cambridge; (iii) vol 73 Report on the records of the city of Exeter; (iv) 4th
report.

Hoak, D. E., *The King's Council in the reign of Edward VI*, Cambridge, 1976.

Hobhouse, Hermione, *The ward of Cheap in the city of London*, London, 1963.

Holinshed, Raphael, *The chronicles of England, Scotland and Ireland*, vols i, iv,
London, 1807, 1808.

Holmes, Martin, (i) *Moorfields in 1559*, London, 1963; (ii) *Elizabethan London*,
London, 1969.

Hooker, John, *The life and times of Sir Peter Carew*, ed. John Maclean,
London, 1857.

Howes, John, *John Howes' MSS 1582*, ed. William Lemprière, London,
1904.

Huggarde, Miles, *The displaying of the Protestants*, London, 1556.

Hughes, Philip, (i) *Rome and the Counter-Reformation in England*, London,
1944; (ii) *The Reformation in England*, vol ii, London, 1953.

Hume, Martin, 'The visit of Philip II 1554', *Eng. hist. rev.*, vii, 1892.

Hurstfield, Joel, (i) 'Corruption and reform under Edward VI and Mary',
Eng. hist. rev., lxviii, 1953; (ii) *The Queen's wards*, London, 1958; (iii) ed.
The Reformation Crisis, London, 1965.

Hutchinson, F. E., *Cranmer and the English Reformation*, London, 1951.

Jarvis, R. C., 'The King's Beam', *Trans London & Mdx Arch. Soc.*, new ser
xix, 1958.

Jones, P. E., 'The Common Crier and Sergeant at Arms', *Guildhall Ass.
Trans.*, iii, 1963.

Jordan, W. K., (i) *The development of religious toleration in England*, London,
1932; (ii) *Edward VI: the threshold of power*, London, 1970.

Kennedy, W. P. M., 'The Imperial embassy of 1553/4 and Wyatt's
rebellion', *Eng. hist. rev.*, vol xxxviii, 1923.

Kingdon, J. A., *Richard Grafton*, London, 1901.

Kingsford, C. L., 'On some London houses of the early Tudor period',
Archaeologia, 2nd ser xxi, Soc. of Antiquaries, 1921.

Kirby, J. W., 'Building work at Placentia 1543–1548', *Trans. Greenwich &*

Lewisham Antiq. Soc., vol iv, pt 6, 1954.

Kitto, J. V., St Martin's in the Fields: the accounts of churchwardens 1525–1603, London, 1901.

Knoop, Douglas and Jones, G. P., *The mediaeval mason*, Manchester, 1933.

Knowles, David, The religious orders in England, vol iii, Cambridge, 1959.

Law, Ernest, *The history of Hampton Court Palace*, vol i, London, 1890.

Loades, D. M., (i) *Two Tudor conspiracies*, Cambridge, 1965; (ii) *Papers of George Wyatt*, Camden Soc., 4th ser v, 1968; (iii) *The reign of Mary Tudor*, London, 1979.

Loseley MSS, ed. A. J. Kempe, London, 1835.

Machyn, Henry, *The diary of Henry Machyn*, ed. J. G. Nichols, Camden Soc., xlii, 1848.

Mackie, J. D., *The earlier Tudors 1485–1558*, Oxford, 1952.

Maclure, Millar, The Paul's Cross sermons 1534–1642, Univ. of Toronto, 1958.

Malfatti, C. V., *Two Italian accounts of Tudor England*, Barcelona, 1953.

Masters, Anthony, *Bedlam*, London, 1977.

Masters, B. R., 'The Mayor's household before 1600', *Studies in London history, presented to P. E. Jones*, London, 1969.

Miller, Helen, 'Subsidy assessments of the peerage in the 16th century', *Bull. Inst. Hist. Res.*, vol xxviii, 1955.

Moore, Norman, *The history of St Bartholomew's Hospital*, vol ii, London, 1918.

Morgan, E. D. & Coote, C. H., *Early voyages and travels to Russia and Persia by Anthony Jenkinson and other Englishmen*, Hakluyt Soc., vol lxxii, 1856.

Mountayne, Thomas, 'Reminiscences', *Narratives of the days of the Reformation*, ed. J. G. Nichols, Camden Soc., lxxvii, 1859.

Mozley, J. F., *John Foxe and his book*, London, 1940.

Muller, J. A., *Stephen Gardiner and the Tudor reaction*, London, 1926.

Mullins, E. L. C., 'The effects of the Marian and Elizabethan religious settlements upon the clergy of London 1553–1564', Univ. of London thesis, 1948.

Naunton, Robert, *Fragmenta regalia*, London, 1641.

Neale, J. E., (i) 'The Commons journals of the Tudor period', *Trans. Roy. Hist. Soc.*, 4th ser iii, 1920; (ii) 'The Commons privilege of free speech in Parliament', *Tudor studies, presented to A. F. Pollard*, London, 1924; (iii) *The Elizabethan House of Commons*, London, 1949.

Needham, R. W. & Webster, Alexander, *Somerset House, past and present*, London, 1905.

Newton, A. P., 'Tudor reforms in the royal household', *Tudor studies, presented to A. F. Pollard*, London, 1924.

Nichols, John, *The progresses and public processions of Queen Elizabeth*, London, 1823.

Nichols, John Gough, (i) *London pageants*, London, 1831; (ii) ed. 'Life of the last Fitzalan, Earl of Arundel', *Gentleman's magazine*, ciii pt 2, 1833; (iii) 'The Lord Mayor's Show', *Gentleman's magazine*, ciii pt 2, 1833; (iv) ed. *The Chronicle of Queen Jane and of two years of Queen Mary*, Camden Soc., lxviii, 1850; (v) ed. *Narratives of the days of the Reformation*, Camden Soc., lxvii, 1859; (vi) *The legend of Sir Nicholas Throckmorton*, Roxburghe Club, 1874.

de Noailles, Antoine & Francois, *Ambassades de messieurs de Noailles en Angleterre*, ed. R. A. Vertot & C. Villaret, Leyden, 1763.

O'Donoghue, E. G., (i) *The story of Bethlehem Hospital*, London, 1914; (ii) *Bridewell Hospital: palace, prison, school*, London, 1923, 1929.

Oman, Charles, *A history of the art of war in the 16th century*, London, 1937.

Outhwaite, R. B., (i) 'A note on *The practice of the Exchequer Court . . . by Sir T. F.*', *Eng, hist. rev.*, lxxxi, 1966; (ii) *Inflation in Tudor and Stuart England*, London, 1969.

Overall, W. H., ed. *The accounts of the churchwardens of the parish of St Michael, Cornhill 1456–1608*, London, 1871.

Parliament (i) *Journals of the House of Commons from 1 Nov 1547 to 2 Mar 1628*, London, 1803; (ii) *The statutes of the realm*, ed. A. Luders, T. E. Tomlins & J. Raithby, vol iv, London 1819; (iii) *Journals of the House of Lords 1510–1614*, London, 1846; (iv) *Official return of members of Parliament*, Parliamentary papers, 1878.

Parsons, F. G., *The history of St Thomas's Hospital*, vol i, London, 1932.

Patent Rolls, Calendar of, Philip and Mary, vols i–iv, London, 1936–9.

Pearce, Arthur, *History of the Butchers' Company*, London, 1929.

Pearce, E. H., *Annals of Christ's Hospital*, London, 1908.

Perks, Sydney, *The history of the Mansion House*, Cambridge, 1922.

Perlin, Etienne, *Description des royaumes d'Angleterre et d'Ecosse 1558*, ed. R. Gough, London, 1775.

Philp, I. E., 'The history of the Thames watermen', *Guildhall Ass. Trans.*, iii, 1963.

Pickthorn, Kenneth, *Early Tudor government*, Cambridge, 1934.

Planché, J. R., *Regal records*, London, 1838.

Pogson, R. H., 'Revival and reform in Mary Tudor's Church', *Jl of eccles. hist*, xxv, 1974.

Pollard, A. F., *The political history of England*, vol vi, 1547–1603, London, 1910.

Ponet, John, *A short treatise of politike power*, Strasburg, 1556.

Prescott, H. F. N., *Mary Tudor*, London, 1952.

Prest, Wilfred, 'Legal education of the gentry at the Inns of Court, 1560–1640', *Past and Present*, xxxviii, Dec 1967.

Privy Council, Acts of, ed. J. R. Dasent, London, 1890–1907.

Proctor, John, 'The historie of Wyate's rebellion 1554', *An English garner*, ed. E. Arber, vol viii, Birmingham, 1896.

Ramsay, G. D., (i) *English overseas trade during the centuries of emergence*, London, 1957; (ii) 'The undoing of the Italian mercantile colony in 16th century London', *Textile history and economic history, in honour of Miss Julia de Lacy Mann*, Manchester, 1973; (iii) *The city of London in international politics at the accession of Elizabeth Tudor*, Manchester, 1975.

Ramsey, P. H., (i) 'Some Tudor merchants' accounts', *Studies in the history of accounting*, ed. A. C. Littleton & B. S. Yoomey, London, 1963; (ii) *Tudor economic problems*, London, 1963; (iii) ed. *The price revolution in 16th century England*, London, 1971.

Raven, Charles, *English naturalists from Neckam to Ray*, Cambridge, 1947.

Read, Conyers, *Mr Secretary Cecil and Queen Elizabeth*, Oxford, 1955.

Recorde, Robert, (i) *The ground of artes*, London, 1543; (ii) *The urinal of physic*, London, 1548; (iii) *The pathway to knowledge*, London, 1551; (iv) *The castle of knowledge*, London, 1556; (v) *The whetstone of wit*, London, 1557.

Rendle, William, *Old Southwark and its people*, London, 1878.

Rich, E. E., *The ordinance book of the merchants of the Staple*, Cambridge, 1937.

Richardson, W. C., *History of the Court of Augmentations 1536–1554*, Baton Rouge, 1961.

Ridley, Jasper, (i) *Thomas Cranmer*, Oxford, 1962; (ii) *John Knox*, Oxford, 1968; (iii) *The life and times of Mary Tudor*, London, 1973.

Robinson, Hastings, ed. *The Zurich letters*, Parker Soc., 1842.

Robson-Scott, W. D., *German travellers in England 1400–1800*, Oxford, 1963.

Rogers, Kenneth, (i) *The Mermaid and Mitre taverns in old London*, London, 1926; (ii) *Old Cheapside and Poultry*, London, 1931; (iii) *Old London: Cornhill, Threadneedle Street and Lombard Street*, London, 1935.

Roseveare, Henry, *The Treasury*, London, 1969.

Rosso, Raviglio Giulio, *I successi d'Inghilterra dopo la morte de Edouardo Sesto*, Ferrara, 1560.

Russell, Conrad, *The crisis of parliaments: English history 1509–1660*, Oxford, 1971.

Rutland papers, ed. W. Jordan, Camden Soc., xxi, 1842.

Rye, W. B., *England as seen by foreigners in the days of Elizabeth and James I*, London, 1865.

Saunders, H. St G., *Westminster Hall*, London, 1951.

Sayle, R. T. D., (i) *Lord Mayor's pageants of the Merchant Taylors' Company in the 15th, 16th, 17th centuries*, priv. circ., 1931; (ii) *The barges of the Merchant Taylors' Company*, priv. circ., 1933.

Schenk, W., *Reginald Pole, Cardinal of England*, London, 1950.

Scott, W. R., *The constitution and finance of English, Scottish and Irish joint stock companies*, Cambridge, 1910–1912.

Simon, A. L., *The history of the wine trade in England*, London, 1906.

Society of Antiquaries of London, *A collection of ordinances and regulations for the Royal Household*, London, 1790.

Somerville, Robert, *The Savoy – manor, hospital, chapel*, London, 1960.

Stanley, A. P., *Historical memorials of Westminster Abbey*, London, 1868.

State Papers, Calendars of, (i) *Domestic*, vol i, ed. R. Lemon, London, 1856; (ii) *Venetian*, vols v, vi (3 pts), ed. Rawdon Brown, London, 1873, 1877, 1881, 1884; (iii) *Spanish*, vols xii, xiii, ed. Royall Tyler, London, 1949, 1954; (iv) *Spanish*, vol i (1558–67), ed. M. A. S. Hume.

Stern, W. M., *The porters of London*, London, 1960.

Stone, J. M., *The history of Mary I, Queen of England*, London, 1901.

Stopes, C. C., (i) 'Mary's Chapel Royal and her coronation play', *The Athenaeum*, Sep 1905; (ii) *William Hunnis and the Revels of the Chapel Royal* (Materialen zur Kunde des alteren Englischen Dramas 29, ed. W. Bang), Louvain, 1910.

Stow, John, (i) *The annales of England*, London, 1592; (ii) *A survey of London 1603*, ed. C. L. Kingsford, London, 1908.

Strype, John, (i) *Ecclesiastical memorials*, London, 1721; (ii) *The life of the learned Sir John Cheke, kt*, Oxford, 1821.

Sturge, C., 'The life and times of John Dudley, Earl of Warwick', Univ. of London thesis, 1927.

Survey of London, (i) vols ii & iv, *Chelsea*, London, 1913; (ii) vol xiv, *The Queen's House at Greenwich*, London, 1937; (iii) vol xviii, *Strand, etc*, London, 1937; (iv) vol xxii, *Bankside*, London, 1950.

Thornley, Keith, 'The destruction of sanctuary', *Tudor studies, presented to A. F. Pollard*, London, 1924.

Thrupp, Sylvia, *A short history of the worshipful company of Bakers of London*, London, 1933.

Tittler, Robert, (i) *Nicholas Bacon*, London, 1976; (ii) *The reign of Mary I*, London, 1983; (iii) with S. L. Bettley, 'The local community and the Crown in 1553: the accession of Mary Tudor revisited', *Inst. of Hist. Res. Bull.*, LVII, 1984.

Tottel's miscellany (1557–1587), ed. H. E. Rollins, Cambridge, Mass., 1965.

Tyler, Royall, *The Emperor Charles the Fifth*, London, 1956.

Tytler, P. F., *England under the reigns of Edward VI and Mary*, London, 1839.

Underhill, Edward, 'Reminiscences', *An English garner*, ed. E. Arber, vol iv, Birmingham, 1882.

Unwin, George, (i) 'The Merchant Adventurers' Company in the reign of Elizabeth', *Studies in economic history*, ed. R. H. Tazney, London, 1927; (ii) *The guilds and companies of London*, London, 1963.

Vicary, Thomas, *The anatomie of the bodie of man*, ed. F. J. & P Furnivall, Early Eng. Text Soc., extra ser liii, 1888.

Vietz (Vincentio), P., *Historical narration of certain events that took place in the kingdom of Great Britain in the month of July in the year of our Lord 1553.*

P. V., ed. J. Ph. Berjeau, London, 1865.

Walker, G., *A manifest detection of the most vyle and detestable use of dice play*, ed. J. O. Halliwell, Percy Soc., 1859.

Walker, G. G., *The Honourable Artillery Company 1537–1947*, Aldershot, 1954.

Walters, H. B., *Church bells of England*, London, 1912.

Westlake, H. F., *Westminster Abbey*, London, 1923.

Willan, T. S., (i) *The Muscovy merchants of 1555*, Manchester, 1953; (ii) 'Some aspects of English trade with the Levant in the 16th century', Eng. hist. rev., lxx, 1955; (iii) *The early history of the Russia Company*, Manchester, 1956; (iv) *A Tudor book of rates*, Manchester, 1962.

Williams, Sheila, 'The Lord Mayor's Show in Tudor and Stuart times', *Guildhall miscellany*, x, Sep. 1959.

Williamson, J. A., (i) *Maritime enterprise 1485–1558*, Oxford, 1913; (ii) *The Tudor age*, 2nd ed., London, 1959.

Wood, Anthony à, *Athenae Oxonienses*, London, 1691, 1692.

Wriothesley, Charles, *A chronicle of England during the days of the Tudors*, ed. W. D. Hamilton, Camden Soc., new ser xi, 1875, 1877.

Index